sin

sin

a history

gary a. anderson

yale university press / new haven and london

The author gratefully acknowledges permission to reprint from the following copy-righted work: *Tanakh: The Holy Scriptures: The New JPS Translation to the Traditional Hebrew Text*, ©1985 by The Jewish Publication Society.

Library of Congress Cataloging-in-Publication Data
Anderson, Gary A., 1955–
    Sin : a history / Gary A. Anderson.
        p. cm.
    Includes bibliographical references and indexes.
    ISBN 978-0-300-14989-0 (cloth : alk. paper)
    1. Sin.   I. Title.
    BL475.7.A53 2009
    241′.309—dc22

                            2009012342

Set in Minion type by The Composing Room of Michigan, Inc.
Printed in the United States of America.

A catalogue record for this book is available from the British Library.

This paper meets the requirements of ANSI / NISO Z39.48-1992 (Permanence of Paper).

10 9 8 7 6 5 4 3 2 1

For my two boys
Christopher Michael and Matthew Tobias

Psalm 127:3–5

Lay not up for yourselves treasures upon earth, where moth and rust doth corrupt, and where thieves break through and steal. But lay up for yourselves treasures in heaven, where neither moth nor rust doth corrupt, and where thieves do not break through nor steal. For where your treasure is, there will your heart be also.

—Matthew 6:19–21

CONTENTS

PREFACE

This book originated many years ago when I was beginning my teaching career at the University of Virginia. While reading the *Damascus Covenant,* one of the most important texts found among the Dead Sea Scrolls, I noticed that its language about human sin was strikingly different from that of the Hebrew Bible. Whereas the Bible's most common metaphor for sin is that of a weight an individual must carry, the scroll I was reading viewed sin as a debt that had to be repaid or remitted. As I pondered those lines, I knew this scroll provided a clear window into a major point of transition in biblical thought. This becomes apparent once one notices that the original Greek form of the Our Father reads: "Forgive us our debts, just as we forgive our debtors." In much of the New Testament, as well as in all of rabbinic literature and Aramaic-speaking Christianity, the primary metaphor for sin is that of a debt. The Dead Sea Scrolls, then, mark an important transition point to what became the dominant emphasis of later Judaism and Christianity.

As my research progressed, I realized that the story I wanted to tell was far bigger than I had imagined. For during the era in which sin begins to be thought of as a debt, human virtue assumes the role of a merit or credit. This first becomes evident in the book of Tobit, where we learn that the giving of alms to the poor creates a "treasury in heaven" for the virtuous person. In times of crisis, that treasury can be used to pay down the debt of one's sin. From this notion will emerge the important Jewish concept of the "merits of the fathers," that is, the idea that the virtuous deeds of Israel's righteous ancestors have produced an enormous treasury in heaven that subsequent Israelites can draw upon in times of trouble. A similar construal arose at the same time among Christians. For them, Christ's life of obedience had funded a "treasury of merits" that was later supplemented by the work of the saints. As students of the Protestant Reformation know, this idea would become controversial in the sixteenth century, for it seemed to put a high value on human works at the expense of faith. Sin, I realized, had a history. The developments in the characterization of sin had an immeasurable effect on how biblical ideas were put into practice. If one wants to address and overcome the theological disputes that arose from the Reformation, one must attend carefully to how the correlative concepts of sin and virtue developed over time. Their meaning and role in the religious life are not univocal over the course of the tradition's development.

In this book I propose to do two things. First, I want to trace the origin of sin as a debt back to those places in the Old Testament where it initially appears. Even though I first stumbled across that idea in the Dead Sea Scrolls, subsequent research led me to see that the idea already appears in the latest stratum of the Old Testament. Part of my task is to account for how the metaphor of sin as a debt replaced that of sin as a burden and how that metaphor slowly worked its way into early Jewish and Christian thought. One of the more striking themes of my book is that one cannot fully appreciate how the early church thought about Christ's atoning act apart from a careful study of the (originally) Jewish metaphor that stands behind it.

Second, I want to tell how almsgiving emerged as such an important spiritual practice among Jews and Christians in the early postbiblical (sc., post–Old Testament) period. I will show how almsgiving and the debt metaphor emerged simultaneously and developed into an ongoing back-and-forth relationship. The subtle dialectic that exists between these concepts has escaped previous interpreters.

The book divides neatly into three sections. In Part 1 I introduce the problem of how sin was viewed in the earlier parts of the Bible and how the image of sin as a debt arose. Crucial to this discussion is the notion that sin in biblical thought possesses a certain "thingness." Sin is not just a guilty conscience; it presumes, rather, that some-"thing" is manufactured on the spot and imposed on the sinner. In the early strata of the Bible it is either a burden that is lowered upon the shoulders of the guilty or a stain that discolors one's hands; in the later strata the image of a stain remains, but the image of the burden is replaced by the idea that a debit has been recorded in the heavenly account books.

In Part 2 I trace how that idea of sin as a debt begins and develops in several late biblical compositions. These include the later strata of the book of Leviticus (often known as the Holiness School), Second Isaiah, and the book of Daniel, all of which can be dated from the fifth to the second century BCE. From there I turn to how the idea unfolds in rabbinic literature and in the early church (the second to the sixth century CE). A subplot within my work is the presumption that one can understand what happens at any single point only by knowing what the grander sweep of time will bring (what the French Annales School has called *la longue durée*). Many scholars have failed to appreciate the full significance of the texts examined here because they have been hemmed in by the straightjacket of their individual disciplines. Only by opening up our temporal horizons can we see what a momentous set of changes is taking place.

Part 3 returns to the biblical period and traces how the meritorious act of giving alms to the poor became a means of securing forgiveness from God. The principal verse for this idea is Daniel 4:24 (v. 27 in many English versions), a controversial text during the Reformation. I trace how this idea winds its way through a number of Jewish compositions of the Second Temple period, including the books of Tobit and Ben Sira. I then turn to rabbinic and early Christian sources to follow its development there. I close the book with a brief foray into the Middle Ages. I thought that a fitting place to end because St. Anselm's *Why God Became Man,* the most influential text in the history of Western Christendom on atonement, takes as its point of departure the concept that the sins of humankind are debts that must be repaid.

Forms of the argument presented here have appeared in a variety of lectures and courses I have given around the country and in Israel, as well as during my teaching positions at the University of Virginia, Harvard, and Notre Dame. Several granting agencies have generously supported my research, and to them I am eternally grateful: the Institute for Advanced Studies at the Hebrew University, the American Philosophical Foundation, the Association for Theological Studies / Lilly Faculty Fellowship, and the Center for Jewish Studies at Harvard University.

Among the individuals who have assisted me along the way by reading portions or all of the manuscript are Khaled Anatolios, Josephine Dru, Katherine Elliot, Kevin Haley, Ronnie Goldstein, Bradley Gregory, Jon Levenson, Bruce Marshall, Tzvi Novick, Mark Nussberger, Jonathan Schofer, Baruch Schwartz, and Michael Segal. I also wish to thank the many others who, over the years, have helped me think through various details of my argument.

Quotations from the Old Testament or *Tanakh* are taken from the *Tanakh* (Philadelphia: Jewish Publication Society, 5746/1985). Passages from New Testament and Old Testament books not found in the *Tanakh* (such as Tobit and Ben Sira) are taken from the New Revised Standard Version of the Bible. Some citations from both the Old and New Testaments, however, are my own and are identified as such in the notes. All postbiblical texts are my translations unless otherwise noted. Any emphasis added to biblical texts is my own.

ABBREVIATIONS

FREQUENTLY CITED SOURCES

AB	Anchor Bible
ACW	Ancient Christian Writers
ANF	Ante-Nicene Fathers
BDB	*The Brown, Driver, Briggs Hebrew and English Lexicon*
BGBE	Beitrage zur Geschichte der biblischen Exegese
BT	Babylonian Talmud
CAD	*Chicago Assyrian Dictionary*
CBQMS	Catholic Biblical Quarterly Monograph Series
CD	*Damascus Covenant*
CSCO	Corpus Scriptorum Christianorum Orientalium
Decal.	Philo, *De Decalogue*
DJD	*Discoveries in the Judean Desert*
DSD	*Dead Sea Discoveries*
EtB	*Etudes bibliques*
FAT	Forschungen zum Alten Testament
FC	Fathers of the Church
HALOT	*Hebrew and Aramaic Lexicon of the Old Testament*
HCOT	Historical Commentary on the Old Testament
HSS	Harvard Semitic Studies
HUCA	*Hebrew Union College Annual*
ICC	International Critical Commentary
JAOS	*Journal of the American Oriental Society*
JBL	*Journal of Biblical Literature*
JJS	*Journal of Jewish Studies*
JPS	Jewish Publication Society
JSQ	*Jewish Studies Quarterly*
JSNTSS	Journal for the Study of the New Testament Supplement Series
JSOTSS	Journal for the Study of the Old Testament Supplement Series
JSSSuppl	Journal of Semitic Studies Supplement
JT	Jerusalem Talmud
LCC	Library of Christian Classics
LCL	Loeb Classical Library
NJPS	New Jewish Publication Society Translation (*Tanakh*)
NRSV	New Revised Standard Version
OTL	Old Testament Library

RQ	*Revue de Qumran*
SBLDS	Society of Biblical Literature Dissertation Series
SJSJ	Supplements to the Journal for the Study of Judaism
Spec. Leg.	Philo, *De Specialibus Legibus*
SVT	Supplements to Vetus Testamentum
TDNT	*Theological Dictionary of the New Testament*
TDOT	*Theological Dictionary of the Old Testament*
TS	*Theological Studies*
USQR	*Union Seminary Quarterly Review*
ZAW	*Zeitschrift fur die alttestamentliche Wissenschaft*

OLD TESTAMENT

I Chron	I Chronicles
II Chron	II Chronicles
Dan	Daniel
Deut	Deuteronomy
Exod	Exodus
Ezek	Ezekiel
Gen	Genesis
Isa	Isaiah
Jer	Jeremiah
Josh	Joshua
Jud	Judges
Lam	Lamentations
Lev	Leviticus
Macc	Maccabees
Num	Numbers
Prov	Proverbs
Ps	Psalms
Sam	Samuel
Sir	Ben Sira (or Sirach; Ecclesiasticus in some Bibles)

NEW TESTAMENT

Col	Colossians
I Cor	I Corinthians
Matt	Matthew
Rom	Romans
I Thess	I Thessalonians
I Tim	I Timothy

RABBINIC WRITINGS

B. Bathra	*Baba Bathra*

Exod Rab	*Exodus Rabbah*
Gen Rab	*Genesis Rabbah*
Ket	*Ketubbot*
Lev Rab	*Leviticus Rabbah*
m.	*Mishna*
Qid	*Qiddushin*
San	*Sanhedrin*
t.	*Tosephta*
Yeb	*Yebamot*

part one:

introducing the problem

1

what is a sin?

It is not easy to define a sin. If we pay attention to how people talk, we notice that metaphors are impossible to avoid. For example, slavery in the United States is said to have left a "stain" upon our hands that still awaits "cleansing." To speak in this fashion is to assume that sin is much more than a violation of a moral norm and that the effects of sin are more extensive than a guilty conscience. A verbal declaration of regret may be fine, but the way a culture grapples with the enduring legacy of sin is another matter. A wrongful deed creates in its wake some sort of "thing" that has to be removed.

It is not always easy to escape sin. The terrible legacy of slavery in the nineteenth century is one example of how the effects of sin can linger long after the perpetrators have left the scene. One could point to many other examples. Take, for instance, the division of the Middle East after the close of the First World War. Before 1917 the entire Arab world from Egypt to Iraq was ruled by a single power, the Ottoman empire. Because the Ottomans made the fateful decision to support the Germans in the First World War, they also suffered the consequences of the German defeat. After 1917 the Middle East was under the authority of the French and the British, who proceeded to divide the land into the countries that we recognize today: Lebanon, Syria, Jordan, Iraq, and so forth. As we have come to realize at the dawn of the twenty-first century, these borders did not always respect the ways discrete peoples were located. Much of the turmoil of the past generation or so has come from an attempt to settle some of these disputes from within. But now, nearly a hundred years after the revision of these territories, there is no going back on the fateful decisions of the French and the

British in the early twentieth century. The sins of the fathers, the Bible records, are visited upon the sons and grandsons up to the fourth generation (Exod 20:5). Like slavery, these unfortunate actions have left an enduring legacy. It is no longer simply a matter of identifying the guilty and seeking a confession. Some "thing" will still be left, even after the wrongdoers have been singled out. Even after a war of emancipation and much corrective legislation, the hands of the American people retain their stain.

It would not be inaccurate to say that committing a serious sin triggers the creation of some sort of thing. In the case under consideration, a stain is spontaneously generated once the fateful act has been accomplished. Once this stain has appeared, it cannot be simply brushed aside. Even contemporary secular speech retains a sense of this when it refers to a guilty person bearing the consequences of an act on his or her shoulders. When the psalmist prays that God will "turn his face" from what he has done, there is a seriousness about his speech. If God "visits his sin," the consequences will be grave. This is because sin has created some thing that God's eyes can truly see. That is why God must reassure the penitent whose sin has been forgiven that the sin has been removed "as far as east is from west." It takes a distance such as this to put the matter out of God's purview.

Sin is not just a thing, however, but a particular kind of thing. When one sins, something concrete happens: one's hands may become stained, one's back may become burdened, or one may fall into debt. And the verbal expressions that render the idea of forgiveness follow suit: stained hands are *cleansed,* burdens are *lifted,* and debts are either *paid off* or *remitted.* It is as though a stain, weight, or bond of indebtedness is created ex nihilo when one offends against God. And that thing that sin has created will continue to haunt the offenders until it has been engaged and dealt with.

METAPHORS MATTER

It is impossible to understand sin and forgiveness in the Bible without attending carefully to the metaphors in which these concepts are embedded. They are an essential feature of biblical thought and embody its intricacies. Often, the emotional, psychological, and theological complexities have been lost in translations that collapse this wide variety of colorful idioms into a single, more monotone rendering. In English, sin has become tethered thus to the word *forgive.* The word *forgiveness,* however, does not explicitly suggest the deeper connotations that the equivalent biblical words possess. Its ubiquitous rendering also fails to reveal the major dialectal shifts that occurred in biblical language over time.

As philosophers of language have come to remind us, metaphors are intrinsic to everyday speech, and as such they structure the way we think, perceive, and act in the world. In their important and oft-cited study of metaphor, George Lakoff and Mark Johnson begin with a consideration of how speakers of English describe the terms of an argument.[1] Consider these sentences:

Your claims are *indefensible.*
He *attacked every weak point* in my argument.
His criticisms were right *on target.*
I *demolished* his argument.
I've never *won* an argument with him.
You disagree? Okay, *shoot!*
If you use that *strategy,* he'll *wipe you out.*
He *shot down* all of my arguments.

Lakoff and Johnson argue that these colorful phrases are not mere verbal filigree. We could not strip away such metaphors from ordinary speech and thereby reveal what Plato would have called the "ideal form" of an argument. In fact, we would do better to proceed from the exact opposite position. It is the details of everyday language that lay bare what an argument is.

In short, the way we conduct arguments is influenced by the way we conceive and talk about them. "Imagine a culture where an argument is viewed as a dance," Lakoff and Johnson propose; "the participants are seen as performers, and the goal is to perform in a balanced and aesthetically pleasing way. In such a culture, people would view arguments differently, experience them differently, carry them out differently, and talk about them differently."[2] Indeed, Lakoff and Johnson conclude that we would probably have a hard time understanding what these individuals were doing. So embedded is our understanding of argument in idioms of attack and aggression that we would find it difficult to label such activity "arguing."

In his seminal work *The Symbolism of Evil,* Paul Ricoeur takes this point one step further.[3] In his view, philosophers have no direct and unmediated access to the semantic content of ideas such as fault, sin, error, and their consequent rectification (that is, what we call "forgiveness"). All that stands at our disposal are metaphors that serve as building blocks for larger narrative complexes. To understand what a sin is, one must begin with the terminology deployed by a particular writer. Once one grasps the concrete nature of these metaphors, one can see how they are deployed in narratives. It is from this process that Ricoeur coined his oft-cited aphorism "the symbol gives rise to thought." By this he meant that through the irreducible meta-phoric content of human language, the philosopher is given the building blocks through which a deeper understanding of the human condition can be ascertained. Indeed the point should probably be expressed more em-phatically: apart from attention to the concrete particularity of human lan-guage there is no access to the categories of sin and forgiveness.

It is impossible to understand forgiveness in the Bible without attend-ing to these metaphors. As Ricoeur has taught us, they are not merely liter-ary ornaments; they are an essential feature of biblical teaching. Many read-ers miss the whole purpose of a narrative because they are deaf to the metaphors that attend the biblical text. Translations are a major stumbling block because they often collapse the wide variety of colorful idioms into a single, plain-vanilla rendering: "to forgive a sin." One of the principal things lost is the way the concept of sin and forgiveness changes over time. I argue that the term *sin* does not have the same meaning in the book of Genesis as it does in the book of Daniel or the Gospel of Matthew. There is a story to be told about how the idea of sin evolves over time and how the manner of forgiving sin adjusts to fit the new circumstances.

SIN HAS A HISTORY

Comparing the Day of Atonement in the book of Leviticus with the Our Fa-ther in the Gospel of Matthew illustrates this metaphorical shift. Scholars differ as to the date of Leviticus. Some believe the text is as early as the monarchical period (ca. 1000–587 BCE); others place it in the exilic period (ca. 550–400 BCE). In any event, it is safe to say that at least half a millen-nium separates these two texts. But we are speaking not only of a large tem-poral gap but of a large linguistic one as well. The dialect of the Judean coun-tryside had changed considerably over this period, and, as a result, so had the definition of what sort of "thingness" adhered to human sin. On the Day of Atonement, the rite for the removal of the sins of the Israelites involved a scapegoat. (Actually it was not a scapegoat at all but, rather, some sort of pack animal.) According to the Bible, the high priest puts both hands on the goat's head, confesses the sins of Israel over it, and then sends the animal into the wilderness, never to return (Lev 16:21–22). The animal has thus as-sumed the *weight* of Israel's sins and carries them to the heart of the desert —an area that was thought to be beyond the reach of God—where the sins will disappear forever.[4] God will not be able to "view" them there. It is not enough for Israel to fast and repent; the physical material of the sin that had rested on the shoulder of every Israelite must be carted away into oblivion.

Jesus, on the other hand, speaks in a completely different idiom. In the Gospel of Matthew, he teaches his disciples to pray "Forgive us our *debts* just as we forgive our debtors." And elsewhere in the Gospel, Jesus provides a parable about a king who wished to settle his accounts (Matt 18:23–34), which serves as a commentary on that particular sentence of the Our Father. All one has to do is think of the monetary debts owed the king figuratively, as sins. The parable begins with the king closing the books on one servant's account, which is in arrears by some ten thousand talents. Because the slave does not have the means to repay this sum, the king gives orders that he, his wife, and his children, along with everything he owns, be sold to raise currency to pay the debt. Only when the slave gets on his knees and begs the king to show mercy does he relent and remit the enormous debt. If a person was not able to cover his debts, however, he was sold as a debt-slave, and the punishment he underwent constituted his payment on the debt. Jesus therefore taught his disciples to pray "Forgive us our debts" so that they might avoid a fate as a debt-slave. But apart from an act of divine mercy, one will have to pay for a misdeed with a form of currency generated by physical punishment.

Debt, of course, was not a specifically Christian innovation. The Jesus we read about in the Synoptic Gospels is representative of the type of thought current among Jews of his day. Scholars have long noted that his affinity for describing sin as a debt derives from the contemporary Hebrew and Aramaic idiom of that time. In first-century Palestine, the word used in commercial contexts to identify debt became in religious contexts the most common word for sin. By contrast, one will rarely find, either in the New Testament or in contemporary Jewish texts, any free usage of the earlier metaphor of sin as a weight. (Of course, that idea will persist in the form of textual citation and allusion, but by "free usage" I mean contemporary speech that is unbound by the legacy of the past. For example, we moderns almost never use archaic constructions such as "thou art" in our everyday speech, yet they are retained in common prayers or hymns such as "How Great Thou Art.")

In studying how debt came to replace the notion of weight with regard to sin, however, we see the fundamental changes in thinking that occurred during the era of Persian rule (538–333 BCE), a time when the Middle East and the eastern Mediterranean were being massively reshaped. Linguistically, these changes were tied to the rise in stature and influence of the Aramaic language. During the Persian period, Aramaic was adopted as the official language of the empire; evidence of its influence can be found from

Upper Egypt to Afghanistan, an enormous geographical reach even by modern standards. Because Jews during the exile and afterward were bilingual in Hebrew and Aramaic, the vocabulary of Aramaic had a marked influence on the development of Hebrew. One of the linguistic items that came on board was the construal of sin as a debt, a metaphor implied in the Aramaic tongue, but not in the Hebrew.

At the same time that the Israelites' language was being reshaped, they were also experiencing exile and enslavement. In biblical texts we see the development of a narrative to explain their misfortune. Second Isaiah imagined that Israel was sold into slavery in Babylon after the destruction of the First Temple in 587 BCE owing to her great sinfulness. Like the servant in the parable from Matthew, the punishment was severe: decades of penal service in the heart of Babylon. There the physical punishment of exile served as the means by which Israel raised "hard currency" to pay off the debt she owed. When her suffering had reached this goal, Isaiah was able to proclaim: "Comfort, comfort my people, says your God. Speak tenderly to Jerusalem, and cry to her that her penal service is ended, that her sin has been paid off, that she has received from the LORD's hand double for all her sins" (Isa 40:1–2).

Physical punishments, therefore, came to be thought of as a means of paying for one's crime. This idea comes directly from the experience of debt-slavery, which had a long legal precedent throughout the ancient Near East. In this tradition, anyone unable to repay a loan could work as a debt-slave for the creditor until the loan was paid off. Similarly, if a sinner committed a serious error and so incurred a "great debt," the penalty imposed upon him was thought to "raise currency" in order to pay down what was owed. Although the punishments remained physical, the metaphors for sin became distinctly economic, having been influenced by the linguistic, legal, and historical specificities of that era. Identifying the subtleties of this metamorphosis explains why, by the Middle Ages, theologians were able to provide a catalog of "prices" (i.e., various penances) for people's misdeeds.

Many would see that medieval practice as distinctly unbiblical. There is some truth to this, for nowhere in the Bible do we find such a catalog. But as we shall see, at the end of the Hebrew Bible period, the penalty for sins was thought of in terms of prices. One thinks, for example, of Paul's famous dictum "the wages of sin is death" (Rom 6:23). In addition, rabbinic texts that date to a period just after Jesus provide a list of "costs" for various sins. As Baruch Schwartz has noted in rabbinic texts, "The sinner is called ḥayyāb, or 'obligated,' because he must repay his debt [ḥôb]. The one who owes [ḥayyāb] a sin-offering or a reparation offering must pay with the respective form of sacrifice; the one who owes a beating must pay with a lashing of his body; the one who owes death must pay with his life; and the one who owes the penalty of extirpation *[kārēt]* must pay after his death."[5]

Between the early biblical eras and the Middle Ages, however, is the life and death of Jesus of Nazareth. The narrative of his life and, in particular, his death provides a key link in the metamorphosis I am describing. His Crucifixion became, in some traditions, the ultimate act of atonement; through his suffering, Christ was paying off the enormous debts incurred through human sinfulness. For those who saw punishment as a means of raising currency to pay down a debt, it was important to magnify the sufferings of Christ. Late medieval portraits of Jesus as a tortured figure on the cross, such as the Isenheim altarpiece, are a good witness to this.

On the earliest Byzantine crosses we possess, however, Christ is not portrayed as suffering. In this book, I shall describe the ways Syriac speaking-Christians (Syriac is the Christian dialect of Aramaic, the mother tongue of Jesus) thought about the saving work of Christ, presenting two competing theories of how Christ atoned for sin and tracing the effect they had on Latin-speaking Christianity in the West.

ALMSGIVING FUNDS A TREASURY IN HEAVEN

One of the most striking developments in biblical religion comes in the wake of this shift in metaphors. Once it becomes a commonplace to think of sin as debt, the idea that virtuous activity generates a credit appears. The very idiom of rabbinic Hebrew supports this, because the antonym for the term *ḥôb* (debt) is *zekût* (credit). No such antinomy existed in the First Temple period—the idiom of "bearing the weight of one's sin" did not have a natural opposite. Nowhere in the Bible do we find virtuous individuals of superhuman moral strength who could carry the sins of others on their backs. But in Second Temple Jewish texts, it becomes common to speak of persons whose moral virtuosity was so remarkable that they were able to deposit the proceeds of their good deeds in a heavenly bank.

This change was revolutionary. For the first time, Jewish thinkers had a vocabulary that could describe moral virtues in a meritorious way. Human beings, by their good works, could store up credit that could preserve them in times of trouble. One of the earliest texts to do this comes from the book of Tobit (probably written between the third and second centuries BCE). In this work Tobit advises his son to continue his practice of generosity to the poor, for one who gives alms on a regular basis "will be laying up a good treasure for [oneself] against the day of necessity" (4:9).

The development of a doctrine of merit leads to an increased role for the agency of human beings in counteracting the ravages of sin. Rabbinic texts illustrate this momentous change with considerable frequency. In Exodus 32, after Moses has heard God say that he is going to destroy all of Israel because of her veneration of the golden calf, he implores him to rethink this verdict. He asks God to "remember Abraham, Isaac, and Israel, how You swore to them by Your Self and said, 'I will make your offspring as numerous as the stars of heaven.'" For the biblical writer, the force of Moses' argument was clear; we could paraphrase the logic of his prayer as follows: remember what you promised our ancestors Abraham, Isaac, and Israel. Moses feared that God had forgotten what he had once affirmed. But in rabbinic Judaism, when virtuous activity was thought of as generating credits, the text was heard differently. For the Rabbis, the issue was not reminding God of what he had once said to the patriarchs; rather, Moses asks God to remember *what* these men had done.[6] By this was meant the great acts of piety they had once accomplished that generated a vast surplus of credit in heaven, credit that was more than sufficient to counterbalance the debt Israel now owed.

Perhaps the most important biblical example of this is found in Daniel 4:24 (4:27 in the Hebrew), in which Daniel tells Nebuchadnezzar, the Babylonian king who destroyed the city of Jerusalem, that he can redeem himself by giving alms. The key term here is *redeem,* the Aramaic original that means "to buy oneself out of slavery." And that is how this king is imagined —his horrible sins having turned him into a lowly debt-slave in the eyes of God. One way out of debt is physical punishment, but Daniel informs us that there is a second option: giving away one's money to the poor.

At this point we stand at the headwaters of one of the most important developments of early Judaism. In Judaism, almsgiving was frequently named *the* commandment *(ha-mitsvah)* or the commandment that was on par with all others. The early church, which inherited this high valuation of alms from the Jews, became famous throughout the Roman world for its generosity toward the poor. The pagan emperor Julian (fourth century CE) noticed how influential this form of generosity toward the poor was. In response to this he wrote to a pagan priest named Arsacius, who served in the province of Galatia. He began his letter by asking Arsacius to note how "benevolence toward strangers" had advanced the cause of the Christian movement. "I believe," Julian wrote, "that we ought really and truly to practice every one of these virtues. And it is not enough for you alone to practice them, but so must all the priests in Galatia, without exception." This exhortation to do as the Christians do was no trivial matter for Julian; harsh measures awaited those who did not prove attentive to Julian's new demands. "Either shame or persuade them into righteousness," Julian commanded, "or else remove them from their priestly office."[7]

Julian was also willing to be specific: he gave instructions to establish hostels in every city and provided the necessary funding from the imperial coffers: "I have given directions that 30,000 pecks of corn shall be assigned every year for the whole of Galatia, and 60,000 pints of wine. I order that one-fifth of this be used for the poor who serve the priests, and the remainder be distributed by us to strangers and beggars." Why was he so committed to this endeavor? Julian was quick to explain: "For it is disgraceful that, when no Jew ever has to beg, and the impious Galileans [his term for Christians] support not only their own poor but ours as well, all men see that our people lack aid from us."

It may surprise the contemporary reader that the emperor would take such extreme measures on behalf of the poor. Was Roman society completely deaf to the care of the less fortunate? Not at all. This emperor's problem was that in Greco-Roman culture the task of feeding the poor fell upon the state. Only in Judaism and Christianity was the consideration of the poor a *religious* obligation. As Rodney Stark has noted, Julian's attempts to transform the pagan temples into distribution centers was doomed to fail. "But for all that [Julian] urged pagan priests to match these Christian practices, there was little or no response because *there were no doctrinal bases or traditional practices* for them to build upon. It was not that Romans knew nothing of charity, but that it was not based on service to the gods. Pagan gods did not punish ethical violations because they imposed no ethical demands—humans offended the gods only through neglect or by violation of ritual standards."[8] Contrary to Roman religion, service to the poor became an indelible marker of one's spiritual status within Judaism and Christianity. As Jesus himself had said, the separation of the sheep from the goats at the end of time would be determined by service to those in need. For at the last judgment God will say to those who will be stationed at his right: "Come, you that are blessed by my Father, inherit the kingdom prepared for you from the foundation of the world; for I was hungry and you gave me food, I was thirsty and you gave me something to drink, I was a stranger and you welcomed me, I was naked and you gave me clothing, I was sick and you took care of me, I was in prison and you visited me" (Matt 25:34–36). Christian preachers had a decided advantage over their pagan counterparts in this regard, for they could preach that those who lacked charity stood in danger of eternal damnation. Pagan religion, on the other hand, did not provide the grounding for such ideas to take root. Because the seeds of reform that Julian tried to sow fell on shallow soil, they had almost no chance of coming to full bloom.[9]

One reason frequently given for the importance of giving alms in Second Temple Judaism was that it funded a treasury in heaven. This idea, first attested in the book of Tobit, became an important theme in the Gospels. According to this teaching, the money that one gives away was thought to be transferred to "a bank account" in heaven. The hand of the poor man who begged for alms became a replacement for the altar, in that it provided an immediate conduit of goods from earth to heaven. The idea of a heavenly treasury casts some unexpected light on the advice that Daniel had given king Nebuchadnezzar. As I have noted, the logic of Daniel was straightforward. He told the king that his debt here on earth was substantial, perhaps beyond repayment by normal means. His only hope was to start making contributions to his creditor to bring this terrible financial burden under control. But how could one convey money to God? The book of Tobit provides the answer: by funding a treasury in heaven.

Part of the story I tell is how the heavenly economy works in early Judaism and Christianity. One might assume that one's sins and deeds of virtue were simply a set of entries on a ledger sheet. God is nothing more than a meticulous accountant whose sole task is to keep the heavenly books in balance. Nothing is further from the truth. Acts of human generosity funded a treasury that did not play by the rules of a zero-sum economy. Giving alms was like being an initial investor in a company that would eventually rise to the top of the market. The returns one could expect from such an investment would be beyond calculation. God has "gamed" the system to the advantage of the faithful.

The importance of human agency for the forgiveness of sins became paradigmatic in the early church. As many writers noted, at baptism the debts of newly minted converts were wiped clean. Their "bonds of indebtedness," to quote Colossians 2:14, had been erased by the cross of Christ. But how was one to benefit from this act? Was there a way one could put faith into action? The church had one consistent answer to these questions: the giving of alms. In sixteenth-century Spain, when the state began to assume the task of caring for the poor, many laypeople were alarmed. How will we be saved, they asked, if we no longer need to give alms?[10] Aside from baptism, there was one sure course for removing ongoing sins: charity toward the poor.

During the Reformation, this sort of thinking came under severe attack, and the importance of alms as a means of assuring the forgiveness of sins fell out of Protestantism altogether.[11] The principal worry of the various Reformers was that almsgiving was a human work and compromised the notion that salvation was due to grace alone (*sola gratia*). Yet a careful reading of early Christian sources reveals that the problem of human agency in the giving of alms is not so easily parsed.

The definition of a sin has proved far more complicated than one might have imagined. As soon as we begin to speak about the topic we find ourselves searching for metaphors that will capture the type of thing we are trying to describe. Sins are like stains that require cleansing, burdens that must be removed, or debts that have to be repaid. All of these metaphors can be found in the Bible. But it was not the case that biblical authors had all these options before them and freely chose among them as the occasion might merit. Quite the opposite was true. During the early periods one particular metaphor dominated, that of sin as a weight. But at the beginning of the Second Temple period a new metaphor emerged that would take center stage, that of sin as a debt. Sin, I wish to claim, does have a history. Near the end of the biblical period, writers are talking about sin in a strikingly fresh manner.

As Lakoff and Johnson could have predicted, the arrival of this metaphor opened up a new world, for metaphors are far more than mere words. How we talk about sin, philosophers would argue, influences what we will *do* about it. One of the most significant changes was the evolution of almsgiving as a fundamental pillar of biblical faith. This new development should not surprise, for as soon as sins are thought of as debits one begins to think of virtuous acts as credits. If God keeps a record of what one owes, then there must be a corresponding ledger sheet that documents what one owns. Because the giving of alms was thought to fund a treasury in heaven, it was altogether natural to presume that these monies might be able to pay down the debts occasioned by sin. In the first few centuries of the Common Era, Jews and Christians were so committed to assisting the poor by giving alms that even their harshest critics within Greco-Roman paganism had to acknowledge the effects.

I am not saying, however, that assistance to the poor was insignificant in earlier biblical periods. Concern for the poor can be found at every level of the biblical tradition. But with the arrival of this new way of correlating sin (as debt) and virtue (as credit), the long-revered practice of providing for the poor assumed an even higher prestige. What had once been simply a single command among others rose to being a command that epitomized one's entire relationship toward God. As the Rabbis would later put the matter: "The giving of alms and works of charity are equal in value to all of the commandments in the Torah."[12]

But the evolution of this new metaphor has also been the source of considerable theological controversy. Many have recoiled from what they perceive to be the overly mechanistic quality of this imagery. A world of debits and credits seems to portend a system of rigid obligation in which there is no room for the mercy of God to shine through. Others have been concerned that focusing on the value of human merits has turned salvation into a human work rather than a gift graciously bestowed by God. The issues at stake are profound and lie at the heart of the Protestant Reformation. For this reason the rhetoric can sometimes get heated. Yet a careful consideration of how Jewish and Christian thinkers deployed these metaphors in their theological writings should dispense with most of these controversies.

2

a burden to be borne

[On the Day of Atonement] the goat shall carry all of Israel's iniquities to an inaccessible region; and the goat shall be set free in the wilderness.

—Leviticus 16:22

Setting the stage for the texts I discuss requires a chronological framework. The majority of events recorded in the Old Testament take place within what is known as the First Temple period, which refers to the era in which the temple erected by King Solomon stood in Jerusalem. The temple was built in the mid-tenth century BCE and was destroyed by King Nebuchadnezzar and his Babylonian armies in 587 BCE. That national tragedy led to a period known as the exile, during which many of Israel's leaders were carried off to Babylon and attempted to refashion Jewish life while bereft of a liturgical center and any form of political sovereignty. About fifty years later, the Babylonian empire succumbed to Persian forces, and a new age dawned in the ancient Near East. The Persians were benevolent conquerors and allowed those who had been exiled to Babylon to return to their native countries. Under the leadership of Zerubbabel and with the active support of the prophets Haggai and Zechariah, the Israelites who had returned from Babylon began to rebuild the temple. In 520 BCE the foundations were laid, and in 515 BCE the new building was formally rededicated. This initiated an era known as the Second Temple period, which lasted until 70 CE, when the Romans invaded the land of Israel and destroyed the temple for the last and final time.

For our purposes it is crucial to note that the Hebrew language changed dramatically from the First to the Second Temple period. Any student of

Hebrew studies who began with the classical dialect of the Old Testament knows that biblical language is quite different from that found in Ben Sira, the Dead Sea Scrolls, and the rabbinic corpus. Both the syntax and the vocabulary have undergone a considerable transformation. One reason for that shift was the growing importance of Aramaic in the Second Temple period. Aramaic became such a significant linguistic force because the Persians had adopted it as the lingua franca of their burgeoning empire.

By the time of Jesus, many Jews would have spoken both Hebrew and Aramaic. Because the two tongues are closely related, there was a strong tendency for each to influence the other. It is often difficult for linguists to know whether the meaning of a rabbinic Hebrew word is native to Hebrew itself or the result of a borrowing from Aramaic. But let me postpone for a moment the importance of Aramaic influence and return to the idiom of classical biblical Hebrew.

SIN AS A WEIGHT

In the Hebrew Bible, there are numerous metaphors that describe the nature of sin. Among the most common are those of sin as a stain from which one must be purified: "*wash me [kibbēs]* thoroughly of my iniquity *[ăwōn]* and purify me from my sin" (Ps 51:4); and of sin as a weight that must be borne: "the goat shall bear away *[nāśāʾ]* all the iniquities *[ʿăwōn]* to an inaccessible region" (Lev 16:22). In both texts the crucial determinant of the metaphorical unit is not the noun for sin (in both cases, *ʿăwōn*) but the verb *(kibbēs,* "wash away," and *nāśāʾ,* "carry away"). Indeed, of the many biblical metaphors, the concept of sin as a burden is by far the most productive one in the Hebrew Bible. The following table illustrates the various verbal roots that are used in conjunction with the most common noun for sin, *ʿăwōn:*

Hebrew Verb	Translation	Number of Occurrences
nāśāʾ	"to bear (or bear away) a sin"	108
sālaḥ	"to forgive a sin" (etymology unknown)	17
kippēr	"to wipe away a sin"	6

Other terms with one or two occurrences include: *heʿĕbîr,* "to make a sin pass away"; *kissâh,* "to cover over a sin"; *kābaš,* "to trample down, destroy a sin"; *māḥâh,* "to wipe away a sin"; *kibbēs,* "to wash away sin"; and *ṭihhēr,* "to purify [someone] from sin."

What is most striking is the frequency of the idiom "to bear [the weight of] a sin" within the Hebrew Bible; it predominates over its nearest competitor by more than six to one. For Hebrew speakers in the First Temple period, therefore, the most common means of talking about human sin was to compare it to weight.

When I mention this fact to both laypersons and scholars, I am often greeted with surprise. Even the most dedicated readers of the Bible would not guess this to be the case, because no translation of the Bible renders the phrase *nāśāʾ ʿăwōn* literally as "to carry away (the weight of) a sin." This is in contrast to other idioms in the Bible, where literal translation is usually the norm—one regularly reads of sins being "washed away" or "covered over," to name just two examples. Instead of bringing out the underlying metaphor, nearly every translation of the Bible renders *nāśāʾ ʿăwōn* rather colorlessly as "to forgive a sin."

Certainly one explanation for the nonliteral translation of the phrase is that the idiom *nāśāʾ ʿăwōn* is more difficult than it might appear at first glance. It has proven a challenge for both lexicographers and commentators because it has two polar opposite meanings. In contexts of judgment it means "to be culpable," or even "to be punished," whereas in contexts of mercy it is best translated "to forgive."

To get a proper purchase on the matter, let us look at some texts that illustrate the problem. The first two concern the use of the idiom to mark culpability, the last two, forgiveness.[1]

1   When [a person] has heard a public imprecation and . . . does not give information, *he shall be subject to punishment [nāśāʾ + ʿăwōn].* (Lev 5:1)
2   Anyone who blasphemes his God *shall bear his guilt [nāśāʾ + heṭʾ].* (Lev 24:15)

For the meaning "to forgive a sin," compare the following:

3   So you shall say to Joseph, "*Forgive,* I urge you, *the offense [nāśāʾ + pešaʿ]* and the guilt of your brothers who treated you so harshly." (Gen 50:17)
4   *Forgive my offense [nāśāʾ + ḥaṭṭāʾt]* just this once, and plead with the LORD your God that He but remove this death from me. (Exod 10:17)

ONE EXPRESSION, TWO INCOMPATIBLE MEANINGS

How should we understand the exactly opposite meanings that are expressed by the single Hebrew expression *nāśāʾ + ʿăwōn, heṭʾ/ ḥaṭṭāʾt,* or *pešaʿ*? One answer has been an appeal to the peculiar *mentalité* of Israelite culture, a culture that some would argue did not always distinguish between an action and its consequences. In this sort of holistic thinking, terms for sin can be rendered two ways, depending on the context: as a simple act of wrongdoing or "sin" (nos. 3 and 4) or its consequential result, "punishment" (nos. 1 and 2).

In a brilliant article, Baruch Schwartz noted some problems with such a perspective.[2] First, even though the development of secondary meanings is well documented with respect to dozens of cultic terms, the production of two idioms that stand as complete opposites is peculiar in the extreme and has no adequate parallel. Second, the manner in which the two extended meanings of the idiom *nāśāʾ ʿăwōn* develop is equally perplexing. One must presume that *both* the verb *nāśāʾ* and the noun *ʿăwōn* develop two distinct meanings, one literal and the other metaphoric.

Term	Primary meaning	Secondary meaning
nāśāʾ	to bear, carry	to forgive
ʿăwōn	sin	punishment

In a context of mercy (nos. 3 and 4), *nāśāʾ* takes on the extended meaning of "forgive," whereas *ʿăwōn* retains its primary meaning of "sin." But in the context of punishment (nos. 1 and 2) the verb retains its original meaning "to bear, carry," whereas the noun *ʿăwōn* assumes its secondary meaning of "punishment."[3] The mixture of primary and secondary meanings in each idiom appears arbitrary. It is an odd way to explain the growth of an idiom.

Schwartz's solution to these inconcinnities is as brilliant as it is ordinary. In his opinion everything depends on attention to how the verb *nāśāʾ* functions in conventional discourse. A casual inspection of a Hebrew lexicon shows that the verb can mean both [A] "to carry [a burden]" and [B] "to remove [a burden]."

For the former meaning [A], let us consider Numbers 11:11–14, wherein the Israelites begin to moan bitterly about their status as travelers in the desert. This causes the LORD to grow angry, which, in turn, prompts Moses to plead: "Why have you dealt ill with Your servant, and have I not enjoyed Your favor, that You have laid the *burden [maśśāʾ*, a noun that derives from *nāśāʾ]* of all this people upon me? Did I conceive all this people, did I give birth to them, that You should say to me, 'Carry them *[nāśāʾ]* in your bosom as a nurse carries an infant to the land that You have promised on oath to their fathers'? . . . I cannot *carry [nāśāʾ]* all this people by myself, for they are *too heavy* for me." Here, the "burden" that Moses must labor under is the responsibility of caring for the people.[4] Not inappropriately, the obligation or "burden" *(maśśā ʾ)* Moses must bear is compared to that of a nurse who must carry a child from one location to another.

For the latter meaning [B] of *nāśā ʾ*, as in "to remove a burden," let us begin with Numbers 16:15. In this text Moses has been accused of improperly discharging his responsibility to lead the people of Israel. Having become incensed over this false charge, he declares his righteousness by confessing: "I have not *taken* from them *[nāśā ʾti]* a single ass."[5] In I Samuel 17:34–35 David describes his actions as a responsible shepherd. He notes that whenever "a lion or bear [would come] and *[carry] off [nāśā ʾ]* an animal from the flock, [he] would go after it and fight it and rescue it from its mouth." In each of these texts the verb *nāśā ʾ* means to take something *away* from someone else.

In both cases, however, we are speaking about a single activity: someone is assuming a burden. In the former context, the emphasis is put on the act of *carrying* the burden so assumed, whereas in the latter the emphasis is on the act of *assuming* a burden that had not been previously in one's possession. In short, there is nothing magical or mysterious about the two meanings. Everything depends on context. If the subject has assumed a burden that was not in the possession of someone else, then one should translate *nāśā ʾ* as "to carry," just as we saw in Numbers 11:14—"I cannot *carry* all this people by myself." On the other hand, should the subject take the object from someone else, then the proper translation will be "to take from," or "carry away" as in Moses' confession: "I have not *taken* from them *[nāśā ʾti]* a single ass," or David's observation that a lion would "*carry off* an animal from the flock."

These two contrasting usages of the verb *nāśā ʾ* are key to understanding the metaphoric usage of *nāśā ʾ ʿăwōn*. Recall that sins in the Bible have a certain "thing"-like quality. God can see them, and should he be inclined to mercy, he can either wash them away, cover them over, or crush them under foot. Whichever metaphor we encounter, we must presume that the offending item has been, as it were, manufactured ex nihilo upon completion of the forbidden act. In the case of *nāśā ʾ ʿăwōn* it is as though a weight was placed on the shoulders of the sinner at the moment of the interdicted act. Even in our own day we are prone to characterize the cares of the world or the guilt of sin as pressing down on one's shoulders. One frequently sees this illustrated by a figure walking around hunched over. The metaphoric weight with which the person is burdened is more than mere metaphor; it has all the appearances of being something real.

So let us return to the biblical usages of this idiom when it refers to human sin. In contexts where the emphasis is on culpability, nāśā' 'āwōn should be translated "to bear the burden of one's sin." The sinner is depicted as a person who bears the full weight of the burden created by his offense; so, for example, "he who blasphemes God shall bear the weight of his sin" (Lev 24:15). But should the context be that of a guilty person begging for forgiveness, the verb marks the act of removing the burden from his or her shoulders. When Pharaoh sees that he has offended Moses by not heeding his cry to let the Israelite people go free, he declares, "Bear away the burden of my offense" (Exod 10:17). In this instance, we must assume that when Pharaoh flouted Moses' request to allow all the Israelites, both young and old, to depart from Egypt to worship the LORD (Exod 10:7–11), a weight was created and imposed on his shoulders. Pharaoh becomes, in some sense, the "servant" of Moses insofar as he bears a load that only his "master" Moses can release. Moses demonstrates the iniquity of Pharaoh's act by sending a swarm of locusts to consume the vegetation of Egypt. Pharaoh quickly summons Moses and confesses, "I have sinned against the LORD your God and you" and then exhorts Moses "to bear away" the burden of his offense and pleads with the LORD to remove the plague of the locusts as well.

In short, there is no need to invoke some mysterious notion of holistic thinking to make sense of this curious Hebrew idiom. The double meaning found in its extended metaphoric usage is not different from the double meaning found in more mundane contexts. With these insights in mind, it is worth returning to the two sets of texts I introduced earlier, but now translating them more literally in terms of the rich metaphoric context they evoke. By attending to the literal sense of the metaphor it will no longer seem peculiar that a single phrase, nāśā' 'āwōn, can mean both the state of culpability ("to bear [the weight of] a sin") and its removal ("to bear *away* [the weight of] a sin").

The idiom nāśā' 'āwōn in the sense of "to bear the weight of one's own sin":

1 When [a person] has heard a public imprecation and . . . he does not give information, *he shall bear the weight of his sin.* (Lev 5:1)
2 Anyone who blasphemes his God *shall bear the weight of his sin.* (Lev 24:15)

The idiom meaning "to remove the weight of sin from someone else's shoulders":

3 So you shall say to Joseph, "*Bear away,* I urge you, *the burden of the sin of your brothers who treated you so harshly.*" (Gen 50:17)

4 *Bear away the burden of my offense* just this once, and plead with the LORD your God that He but remove this death from me. (Exod 10:17)

NARRATIVES ABOUT SIN AS A BURDEN

Thus far I have considered the semantic puzzle that underlies the Hebrew idiom *nāśā' 'āwōn*. But it is not sufficient merely to see how the phrase developed semantically. Lakoff and Johnson as well as Ricoeur, showed us that metaphor is the crucial variable in understanding how a culture thinks about sin and forgiveness. We can see this by attending to the larger literary settings in which the metaphor is deployed.

The prophet Isaiah, who lived in the eighth century BCE, uses the idiom twice to depict the nature of Israel's sin. The first instance appears in the opening verses of the book:

> *Hear, O heavens and give ear,*
> *O earth, for the LORD has spoken:*
> *I reared children and brought them up—*
> *And they have rebelled against Me!*
> *An ox knows its owner, an ass its master's crib:*
> *Israel does not know, My people takes no thought.*
> *Ah sinful nation!*
> *People* heavy laden with iniquity [kebed 'āwōn]
> *Brood of evildoers!*
> *Depraved children!*
> *They have forsaken the LORD,*
> *Spurned the Holy One of Israel,*
> *Turned their backs [on Him]. (Isa 1:2–4)*

The prophet begins with a comparison of children to domesticated animals. Both are dependent on those who raise them for sustenance. One would think that children, who possess a higher form of intelligence, would be the ones most likely to know this. Yet "Israel does not know," Isaiah exclaims, "My people takes no thought." It is rather the ox and the ass, he charges, who have acknowledged their owners. Then comes another startling reversal. Although animals are by nature "beasts of burden," it is not they, Isaiah contends, but Israel that is heavily laden—with sin, a peculiar cargo indeed! Just a few chapters later, the prophet takes this metaphor further. Israel is so wicked that the sins she has committed are compared to a burden that must be loaded onto a cart and hauled with oxen: "[They] haul sin as though by roped [oxen],[6] and iniquity as with cart ropes" (Isa 5:18).

One of the well-known symbolic acts of the prophet Ezekiel reflects graphically the underlying image of this metaphor: "[O mortal] lie on your left side and let it *bear [the weight of]* the sin of the House of Israel; for as many days as you lie on it you shall *bear [the weight of] their sin.* For I impose upon you three hundred and ninety days, corresponding to the number of years of their punishment; and so you shall bear the punishment for the House of Israel. When you have completed these, you shall lie another forty days on your right side, and *bear [the weight of] the sin* of the House of Judah. I impose on you one day for each year" (Ezek 4:4–6). In this text the prophet Ezekiel is enacting in his own person the state of the nation as a whole. In this example it is significant that the prophet must lie on his side and bear the punishment that has accrued to both Israel and Judea. By acting in this fashion, the prophet both symbolically enacts the fate of the nation and identifies with it. The sins of Israel are clearly construed as a burden that must be borne.

Last, we should mention the goat in the ritual Day of Atonement (Lev 16). On that day the people of Israel are instructed to bring two goats to the temple in Jerusalem. Aaron, the high priest, receives the animals and casts lots over them. One will be marked for sacrificial slaughter; the other will be sent into the wilderness. The animal to be banished has come to be known as the scapegoat. The term originally signified the animal that had "(e)scaped" the verdict of slaughter, but it has come to have the extended meaning of someone who bears the blame for something he or she has not done or even someone who is the focus of an irrational hatred. But in the Bible, the goat has a far more pedestrian function. It has one simple task: to carry the burden of Israel's sins. According to the book of Leviticus, once the high priest receives this animal, he is to "lay both his hands upon the head of the live goat and confess over it all the iniquities and transgressions of the Israelites, whatever their sins, putting them on the head of the goat; and it shall be sent off to the wilderness through a designated man" (16:21). Through this ritual act, Aaron symbolically puts the *weight* of Israel's sins upon the animal. Once the animal has assumed this burden, it can carry out its responsibility. As in much of the ancient Near East, the wilderness could serve as a portal to the underworld, the domain of the demonic. As Jacob Milgrom, the great scholar of the book of Leviticus, has argued, the goat that has been burdened with these sins "is in reality returning evil to its source, the netherworld."[7] Because this area was thought to be beyond the reach of God, the sins would fall outside the range of his supervisory powers. Once God could no longer see them, it is as if they ceased to exist. The forgiveness of sins in ancient Israel was not simply a matter of feeling contrite for what one had done wrong; the physical material wrought by the sin (its "thingness") had to be removed.

The ritual of the scapegoat, therefore, is dependent on the imagery of sin as a heavy burden that requires a beast of burden to bear it away from the realm of human habitation. The weight of iniquity, our text presumes, cannot be annihilated after it has been created, but it can be banished. One thinks of the oft cited line from Psalms: "As far as east is from west, so far has He removed our sins from us" (103:12), or the closing lines of Micah: "He will take us back in love; He will crush [under foot] our iniquities and cast [them] into the depths of the sea (7:19)."[8] In both these poetic texts, as well as in Leviticus, the sins of Israel are imagined as concrete things that must be removed from God's purview altogether. Once the sins of Israel have been borne away into the wilderness, they leave the domain of the habitable and enter a land that was thought to be God-forsaken. Indeed, the book of Leviticus deems the wilderness to be the habitation of the demon Azazel.[9] As with the example from the Psalm or Micah, the sins of Israel are now outside God's immediate purview.

As Ricoeur could have predicted, a culture that imagines sin as a concrete object with mass and weight would have to develop some mechanism for its removal. Viewed retrospectively, it is not surprising that Israel's foundational narrative about the forgiveness of sins involves a pack animal that bears them away. It is not the case, however, that a narrative about the pack animal in Leviticus 16 was *necessitated* by the metaphor. That would be saying too much. One can imagine other ritual and narrative realizations of the process of forgiveness. At the same time, it would be difficult to imagine such a ritual if the underlying language of the culture in question did not conceive of sin as a heavy burden to be carried away.

Lakoff and Johnson suggested that a culture that structures its discourse about arguments in an idiom other than war may not be intelligible to us. Similarly, one could say that biblical interpreters who fail to appreciate the metaphoric character of "bearing the weight of one's sin" as a marker of culpability will also fail to delineate precisely when the idiom *nāśā᾽ ῾ăwōn* means the act of bearing up under a particular burden (to *put up* with someone; recall Num 11:11–15, above) and when it conveys forgiveness (to *remove* the source of offense).

One text that has numerous problems is Cain's response to the judgment of God for the murder of Abel. After Cain murders his brother in the field, the Lord appears before him and asks, "'Where is your brother, Abel?' And he said, 'I do not know. Am I my brother's keeper?' Then he said, 'What have you done? Hark, your brother's blood cries out to Me from the ground! Therefore, you shall be more cursed than the ground, which opened its mouth to receive your brother's blood from your hand. If you till the soil, it shall no longer yield its strength to you. You shall become a ceaseless wanderer on earth'" (Gen 4:8–12). The interrogation and punishment of Cain both echoes and goes beyond the interrogation and punishment of Adam and Eve just one chapter earlier (2:9–19). But our focus is Cain's response to the punishment that God metes out: "My punishment is too great to bear! Since You have banished me this day from the soil, and I must avoid Your presence and become a restless wanderer on earth—anyone who meets me may kill me!" (Gen 4:13). Commentators are divided as to how the first sentence of Cain's response should be translated. Most would follow the translation of the Jewish Publication Society, "My punishment is too great to bear," though some prefer "My sin is too great to be forgiven."[10] The ambiguity depends on how we understand the noun *ʿăwōn* ("punishment" or "sin") and the verb *nāśāʾ* ("to bear" or "to be forgiven"). In the first case Cain becomes something of a whiner who cannot come to grips with the magnitude of his offense, whereas in the second Cain exhibits a certain remorse for what he has done. A late rabbinic midrash picks up on this latter possibility: Whence do we know that Cain repented? "And Cain said to the LORD, 'my sin is too great to be forgiven.'"[11]

Yet Cain's words need not be puzzling if we attend to the content of the metaphoric expression. Things become clearer if we translate Cain's response as follows: "The weight of my sin is too great for me to bear." As Schwartz notes, Cain does not confess that his sin is beyond forgiving, nor does he complain that his punishment cannot be borne. Rather, Cain owns up to the severity of his offense. When first confronted by God about his crime, Cain is asked: "Where is Abel, your brother?" He dismisses this question in a perfunctory way: "I have no idea. Am I my brother's keeper?" This is a man who does yet not feel the weight of his crime. God then imposes a severe penalty on Cain—the land he works shall be accursed and Cain will be reduced to a wandering refugee. Only now does Cain take the true measure of what he has done. No longer does he belittle his crime ("Am I my brother's keeper?"); he owns up to his culpability.

In this fashion, the response of Cain can be compared to the way the idiom "bearing a sin" works in legal texts. In Leviticus 5:1, one encounters the case of an individual who does not provide testimony in court even though he is obliged to. This individual, our text concludes, "shall bear the weight of his sin." It is important to note that this statement is not an account of a specific punishment or liability. That is detailed later, in the prescription that the sinner must confess his sin and bring an animal for sacrifice (Lev 5:5–6). The function of the clause "he shall bear the weight of his sin" has a different subject matter in mind; it marks the person in question as culpable for the crime that has been committed. And so I have argued for Cain. When he cries out that his sin is beyond bearing, he is referring not to the punishment per se but to the extent of his culpability. The severity of the punishment is an index of the degree of guilt he has incurred for his crime.

Most readers of the Bible have not realized how important the metaphor of sin as a burden is in the Old Testament. As I have shown, this is because translators have almost never rendered the idiom literally. Whereas other verbal metaphors are rendered transparently—to wash away, cover over, or wipe away a sin—the idiom "bearing a sin" has almost always been given a nonliteral equivalent, with two very different meanings. On the one hand, it can be translated "to bear (the weight of one's) sin"; on the other, it can mean "to bear *away* (the weight of one's) sin." To avoid confusion, translators have chosen to render the former "to be culpable, guilty" and the latter "to forgive." Although the basic sense of the text is not harmed by this choice, there are a number of advantages to a more literal translation. First, it allows us to see the reason why the central rite of atonement involves a pack animal carrying sins into the wilderness. The stories that a culture tells about how sins are forgiven are intimately connected to the idioms it uses to express what a sin is. Second, a host of poetic texts become clearer once we see how important this idiom was. It is not by accident that Isaiah declares that the people of Israel are "heavy laden with sin" or that God loads the weight of Israel's sin upon the side of a recumbent prophet. Third, it allows us to interpret more accurately texts such as Cain's response to God that his sin is too heavy to be borne. Standard translations are not terribly in error when they translate the complaint as "my punishment is too great to be borne." But the emphasis of the biblical text, as Schwartz rightly noted, is not on the harsh nature of the punishment that God has just meted out but, rather, on the depth of Cain's personal guilt or culpability. The standard translation allows us to see Cain as complaining about the punishment. Our proposal puts the focus on Cain's honest grappling with the terrible nature of his offense—a subtle, but not insignificant difference. Finally, we should reiterate that both the Day of Atonement ritual and the story of Cain point out yet again that sin has a certain "thing"-like quality. When Cain murdered Abel, it was as if a weight was created ex nihilo and placed on his shoulders. At first Cain did not realize the amount of weight he would be forced to bear, but once confronted by God, the full extent of his crime came into view. In Cain's case, it is not clear whether the burden can ever be removed. Although the mark that God puts on him will preserve him from blood avengers, it appears that culpability for the sin does not disappear. But in Leviticus 16, after God enters into a covenantal relationship with Israel, arrangements are made for removing the burdens that individual Israelites have had to bear. Through the mediation of the high priest Aaron, those sins are loaded onto a goat and sent away, never to be seen again.

3

a debt to be repaid

Forgive us our debts as we forgive those who hold debts against us.

—A literal rendering of the Our Father

Sin, I wish to argue, has a history. As we saw in the previous chapter, the Old Testament contains a number of metaphors for sin, the most predominant being that of sin as a burden. This concept changed dramatically, however, during the Second Temple period, an era in which some of the youngest books of the Old Testament were written, as well as a number of nonbiblical books. During this time the metaphor of sin as a burden was replaced by that of sin as a debt.[1] Although there is little evidence in the Hebrew texts of the First Temple period for such an idea, the explanation is not difficult to pinpoint: the influence of Aramaic.[2] The adoption of Aramaic as the official language of law and commerce by the Persian rulers had a deep impact on the dialect of Hebrew spoken in Israel in the Second Temple period. Many of the books written during that time show the extensive influence of Aramaic on both vocabulary and syntax.

In Aramaic the word for a debt that one owes a lender, ḥôbâ, is the standard term for denoting sin.[3] This term comes into Second Temple Hebrew and has the same double meaning. The idea of sin as a weight is rarely found in rabbinic Hebrew, having been replaced by the idea of sin as a debt. One can clearly see this transformation by examining how the various Aramaic translations of the biblical text (Targums) treat the phrase nāśāʾ ʿăwōn.[4] In almost every instance where nāśāʾ ʿăwōn means "to bear the weight of a sin," we find the Aramaic idiom *qabbēl ḥôbâ*, "to assume a debt." Consider these two texts, which I translate as literally as possible:

Hebrew Bible

1. If a person should sin [*teḥĕṭâʾ*]. . . he shall bear the weight of his sin [*nāśāʾ ʿăwōnô*]. (Lev 5:1)

2. Anyone who blasphemes his God *shall bear the weight of his sin* [*ḥēṭʾô nāśāʾ*]. (Lev 24:15)

Aramaic Targum

If a person becomes obligated [by sin] [*yeḥôb*] . . . he assumes a debt [*yĕqabbēl ḥôbêh*].[5]

Anyone who brings about wrath before his God *shall assume a debt* [*yĕqabbēl ḥôbêh*].

Conversely, everywhere we find *nāśāʾ ʿăwōn* with the meaning "to bear away a sin," we find the Aramaic idiom *šbaq ḥôbâʾ*, "to remit a debt." Like its English equivalent, the Aramaic verb denotes an individual who refrains from collecting on an obligation or payment that is due him. As such it connotes a gracious deed in that a right holder graciously waives his right to collect what is due.

Hebrew Bible

1. So you shall say to Joseph, "*Bear away . . . the burden of the sin* [*śāʾ . . . lappešaʿ*] of your brothers who treated you so harshly." (Gen 50:17)

2. *Bear away the burden of my offense* [*śāʾ . . . ḥaṭṭāʾtî*] just this once, and plead with the LORD your God that He but remove this death from me. (Exod 10:17)

Aramaic Targum

So you shall say to Joseph, "*Remit . . . the debt of the sin* [*šbôq . . . le-ḥôbê*] of your brothers who treated you so harshly."

Remit the debt of my sins [*šbôq . . . le-ḥôbây*] just this once, and plead with the LORD your God that He but remove this death from me.

This linguistic move is not simply that of the Aramaic Targum; it is equally well grounded in rabbinic Hebrew. In the Mishnah one who is at fault is said to be *ḥayyāb*, that is, in possession of a particular *ḥôb*, or debt, that must be repaid.[6] In fact, so complete is this linguistic revolution that usage of the idiom *nāśāʾ ʿăwōn* practically comes to an end in the rabbinic period. To illustrate this, consider how Psalm 32:1, "Happy the one whose wrongdoing is borne away, whose sin is covered over," is understood in *Pesiqta Rabbati*.[7] Within the culture of the Bible it is clear that the sin in question is some form of weight or burden that rests upon the offender's shoulders. The rabbis, however, understand the item that is borne away in a different manner: they assumed that the background for the Psalm is the Day of Atonement and that as God weighs the sins of Israel he finds that the debits and credits are evenly balanced. Satan, the avowed enemy of Israel, attempts to find further notes of indebtedness so that Israel can be condemned. While he is searching, however, God removes some of the sins from the scale and hides them under his robe. When Satan returns, he cries out: "Lord of the World, *you have borne away the wrongdoing of your people and covered over all their sin*'" (Ps 85:3). To which David, the author of the Psalms, replies: "*Happy is the one whose wrongdoing is borne away, whose sin is covered over*" (Ps 32:1). This midrashic interpretation fashions a rather colorful narrative to explain the biblical idiom of having one's sin "borne away." To make sense of this ancient metaphor, the rabbis imagine a set of scales with debits and merits in the respective pans. To have one's sins borne away no longer refers to the removal of a weight from one's back but to a bond of indebtedness deducted from one's balance sheet.

SOME LEXICAL EXAMPLES

Perhaps the best way to understand the significance of this idiom for rabbinic thought is to tour the lexicon of rabbinic Hebrew. Let us consider four representative examples: (1) the payment of a bill, (2) the act of collecting payment, (3) the state of being indebted, (4) and the act of releasing someone from the obligation to repay a debt. What we will find is a complete interchangeability between commercial and theological terminology. The significance of the latter is intelligible only in light of the former.

(1) The payment of a bill: The verb *pāraʿ* normally means "to pay for something," that is, to provide a cash equivalent for what one owes: "*I have repaid you [pāraʿtîka]* [the money I previously owed] within the time frame [of the contract]."[8] In the reflexive conjugation (known in Hebrew as the *niphal*), this same verbal root has the literal sense of "to collect payment from someone." But because physical punishment is considered a form of currency with which to repay a debt, the verb can be translated more simply as "to punish." Consider how the rabbis interpret this verse from the book of Exodus: "The LORD drove back the sea with a strong east wind all that night and turned the sea into dry ground" (14:21). Of course, the purpose of this divine act was to provide a dry path on which the Israelites could flee, along with a deluge that would destroy their pursuers. In a rabbinic commentary on the book of Exodus, known as the *Mekhilta deRabbi Ishmael,* we learn that God separated the waters of the Sea of Reeds so that

he could lead Israel to safety and *take payment* (*nipra*ᶜ) from those bent on destroying Israel.⁹ The reflexive form of the verb (*nipra*ᶜ) implies that God took payment on the debt that Pharaoh and his accomplices owed him. The terms of their payment was death.

I might add that the most commonly used noun for *punishment* in rabbinic Hebrew, *pûr*ᶜ*ānût*, derives from the same stem. So when the rabbis declare that "the measure of God's goodness is greater than that of his retribution [*middat hap-pûr*ᶜ*ānût*]," we must recall that the literal sense of the term *retribution* is to "collect payment on what someone owes."¹⁰ God, then, is compared to a creditor who holds a bond of indebtedness in his possession that was drawn up when a sin was committed. He is free to call in this bond at his discretion, which will entail some sort of punishment.

(2) The act of collecting payment: The verb *gābâh*, which normally means "to collect payment due on a bill," also has the extended meaning "to punish." For the former sense, consider this line from the Babylonian Talmud: "If a latter creditor collected first [*qādam we-gabâh*], what he collected is his own."¹¹ For the extended metaphoric sense, consider this text from *Genesis Rabbah* (which I discuss in a subsequent chapter): "When could God collect [*gābâh*] the debt [of the sinner] that was owed on his bond?"¹²

(3) The state of being indebted: The most common verbal root for conveying the sense of obligation is *ḥāb*, which normally means "to owe." It has a substantivized adjective *ḥayyāb*, which means "one who owes," and a noun *ḥôb*, which refers to the item owed, that is, a debt. Because a monetary debt always involves a contract, the term for a creditor is one who is in possession of a debt instrument (*ba*ᶜ*al ḥôb*), that is, the document (*šṭar*), that was executed when the loan was formally issued and signed in front of witnesses. The presumption is that as long as the creditor holds this bond, he is entitled to collect what is due him. As a result, when a bond was paid off, it was either torn in two to mark its cancellation or it was returned to the borrower, who could dispose of it as he chose. But in a larger metaphoric sense it was thought that the punishment of a sinner by God was nothing other than the act of the divine creditor's collecting payment (in the form of punishment) on what was due: When an individual was about to be punished, R. Isaac said, "The creditor [*ba*ᶜ*al ḥôb*] found the opportunity to collect on his bond [*šṭar*]."¹³

(4) The act of releasing someone from the obligation to repay a debt: The verb *māḥal* means "to cancel a bond of indebtedness" in its literal sense (*šbaq* is its equivalent in Aramaic) and "to forgive a sin" in a metaphoric sense. For the former, consider this text from the Babylonian Talmud: "If a

man provides a bond *[štar]* for a loan then pays it off *[pāraʿ]*, he cannot provide this bond again because the security which it contains has been cancelled *[nimḥal]*."[14] For its metaphoric sense, compare this text: "R. Tanhum b. Hanilai said: 'No rain shall fall unless the sins of Israel are forgiven (*nimḥălû*) for scripture says, O LORD, *You have favored Your land, restored Jacob's fortune; You have borne away Your people's iniquity, and covered all their sins; You have withdrawn all your anger, and turned away from your rage*'" (Ps 85:2–4).[15] It is striking that the biblical idiom of sin as a weight ("You have *borne away* Your people's iniquity") has been ignored in favor of sin as a debt. This is good evidence of how the metaphor of sin as a weight dropped out of common speech in later Hebrew. Its replacement by the metaphor of debt is practically complete.

JESUS AND THE OUR FATHER

In the New Testament the metaphor of sin as debt was ubiquitous. Jesus frequently told stories about debtors and creditors as a way of illustrating the dynamics of sin and forgiveness. Given that he spoke a form of Hebrew close to that of the rabbinic dialect, this is hardly surprising. As Lakoff and Johnson documented, metaphors determine how we think, act, and tell stories in the everyday world.

Consider, for example, the famous line from the Our Father as found in Matthew's Gospel: "Remit us our debts as we remit those who hold debts against us" (6:12). Forgiveness here is imagined as a gracious act of refusing to collect on an obligation. The person praying asks that God act this way, while at the same time affirming an intention to do the same. Nearly all scholars would concede that the Greek form of this prayer, which we now have in the New Testament, only makes sense when we translate it back into its original Semitic environment. "The Matthean use of 'debts' has a Semitic flavor," observes the New Testament scholar Fr. Raymond Brown, "for, while in secular Greek 'debt' has no religious coloring, in Aramaic *ḥôbâ* is a financial and commercial term that has been caught up into the religious vocabulary. . . . The idea of remitting *(aphiemi)* debts which appears in our petition is also more Semitic than Greek, for 'remission' has a religious sense only in the Greek of the LXX [the 'Septuagint,' or the Greek translation of the Bible], which is under Hebrew influence."[16]

Brown's observation is worth underscoring. The terms that Matthew uses to describe the forgiveness of sins would have struck a Greek speaker as unusual. This is the reason, most New Testament scholars have assumed, that the version of the Our Father in Luke's Gospel differs from that in

Matthew's. In Luke's version we find "forgive us our sins" (11:4). In contemporary Greek the words "remit" *(aphiemi)* and "debt" *(opheilema)* did not have the secondary meaning of "forgive" and "sin." Matthew's version of the Our Father makes sense only if we assume that the wording reflects an underlying Semitic idiom. Thus, in the case of the Our Father it is safe to assume that Jesus' original words would have been expressed in Hebrew or Aramaic. The author of Matthew's Gospel, in contrast to Luke, chose to provide a literal translation. The result was a linguistic formulation that would have sounded odd to a native Greek speaker who did not recognize the underlying Semitic idiom.

The significance of "debt" language is not limited to the Our Father. We find our best illustration of this sort of symbolism in the parable of the unforgiving servant (Matt 18:23–35), in which a king wishes to settle his accounts with various servants:

> For this reason the kingdom of heaven may be compared to a king who wished to settle accounts with his slaves. When he began the reckoning, one who owed him ten thousand talents was brought to him; and, as he could not pay, his lord ordered him to be sold, together with his wife and children and all his possessions, and payment to be made. So the slave fell on his knees before him, saying, "Have patience with me, and I will pay you everything." And out of pity for him, the lord of that slave released him and forgave him the debt. But that same slave, as he went out, came upon one of his fellow slaves who owed him a hundred denarii; and seizing him by the throat, he said, "Pay what you owe." Then his fellow slave fell down and pleaded with him, "Have patience with me, and I will pay you." But he refused; then he went and threw him into prison until he would pay the debt. When his fellow slaves saw what had happened, they were greatly distressed, and they went and reported to their lord all that had taken place. Then his lord summoned him and said to him, "You wicked slave! I forgave you all that debt because you pleaded with me. Should you not have had mercy on your fellow slave, as I had mercy on you?" And in anger his lord handed him over to be tortured until he would pay his entire debt.

This parable brings stunning clarity to what Jesus meant when he advised his disciples to pray that their debts be forgiven just as they forgave the debts of others. According to the logic of the metaphor this prayer employs, we are in danger of becoming debt-slaves when we sin. Should the act go uncorrected, then one will have to "pay" for the "cost" of the misdeed through the "currency" of physical punishment. Fortunately God is merciful and will remit the debt we owe if we humbly beseech him.

As Brown concludes, "The king who wishes to settle debts with his servants is obviously God, and the atmosphere is that of judgment. The parable points out that God's forgiveness of the servant has a connection to that servant's forgiveness of his fellow servant. When this brotherly forgiveness fails, he is given to the torturers until he pays his debt."[17] In this fashion the parable illustrates that petition in the Our Father, where we see not only a request from a servant to his master for debt remission ("remit us our debts") but a remission made contingent on how the servant acts toward a peer who is indebted to him ("as we remit those who hold debts against us").

Note that Jesus does not compare a sinner to individuals who are struggling under a heavy burden. Stories like the scapegoat in Leviticus 16 or the injunction that Ezekiel lie on his side while God loads upon him the sins of Israel simply do not appear in the New Testament. But neither do they occur in rabbinic literature. This is ample testimony to the wholesale replacement of the weight image in favor of debt. The Targum's habit of translating the idiom *nāśā᾿ ῾ăwōn* into financial terms turns out to be a good window into what takes place in the Second Temple period.

DEBT IN THE DEAD SEA SCROLLS

When we turn to the literature of the sect that lived at Qumran and wrote the Dead Sea Scrolls, things become a bit fuzzier, though not because of linguistics. I do not think it overly daring to claim that the Hebrew speakers of Qumran would have *spoken* a language close to that of Jesus and his disciples. Although a good proportion of the scrolls found at Qumran date to a century or two before the birth of Jesus, the community that lived there and copied those scrolls was active well into the first century of the Common Era. Some of the covenanters at Qumran, then, were the contemporaries of John the Baptist and Jesus and even some of the older rabbinic figures mentioned in rabbinic writings. (Some have argued that John the Baptist was familiar with the sect, if not a member at one time.)[18]

What separates the literature at Qumran from later rabbinic traditions is their stance toward the biblical world. The rabbis understood themselves as standing outside the realm of the Bible. This is obvious from the fact that they record their teachings in the contemporary idiom of the day, a dialect of Hebrew that we now label Mishnaic Hebrew. This particular dialect differs both syntactically and lexically from that of the Bible. The texts from

Qumran, on the other hand, were written in a language with closer affinities to the Hebrew Bible. As James Kugel has noted, the scribes at Qumran sought to bring their life and times "under the coverage" of the biblical era.[19] This motivation led to a desire to imitate biblical idiom and conventions of writing. As a result, the pronounced and nearly ubiquitous usage of debt language like that found in rabbinic literature or the New Testament is not found at Qumran. Indeed, whereas rabbinic literature makes regular use of the root ḥôb to describe human culpability for sin, at Qumran this root is rather rare, which might lead one to believe that the metaphor of sin as debt would have been unknown there. This is not the case, however, as a close reading of these texts will reveal.

In the third column of the *Damascus Covenant,* one of the Dead Sea Scrolls, there is a summary of the sins of Israel. This litany of wrongdoing provides a justification for why God allowed the Babylonians to destroy the First Temple in 587 BCE and lead much of the population into exile. The list begins with the sins of the sons of Noah and then stops to recount the righteousness of Abraham, Isaac, and Jacob. After Jacob's death, however, the rebellion against the law of God continues. At the conclusion of this catalogue of Israel's perfidy, the writer observes, stands the apostasy of the final generation of Israelites: "Their kings were cut off because of it, their mighty men perished because of it, and their land was laid waste because of it."[20] But no sooner is the end of the Israelite kingdom accounted for than the writer revisits the matter in a more theological fashion. Why did the Israelites meet such an unhappy end one might ask? "Because," the author continues, "[all] the first members of the covenant *fell into debt [ḥābû,]*, they were given over to the sword. They had forsaken the covenant of God and chosen their own will" (*CD* 3:10–12).[21] Up to this point in the text, the Hebrew of the *Damascus Covenant* has been close to the biblical dialect. A beginning biblical Hebrew student would have no trouble making his or her way through this text. But suddenly in the last line we have cited, the author slips. Instead of following the idiom of conventional biblical Hebrew and writing "because the first members of the covenant had sinned [ḥăṭĕʾû]" or perhaps "rebelled" [pāšĕʿû], the writer introduces an expression familiar from the Hebrew of rabbinic Judaism, "they fell into debt," to describe their state of culpability before God. With this little slip of his pen, the scribe from Qumran reveals that his imitation of the biblical dialect is not complete; evidence of his contemporary idiom has risen to the surface.

The next text from Qumran that I consider is 11QMelchizedek, an enigmatic narrative about the figure of Melchizedek.[22] In the Jewish scriptures

Melchizedek appears twice. In Genesis 14 he is the priest-king of Salem (most likely an alternative name for Jerusalem) who blesses Abram after he has successfully vanquished a group of marauding armies. Abram, in return, offers this righteous king a tenth of all the booty he has captured in battle. In Psalm 110 this king is mentioned again, but his persona there is difficult to outline. It is possible, however, to understand the Psalm as ascribing an important role to this priest-king on the day of divine judgment. It is this eschatological role that surfaces at Qumran. In 11QMelchizedek we read about the events of the final days wherein Melchizedek rouses the armies of light to engage and defeat his demonic adversary, Belial, and the forces of darkness.

The text, like many from Qumran, is fragmentary, so it is impossible to piece together the whole story. But fortunately, the moment of redemption that Melchizedek ushers in is found in more or less readable form. Consider the opening lines of the second column of this document:

> And as for what he said: "in [this] year of the Jubilee [each of you will return to his property" (Lev 25:13), concerning it, he said, "Now th]is is the ma[nner of the release:] Let every creditor remit what he has lent [to his neighbor. He shall not press his neighbor or his brother for repayment, for] God's release [has been proclaimed" (Deut 15:2–3). The interpretation of it concerns] the end of days when the captives (Isa 61:1) who [. . .] and whose teachers have been hidden and kept secret, and from the inheritance of Mechizedek, fo[r . . .] . . . and they are the inheritance of Melchizedek, who will make them return. And liberty (Lev 25:10) will be proclaimed for them, to free them from [the debt of] all their iniquities. And this [wil]l [happen] in the first week of the Jubilee which follows the ni[ne] Jubilees. And the d[ay of aton]ement is the e[nd of] the tenth [Ju]bilee in which atonement shall be made for all the sons of [light and] for the men [of] the lot of Mel[chi]zedek [. . .] for it is the era of the "year of favor" (Isa 61:2) for Melchizedek and [his] arm[ies, the nat]ion of God's holy ones and the era of the rule of judgment as it is written in the songs of David [. . .][23]

The picture is striking: Israel has been suffering under the unjust rule of Belial for some nine Jubilees. During this time she has been deprived of her just inheritance in the Holy Land. But her period of penitential waiting, though lorded over by an unjust despot, is not without its rationale. Israel's sins have put her in the position of a slave sold into slavery because expenses could no longer be covered. At the dawn of the tenth Jubilee, the messianic figure of Melchizedek appears, announces the year of God's favor (šěnat rāṣôn), a year in which all of Israel's former debts are rescinded and the captive nation is restored to her rightful place in the land. Like the tribes under the leadership of Joshua, Israel will march back and assume dominion over her God-given inheritance, the land of Israel.[24]

But the key theme, for our purposes, is how 11QMelchizedek understands the first two texts it cites, Leviticus 25:8–17 and Deuteronomy 15:1–11. Both texts, it must be emphasized, deal solely with the problem of *monetary* debt. Deuteronomy 15 mandates that every seven years the wealthy must remit the debts they hold against those of lesser means. Leviticus 25 is slightly different in that it mandates that every forty-nine years (during the Jubilee year) the Israelites can return to their original landholdings. But because the only reason an Israelite would be alienated from his property would be an inability to fulfill a financial obligation (see Lev 25:25–55), the Jubilee year is also about the forgiveness of debts. In Leviticus the year of release is called děrôr (25:10). This term has an exact cognate in Akkadian, *andurāru*. In Mesopotamian culture, when a new king ascended the throne, he would often grant a one-time cancellation of debt. This resulted in the freedom of many who suffered as debt-slaves and also the release of lands the crown had confiscated for various reasons. The biblical institution of the Jubilee clearly assumes this model but makes at least two significant changes. First, it was no longer a human king who is responsible for this generous deed but the divine king. Second, the act of debt release was not dependent on the whims of a newly crowned monarch but, rather, was subject to the regulations of covenantal law that were imposed by a divine suzerain: debts would be remitted every seven years according to the legislation of Deuteronomy 15, every forty-nine years according to Leviticus 25.

But most important, there is no hint in either Deuteronomy 15 or Leviticus 25 that the forgiveness of sin is at issue. Indeed I think one could say that out of the hundreds of articles and books that have been written over the past century or so on these two texts, not one would make such a claim. They would not even feel the need to argue against such a construal, so far would it be from their imagination. Leviticus 25 and Deuteronomy 15 have nothing to say about sin.

It is on this point that 11QMelchizedek is so interesting. The author of this document is supremely confident that the formulas of debt release found in Deuteronomy 15 and Leviticus 25 have a different purpose. "Liberty will be proclaimed for [the inheritance of Melchizedek] to free them from [the debt of] all their iniquities." Like our text from the *Damascus*

Covenant, 11QMelchizedek is steeped in the idiom of the Bible. Indeed, a good proportion of the text is a pastiche of biblical quotations. But when the writer makes one of his central points—that at the close of the ninth Jubilee liberty *(děrôr)* will be proclaimed and sins will be forgiven—in rushes the colloquial Hebrew from the Second Temple period.

Let us consider more closely the grammar of lines 6–7: "Liberty will be proclaimed to them to free them *(la-ʿăzôb)* from the [debt of] their sins [*ăwōnôtêhemah*]."[25] Set against the background of conventional biblical Hebrew, this sentence is bizarre. In the Bible the verb *la-ʿăzôb* means "to leave, abandon," or even "to forsake." It never means "to free one from sins" or "to forgive." How do we account for this? Let us recall what we learned earlier from the Our Father. New Testament scholars observed that the Greek verb *aphiemi* never means "to forgive [sins]" in conventional Greek texts. The only way to understand its usage in Matthew is to assume that the Gospel writer is trying to find the most literal Greek equivalent to the Aramaic verb *šbaq*.

The same linguistic "error" that informed the Our Father is in evidence at Qumran! The only way to make sense of this usage of the Hebrew verb *ʿāzab,* "to forsake, abandon," in 11QMelchizedek is to understand it as an awkward translation of the underlying Aramaic verb *šbaq*.

ʿāzab	*šbaq*
1. to leave, forsake	1. same meaning
2. to forsake a legal responsibility (e.g., to support a wife) or claim (e.g., to collect on a debt)	2. same meaning
	3. to forgive a sin (imagined as a debt)

From this table one can see that Hebrew and Aramaic overlap completely at the first and second levels of meaning. The fact that the Aramaic root goes one step further and means "to forgive a sin" provides ample room for confusion for the person fluent in both languages. In this instance, our scribe has found himself in a dilemma because he needs a verb for forgiveness that will match his underlying metaphor that sin is a debt. The solution was logical: expand the semantic field of the verb *ʿāzab* on the basis of its cognate in Aramaic. Linguists refer to this sort of error in which a bilingual speaker mixes up the semantic fields of two verbal roots that are closely related as a calque. [26]

It is significant that the scribe at Qumran would invoke such an idiom, for in general he tries hard to stay within the traditional vocabulary of the Bible. That the scribe invokes the idiom of the Second Temple period at this point—when the sins of Israel are at stake—indicates how deeply this metaphor had penetrated. The identification of sins with debts was not the unique heritage of a single Jewish sect or two; it was shared by all Jews of that time. And just as the metaphor of sin as a burden led to the construction of a ritual for the riddance of sin through a scapegoat, so the metaphor of sin as a debt permitted early biblical interpreters to see a level of meaning in the biblical laws about debt release that would have been lost on the original biblical authors. Although it is clear that Deuteronomy 15 and Leviticus 25 had nothing to do with sin when they were composed, it was altogether natural for a biblical interpreter to understand them in this way.[27]

In Chapter 1 I discussed the claim of Paul Ricoeur that religious symbols or metaphors are significant because they "give rise to thought." By this he meant that idioms for sin provide the semantic building blocks upon which narratives about the punishment for or forgiveness of sin are built. With the slightest adjustment we can apply this principle to the exegetical efforts of the scribe from Qumran. This writer, formed by the spoken Hebrew of his day to think of sin as a form of debt to be repaid, was drawn almost inexorably to biblical texts about debt release. If the Jubilee year was that point when all debt related to the land was released, then no enormous hermeneutical leap was required to go one step further and declare that God would also announce the forgiveness of sin on that day. For those sins, like other monetary debts, had been slowly but inexorably accumulating over time.[28]

As Lakoff and Johnson as well as Ricoeur have argued, there can be no discourse about sin and forgiveness apart from the use of specific metaphors. The beliefs we hold about the atonement process are shaped by the stories we tell, which, in turn, are molded by the language we use. For the biblical writer of Deuteronomy, the law about release from debt was a statute about the remission of monetary debts every seven years. Nothing more. But for the author of 11QMelchizedek it illustrated a moment of greater magnitude. Because Israel had gone into exile owing to spiritual indebtedness, the more profane level of this earlier law must have hinted at some larger theological truth. Lakoff and Johnson asked whether a culture that knew of arguments only in the form of war could make sense of a culture that thought of arguments in terms of dance. Perhaps we could rephrase that question: Could the Deuteronomist have seen the laws of debt release as an analog to Israel's past sin and her hope for future redemption? I think the answer can only be negative. His was a culture for which a different metaphorical picture obtained. All of which confirms the thesis I put forward in Chapter 1: sin has a history. And one stage of that history is the change in metaphors from the First Temple period to the Second. What remains to be seen are the implications that follow historically from this transformation.

part two:

making payment on one's debt

4

redemption and the satisfaction of debts

Speak tenderly to Jerusalem, and declare to her that her term of service is over,
that the debt owed for her iniquity has been satisfied.

—Isaiah 40:2

I resume the exploration of sin as a debt by returning to the Hebrew Bible.
By the time we get to materials from the later Second Temple period, such
as those at Qumran (second century BCE through the first century CE), the
metaphor of sin as a debt has become well established. The dialect of Mishnaic Hebrew, which I assume is close to the Hebrew Jesus would have spoken, illustrates how complete the transformation had become. The usage
of nās'ā' 'ăwōn as an idiom to describe culpability has by and large fallen out
of use in these works.[1] One does not have to wait, however, until the emer-
gence of postbiblical Hebrew before the metaphor of sin as debt appears.
The change is already present in one of the later texts of the Hebrew Bible,
the document known as Second Isaiah.

The first element of this financial metaphor is Isaiah's construal of how
Israel has made "satisfaction" for her sins—a deeply significant idea in the
history of Christian thought, especially in regard to the matter of penance
and the doctrine of the atonement. Yet few thinkers have realized how
deeply rooted this idea is in the Bible. The Lutheran theologian (and later
bishop) Gustav Aulén is an excellent example. His landmark work, *Christus
Victor: An Historical Study of the Three Main Types of the Idea of the Atonement,* has informed virtually every discussion of atonement since its pub-

lication in Swedish in 1931 (as an index of its significance, an English translation was issued a year later). For Aulén, the association of penance and atonement is problematic, for it depends on a uniquely Latin (read, Catholic) construal of the human condition. In his mind, this pernicious error in the church's thinking can be traced back through Anselm to Cyprian and eventually to its originator, Tertullian. "How absurd it is," writes Tertullian, "to leave the penance unperformed, and yet expect forgiveness of sins! What is it but to fail to pay the price, and nevertheless, to stretch out the hand for the benefit? The Lord has ordained that forgiveness is to be granted for this price: He wills that the remission of the penalty is to be purchased for payment which penance makes."[2] One can see how this picture of human culpability will eventually lead to the medieval practice of codifying punishments to fit specific crimes and then administering the penance in the confines of the confessional box. In Aulén's view, this is lamentable, because satisfaction, like its near correlate, meritorious action, puts too much emphasis on the human contribution to atonement. Rather than being a work of divine mercy, the forgiveness of sins amounts to a human endeavor.

I shall explore Aulén's deeper reservations about the doctrine of satisfaction in Chapter 12. For now, I wish to show that the doctrine of satisfaction is already present in later books of the Hebrew Bible and that this idea is inextricably linked to the concept of sin as debt. As soon as sin is perceived in this fashion, the doctrine of satisfaction emerges. If this is true, then the argument that this train of thought begins with Tertullian and is dependent on a uniquely Latin understanding of human culpability for wrongdoing will be proven incorrect. I hope to show, instead, that the idea of making satisfaction for one's sins emerges within the writings of an author whom biblical scholars have come to identify as Second Isaiah.

COMFORT YE, COMFORT YE MY PEOPLE

One of the more assured results of modern biblical study is that the book of Isaiah divides into at least two and perhaps three separate works.[3] The first portion of the book (chaps. 1–39) is thought to be the result of a prophet named Isaiah who lived in the eighth century and carried out his prophetic ministry in Jerusalem. The second part of the book (chaps. 40–66) is the work of an anonymous individual who wrote under the pseudonym of Isaiah but lived during the period of the Babylonian exile (the mid-sixth century).[4] This author is referred to as Second Isaiah. It is significant that one of the first examples of the metaphor of sin as debt is found in the writings of this later biblical author. Given that this writer was living in Babylon—and so must have been heavily influenced by the use of Aramaic in this part of the world—it is not surprising that this idiom shows up in his writings.

After the fall of the First Temple in 587 BCE, the Babylonian armies exiled numerous persons of means from Jerusalem and the surrounding Judean countryside to Babylon. There, as Second Isaiah describes the matter, the people sat in mourning over their culpability for the devastation of their homeland and eagerly awaited word that they might return. Around the middle of the sixth century the Babylonian empire began to decline, leaving a void in the ancient world that was quickly filled by the Persians. In 539–538 BCE the Persian emperor Cyrus issued a decree that allowed the Israelites to return to the land of Israel and begin rebuilding the temple. This astonishing event, our biblical writers imagined, could not have occurred apart from the hand of God. The book of Ezra declares that it was the Lord himself who "roused the spirit of King Cyrus of Persia to issue a proclamation throughout his realm by word of mouth." The royal decree declared: "The LORD God of Heaven has given me all the kingdoms of the earth and has charged me with building Him a house in Jerusalem, which is in Judah. Anyone of you of all His people—may his God be with him, and let him go up to Jerusalem that is in Judah and build the House of the LORD God of Israel, the God that is in Jerusalem" (Ezra 1:1–4).

This event made a considerable impression on Second Isaiah. Indeed his language is extravagant and has no parallel elsewhere in the Hebrew Bible. For Second Isaiah, Cyrus is not simply an exemplary king of an emerging superpower; he is both God's shepherd and his anointed.

> [I a]m the same who says of Cyrus, "He is My shepherd,
> He shall fulfill all My purposes!
> He shall say of Jerusalem, 'She shall be rebuilt,'
> And to the Temple: 'You shall be founded again.'"
> Thus said the LORD to Cyrus, His anointed one—
> Whose right hand He has grasped,
> Treading down nations before him,
> Ungirding the loins of kings,
> Opening doors before him
> And letting no gate stay shut:
> I will march before you
> And level the hills that loom up;
> I will shatter doors of bronze
> And cut down iron bars.

I will give you treasures concealed in the dark
And secret hoards—
So that you may know that it is I the LORD,
The God of Israel, who calls you by name.
For the sake of My servant Jacob,
Israel My chosen one,
I call you by name,
I hail you by title, though you have not known Me. (Isa 44:28–45:4)

The release of Israel from captivity was greeted with jubilation by those in Babylon. Second Isaiah was convinced that the time for mourning over Israel's traumatic past had come to its conclusion; the age of redemption was at hand. He opens his literary work with one of the most famous oracles in the Bible:

Comfort, oh comfort My people,
Says your God.
Speak tenderly to Jerusalem,
and declare to her that her term of service is over,
that [the debt owed for] her iniquity has been satisfied;
For she has received at the hand of the LORD
Double for all her sins. (Isa 40:1–2)

Many readers of this text will recognize these words as part of the libretto of Handel's *Messiah*. For our purposes, however, it is important to understand the typological interpretation Second Isaiah has given to Israel's experience of captivity. For this prophet, Israel's exile in Babylon called to mind the slavery Israel had experienced in Egypt many centuries before. This point is made time and again by the writer when he declares that God's saving act should be characterized as an act of redemption *(gĕʾullâh)*, that is, a release of individuals from their bondage in slavery. Indeed, this word in its nominal and verbal forms occurs some twenty-two times within the book. It becomes the central term of Second Isaiah's vocabulary for describing Israel's deliverance from exile. No other book of the Bible, aside from Leviticus (which details the laws for redeeming a slave), comes close to this usage.

Against this background, several colorful expressions in Isaiah 40:2 come into greater clarity, specifically the following three: (1) Israel's term of service is over; (2) she received double for all her sins; and (3) her debt has been satisfied.

Let me begin with the idea that Israel's term of service *(ṣābāʾ)* has come to its fitting end. The Hebrew word for "service" often refers to one's obligation to serve in the army. But it can also be used with respect to fulfilling the terms of one's priestly obligation: "The LORD spoke to Moses and Aaron, saying: Take a [separate] census of the Kohathites among the Levites, by the clans of their ancestral house, from the age of thirty years up to the age of fifty, all who are subject to *service,* to perform tasks for the Tent of Meeting" (Num 4:3).[5] The key clause is "all who are subject to service," where service clearly means performing a set of obligatory tasks. The term can also refer to the general set of obligations of the day laborer as well: "Truly man has a *term of service [ṣābāʾ]* on earth; His days are like those of a hireling—Like a slave who longs for [evening's] shadows, Like a hireling who waits for his wage" (Job 7:1–2, cf. 14:14). This image of the day laborer in the book of Job is crucial, I believe, for understanding the term in Second Isaiah. The laborer is hired for a specific unit of time, and at the end of that time, a commensurate wage will be owed for his service. Such is the situation in the book of Second Isaiah, wherein the debt-slave is also obligated to fulfill a term of service. When the debt-slave has worked for a sufficient amount of time, the debts will be considered repaid and the term of slavery will end.

Indeed, according to Second Isaiah, Israel has done even better than that: she has paid a sum that exceeds what she owed, "For she has received at the hand of the LORD double for all her sins." Scholars have correctly paused over this image of a double payment (*kiplayim*), though nearly all are agreed that the Hebrew term is both legal and financial. It seems to mean that Israel's suffering was sufficient to cover double what she owed. This has troubled some commentators because of the implication that God has been unjust in his punishment. Was God so angry at Israel that he lost all sense of control and subjected his chosen people to double the punishment they deserved? In response to this problem, Gerhard von Rad has argued that the term *kiplayim* should be translated "equivalently."[6] Jan L. Koole, on the other hand, suggests that the reference to a double payment should not be taken literally. What Second Isaiah wishes to convey is that Israel has suffered more than enough; the use of such hyperbole simply conveys the fact that Israel has fully satisfied the terms of her punishment.[7] However one might parse this term, it is clear that Second Isaiah has struck a financial image and that Israel is described as a nation that was sent to Babylon to repay a debt. Joseph Blenkinsopp puts the matter accurately in his terse summary: "She has satisfied her obligations and paid off her debts."[8]

The idea that Israel owed a sum that necessitated exile to Babylon implies that her sins are being conceived of as a debt. It also seems clear that this metaphysical debt cannot be repaid with a conventional form of currency. The only means of understanding the situation is to assume that it will be the sufferings of Israel in her servitude that will raise the currency she requires to set her spiritual house in order. Although no biblical text is explicit on this matter, the history of interpretation provides ample justification for such a reading. As an example, in an early rabbinic commentary on the book of Deuteronomy known as the *Sifre* (third century CE), R. Nehemiah declares: "Beloved are bodily sufferings, for just as sacrifices *repay [mĕraṣṣim]*, so sufferings *repay [mĕraṣṣim]*."[9]

Israel is described as a debt-slave in Babylon not only in Isaiah 40:2 but also later in the book:

> *Thus said the LORD:*
> *Where is the bill of divorce*
> *Of your mother whom I dismissed?*
> *And which of My creditors was it*
> *To whom I sold you off?*
> *You were only sold off for your sins,*
> *And your mother dismissed for your crimes. (Isa 50:1)*

As Benjamin Sommer has noted, this text builds on the presumption that Israel is both the spouse and child of God.[10] Let me begin with the first image. Although the exile appeared to be the result of a successful divorce proceeding, in fact God never carried it through in a final, legal sense because he did not provide Israel with the proper papers ("Where is the bill of divorce?"). Had God carried through with the divorce proceedings, Israelite law would rule out the possibility of the wife being taken back into the household (Deut 24:1–4; Jer 3:1). Given that the legal papers had never been drawn up and signed, however, the option remains that God can take Israel back.

As for the second image, that Israel is a child of God, Second Isaiah has in mind the tragic circumstances in which a parent must sell an offspring into slavery to ensure both his or her own survival and that of the child. The child will be supported by the purchaser, while the parents will eke out a living on the proceeds of the sale. The frightful emotional cost of such a circumstance is illustrated in an episode from the life of Elisha the prophet (II Kings 4:1–7). In that story a wife of one of the disciples of Elisha falls into terrible straits when her husband dies and is left with no means to support herself. Soon the loans he had taken prior to his death begin to fall due, which she is unable to repay. A creditor arrives at her doorstep and threatens to seize the two children as slaves.[11] Should the children be taken, their forced labor will provide the means of making good on the debt. In Second Isaiah, however, there is an important distinction. The mother, who pleads her case to Elisha, is distraught because her husband's tragic death has left her unable to pay her debts and has put the lives of her children in danger. Israel, on the other hand, can make no similar appeal. It is not God's fault that Israel has become a debt-slave; God has no creditor to whom he is answerable. Rather, Israel's current status as a debt-slave is due to her own financial debacle—that of the onerous debt she has assumed.[12]

Let us return to the words of comfort that Second Isaiah addresses to Jerusalem. In these verses Second Isaiah tells Israel that "her service is over, that [the debt owed for] her iniquity has been satisfied; For she has received at the hand of the LORD double for all her sins" (40:2). The translation I provided followed fairly closely that of the Jewish Publication Society. I did alter one crucial clause, however. Whereas the JPS reads, "That her iniquity is expiated," I preferred "that [the debt owed for] her iniquity [ʿawōn] has been satisfied [rāṣâh]."[13] Everything turns on the translation of the verb rāṣâh. Based on standard Hebrew usage one should translate the phrase as "her sin was accepted." This is how rāṣâh in the passive conjugation is consistently rendered in the Hebrew Bible. Consider, for example, the following:

> He shall lay his hand upon the head of the burnt offering, that it may *be acceptable* in his behalf, in expiation for him. (Lev 1:4)
> If any of the flesh of his sacrifice of well-being is eaten on the third day, it shall not *be acceptable*. (Lev 7:18)
> You may, however, present as a freewill offering an ox or a sheep with a limb extended or contracted; but it will not *be accepted* for a vow. (Lev 22:23)

But no one translates Isaiah 40:2 in a literal manner—"that her iniquity has been accepted"—because it would make no sense.[14] To modern ears, accepting iniquity implies getting used to it or even inured to it. Blenkinsopp catches the basic contextual sense of the metaphor: "Jerusalem, representing the people, has served its time of indentured service (ṣābāʾ understood in this sense rather than the military draft, or doing time in prison for nonpayment of debts). She has satisfied her obligations and paid off her debts." In so doing, Blenkinsopp is following a path already charted by the Aramaic Targum: "her debt was remitted [by the one who held it]."

The question returns: How do we understand this usage of the root rāṣâh, "to pay off [a debt]"? Modern commentators such as Driver, Elliger, and Milgrom have followed a trend marked out by the rabbis and seconded by the medieval commentators Ibn Ezra, Hizquni, and, a few centuries later, Seforno and Luzzato.[15] All these premodern figures gloss the usage of *rāṣâh* in Leviticus 26 with the Mishnaic verb *pāraʿ* "to pay off (a debt)."

On the basis of the rabbinic usage of *rāṣâh* (in the causative stem) to mean "to count coins, to pay," it has been suggested that at origin we have two roots, one that originally meant "to accept, be satisfied with" and another that meant "to count [money], to pay."[16] I think, however, that there is a simpler explanation of this conundrum. In my opinion these two different meanings derive from a single ancestor. By tracing this development, we will learn how Israelites in the Second Temple period thought about human sin and its rectification.

To begin this linguistic exploration, recall that the technical usage of *rāṣâh* in the sacrificial laws of Leviticus most commonly denotes the acceptance of the well-being offering *(šĕlāmîm)*. This offering was used in three circumstances: in the presentation of a thank-offering *(tôdâh)* for an unexpected blessing received from God; to fulfill a vow *(neder)* made previously to God; and as a freewill offering *(nĕdābâh)* that is a spontaneous gift brought to the temple (Lev 7:12–18). In all these forms of sacrifice the Bible emphasizes that the ritual be done properly so that the sacrifice can be accepted. In Leviticus we see that the *acceptance* of a sacrifice is tantamount to its being *credited* to one's account: "If any of the flesh of the sacrifice of well-being is eaten on the third day, it shall not be *acceptable [yērāṣeh; niphal imperfect of rāṣâh]; it shall not be *credited [yēḥāšeb]* to the account of the one who offered it. It is an offensive thing, and the person who eats of it shall bear his guilt" (Lev 7:18). The same point is repeated several times in the book, signifying how important it is for God to indicate his acceptance of a sacrificial gift. Consider, for example, the following: "When you sacrifice an offering of well-being to the LORD, sacrifice so that it may be *accepted* on your behalf. . . . If it should be eaten on the third day it is an offensive thing, it will not be *acceptable*" (Lev 19:5, 7).[17]

Note that in these texts the subject is the well-being sacrifice. There is no interest in marking sacrifices that have to do with atonement (the *ʾāšām* and the *ḥaṭṭāʾt*) as "acceptable." In fact, the term is never found in texts that concern sacrifices of atonement. This makes the diction of Isaiah 40:2 all the more striking. The writer sees no problem in linking a term that speaks to the acceptance of sacrifices with the notion of atonement. And this brings us back to the central question: Why does Second Isaiah use the term in such an unprecedented fashion?

FULFILLING ONE'S VOWS

To answer this, consider the contexts in which one would offer a well-being sacrifice. As I noted, the two most common circumstances would be the expression of thanks for the gracious intervention of God on one's behalf and the fulfillment of a vow. What is common to both is that they constitute a form of economic exchange. In return for a specific divine benefaction, the worshiper promises to provide payment in the form of a sacrifice, hence the formulaic expression "I will *pay off [šillēm]* the terms of my vow."[18]

Psalm 22 is an excellent example of this. It begins with an expression of horrific pain on the part of the supplicant: "My God, my God, why have you abandoned me; why are you so far from delivering me and from my anguished roaring?" (22:2). In the middle of his prayer a vow is made: should God rescue him from his plight (vv. 20–22), he will praise God in the sanctuary amid a throng of worshipers (v. 23). At the close of the psalm, after God has responded to the prayer, the psalmist recounts his fulfillment of the vow:

> *Because of You I offer praise in the great congregation;*
> *I pay my vows in the presence of His worshippers.*
> *Let the lowly eat and be satisfied;*
> *Let all who seek the LORD praise him. (Ps 22:26–27)*

Now we can see why the sacrifice of well-being was the appropriate vehicle for the context of a vow. The natural fulfillment of the vow took place around the altar amid a great festive celebration. A large crowd was appropriate because the slaughter of a sheep or goat (or even a cow) provided a tremendous amount of meat, far more than one individual or family could consume.[19] It was therefore appropriate to invite others to join one for a rather significant feast. While enjoying the freshly roasted meat ("let the lowly eat and be satisfied"), the psalmist would recount his deliverance from adversity through words of praise to his God ("I offer praise in the great congregation"). It was, in short, a moment of great celebration.

For our purposes, it is significant that the idiom used to signify the fulfillment of the vow comes from the world of commerce: "My vows *I will pay* in the presence of those who fear him" (Ps 22:26).[20] Consider the formal similarity between the completion of a vow and a sale of merchandise. Both cases involve goods: the psalmist desires deliverance, whereas the purchaser seeks a material good. In both cases we have a provider of goods (God or a seller) and contractual terms that must be met (by the buyer or the one who made the vow). In the case of a vow, the supplicant must provide the deity with the goods that he has promised, whereas the purchaser must provide an item that is equal in value to the merchandise he hopes to acquire. Because both a deed of sale and a vow involve legal obligations, there must have been some means for the seller or God to mark the acceptance of the payment. In the modern era, a cash register receipt fulfills this function, because it signifies that the owner of a store is satisfied with the money he or she has received and that the sale is final. With the receipt in hand the purchaser can take the goods out of the store without fear of being apprehended for theft and, in the future, can demand fulfillment of his or her rights (such as a warranty) by presenting the receipt at a customer-service desk. The importance of a document such as this was also appreciated in the ancient world. As Yochanan Muffs has shown, Akkadian and Aramaic deeds of sale highlight that a purchase price was both received and acknowledged as final. This portion of a contract has come to be known as a "quittance clause," perhaps because the German term for receipt is *Quittung*.[21]

It is worth considering Muffs's discussion of this idea in full, because he provides us with the key to understanding the technical sense of *rāṣâh* in Leviticus. A deed of sale must be clear about the seller's satisfaction with the money he receives lest the seller raise a claim in the future and demand additional monies. The way to make a deed of sale final and incontestable was to have the seller document that he had been "satisfied" by the payment received. Satisfaction, Muffs observed, "indicates the cessation of desire: nothing more is wanted and nothing more can be demanded in the future. In this context, therefore, [when a seller declares:] 'my heart is satisfied with the money you have given me,' [he] means: 'I am quitted after the receipt of full payment or performance.'"[22]

This observation about the role of satisfaction in a deed of sale has immense ramifications for the development of Israelite religion. To assure the person who has paid his vow that the deity has been satisfied and will not require anything additional in the future, the biblical writer takes pains to declare solemnly and in a legally binding fashion that God has "accepted" the sacrifice in question. Consider again the usage of the verb *rāṣâh* in Leviticus 7:18: "If any of the flesh of this sacrifice of well-being is eaten on the third day, *it shall not be acceptable [lo' yērāṣeh]*, it shall not be credited [*yēḥāšēb*] to the account of he who offered it. It is desecrated meat, and the person who eats of it shall bear his punishment." In this instance, improper consumption of the sacrifice will spoil the ability of the Israelite to complete—or "pay off"—his vow. The parallelism between "acceptance" (yērāṣeh) and having one's account duly accredited (yēḥāšēb) seems to settle the matter. Should the payment of a vow not be carried out properly, the deity who provided the "goods" of an answered prayer will not be "satisfied" with the payment in kind. This idiom of acceptance does not occur in sacrificial contexts related to atonement because for most of the biblical period, sacrifices of atonement have little to do with the world of commerce. As Jacob Milgrom has shown, the so-called sin-offering (ḥaṭṭāʾt) does not repay a debt. Rather, its function is to *cleanse* the sanctuary from the impurities that have accrued to it because of sin.[23]

As we have seen, however, during the Second Temple period a new metaphor takes hold in biblical soil—that of sins construed as debts. If this holds, then the meaning of rāṣâh in Isaiah 40:2 is altogether logical. Once this metaphor filters into Israelite thought and speech, it takes only a slight semantic shift to move all this language concerning the obligation to pay in satisfactory terms from the realm of a vow into the realm of atonement. *A verb (nirṣâh) that once described an individual as quit of his obligation to pay a vow naturally comes to mean someone who is quit of his obligation to repay a debt that has accrued through sin.* There is no reason to posit two different roots after all; the root in Isaiah 40:2, "her sin [conceived of as debt] has been repaid," emerges naturally.

One may wonder what sort of currency Isaiah imagines was used to pay down the debt Israel owed. The answer would seem to be the physical suffering Israel endured as debt-slaves in Babylon. As noted earlier, R. Nehemiah declared that bodily suffering repays a debt. But he goes even further and says that suffering provides a better form of atonement than animal sacrifices, because "animal sacrifices are acquired with money whereas sufferings come at the price to the body."[24] And as the book of Job testifies, one's physical well-being is one of life's highest values: "Skin for sin, all that a man possesses he will give on account of his life" (Job 2:4).

All scholars would agree that the usage of rāṣâh in Isaiah 40:2 is highly unusual. The lexicon of Brown, Driver, and Briggs gets the meaning right ("her punishment is accepted as satisfactory") but has to list this text in a separate section.[25] The user of the dictionary is left puzzled as to how the idea of satisfaction for sin evolved. Koehler and Baumgartner, building on the work of Fraenkel, believe there are two roots in play, one of which means to be acceptable, the other to repay (rāṣâh I and rāṣâh II in their nomenclature).[26] Yet it is a basic principle of lexicography that one should opt for two roots only as a last resort. It is for this reason that I desired to show that the putative root *rāṣâh* II is nothing other than a logical development of *rāṣâh* I.

But my point here is hardly limited to philology. Linking these two meanings reveals quite a bit about how sin was viewed in the early Second Temple period. For the author of Second Isaiah, Israel's sins at the close of the First Temple period had put her over her head in debt. Decades of penal service in Babylon would be required to satisfy its terms.

For some readers, the solution to this philological puzzle will create a theological problem. If Israel falls into debt as a result of her sins and must suffer for a specified period in order to satisfy that debt, then God looks like a small-minded accountant whose relationship to Israel is somewhat vindictive. Blenkinsopp remarks, at the close of his comments on the debt imagery of Isaiah 40, that for many these "metaphors [will] sound too legalistic."[27]

I agree with Blenkinsopp that this is a perceptual danger. But at the same time, I think it would be an unfair reading of the materials we have examined. Human sins have consequences. When individuals disobey moral law, a tangible form of evil is created in the world that must be accounted for. And this is even more true when a whole society goes astray. One recalls the horrible sin of slavery in this country in the seventeenth and eighteenth centuries. It is a demonstrable fact that American culture has paid deeply for this travesty and continues to do so. Would it not be a word of grace to hear that our communal suffering has been brought to closure, the debt satisfied? In my mind, this is the type of reality that biblical authors are trying to express. Human wickedness does have a cost, but those costs are not infinite. Second Isaiah can speak his words of comfort because the term of punishment that God has permitted Israel to suffer has come to a close. "Her debt has been satisfied; she has received double for all her sins."

5

ancient creditors, bound laborers,
and the sanctity of the land

In the previous chapter I traced the origins of the metaphor for sin as a debt back to the prophet Second Isaiah. I did not mention, however, that the root *rāṣâh* also occurs in Leviticus 26. Although the usage is similar, Leviticus 26 adds one important detail: it assumes that not only Israel but the land as well must repay a debt. The responsibility of the land for its own debt comes as a surprise, for the main concern has been Israel's responsibility to the commandments she has been given.

To make sense of this new concept, I turn to Leviticus 25, where the role of land in the accumulation and discharge of debt is given considerable emphasis. In this chapter, I explore the complex relationship between these two chapters of Leviticus. I hope to show that both originated as independent entities and that a later editor made a few key adjustments so that the theme of Israel's indebtedness would be the common thread holding them together.

The dating of these two chapters is important. Biblical scholars generally agree that the book of Leviticus divides into two units: chapters 1–16, which come from the Priestly School, and chapters 17–26 (27, the last chapter, is a late supplement to the whole book), which comes from the Holiness School. It had traditionally been thought that the Holiness School preceded the Priestly School, but recent research has shown rather conclusively that the opposite was the case.[1] It is difficult to provide an absolute date for either of these collections, and scholars vary considerably. But suffice it to say that many of the traditions found in the Priestly School date to the First Temple period (the goat that bears away the sins of Israel would be one), even if the final form of the text does not. As to chapters 25 and 26, it is my opinion that both in their original form would have been composed in the First Temple period but that their final redaction took place during the exile or even later. The fact that Israel's sins are conceived of as debts in the latest redactional layer of Leviticus 26 is sound proof of its exilic provenance. But before turning to the question of how these texts were redacted, I wish to examine their structure and show how they work as independent literary units.

LEVITICUS 25

After a brief introduction in the first verse, chapter 25 divides into three parts: (1) the law of the Sabbatical year (vv. 2–7); (2) the law of the Jubilee year (8–22), which is immediately followed by a short description of the principle upon which the Jubilee year rests (23–24); and (3) a set of laws regarding real estate transactions that take place in between the Jubilees (25–55). The Sabbatical year occurs every seven years, the logic of this law following from the observance of the weekly Sabbath. The Israelite farmer is allowed to work his land for six consecutive years, but in the seventh the land must be left fallow: "When you enter the land that I assign to you, the land shall observe a Sabbath of the LORD. Six years you may sow your field and six years you may prune your vineyard and gather in the yield. But in the seventh year the land shall have a Sabbath of complete rest, a Sabbath of the LORD: you shall not sow your field or prune your vineyard" (Lev 25: 2b–4). It is striking that the law is introduced not on an anthropocentric but rather on a "terracentric" principle. It is the land that must rest, and Israel is enjoined to respect this God-given right of the land. Contemporary readers will immediately think of the scientific need of land to replenish itself after being farmed. This is no quaint prescription from the ancient world; every modern farmer employs a similar procedure. But there is more to this law than simple science, which I shall discuss later in the chapter.

The law for the Jubilee (8–22) assumes this seven-year unit and extends its logic. It declares that at the end of seven consecutive Sabbatical cycles— that is, forty-nine years—one must observe the Jubilee year. In that year, that is, the fiftieth, the land shall continue in its fallow state, and everyone who has been forced to sell land for whatever reason returns to the original holding. The reason for this extraordinary procedure is grounded in the fact that God is the true owner of the land, so that any sale of the land is really only a lease that allows the "purchaser" to turn a profit from the crops he raises for whatever time remains until the next Jubilee: "But the land must not be sold beyond reclaim, *for the land is Mine;* you are but strangers resident with Me. Throughout the land that you hold, you must provide for the redemption of the land" (Lev 25:23–24).

The laws for the redemption of property follow naturally from the Jubilee legislation. If the land is truly the property of God, then no "sale" can ever be final. Provision must be made to enable persons to whom God originally deeded the land to return to their patrimony. The land was originally bequeathed to the various tribes of Israel, and within those tribal units it must remain in perpetuity.

The remainder of the chapter (vv. 25–55) addresses the different levels of poverty an Israelite might fall into and the options available to him. The first situation concerns an individual who has been forced to sell a portion of his property (vv. 25–34). Perhaps he borrowed money at the beginning of the planting season to buy seed and then experienced crop failure. Unable to repay the cost of his seed, he is forced to make amends by putting up a portion of his land for sale. After the sale has been made, three options exist for the restoration of the property. First, a near relative can come forward and buy the land from the purchaser. This is the classic definition of redemption in the Bible, and an individual who acts in such a way is known as a redeemer.[2] Second, a seller may buy himself out of his predicament. For example, during the next planting season his fields might produce a large yield. (He has not, after all, sold all his land and thus retains the ability to secure an income.) Should neither of these solutions eventuate, the land will naturally return to the seller or his children at the Jubilee.

The second scenario (vv. 35–38) is worse than the first. In this case the debt the Israelite farmer has assumed requires him to sell all of his land.[3] He thereafter becomes a tenant farmer under the supervision of his creditor. Although it appears as if he has lost everything, this law requires the creditor to allow him the opportunity to make an income. Milgrom suggests, with good reason, that the injunction to allow the debtor to subsist under the creditor's authority (v. 35) means that the creditor must continue to provide the necessary funds to allow the impoverished farmer to seed his land.[4] In light of this, the Bible strictly admonishes the creditor that he must not exact any interest and so cause further hardship for the debtor: "Do not lend him your money at advance interest, or give him your food at accrued interest" (v. 37). Why is such generosity required? It is grounded in the saving act that secured the possibility of owning the land in the first place: "I the LORD, am your God, who brought you out of the land of Egypt, to give you the land of Canaan, to be your God" (v. 38). This section, unlike the

first, does not speak to the possibility of the indebted farmer being redeemed by a near kinsman or coming upon sufficient funds to redeem himself. But it seems fair to assume that those options carry forward from the
first to the second situation.

The third section (vv. 39–55) takes up a different sort of situation, in
which the focus is no longer on the loss of land but on the process of becoming a debt-slave. (Of course the two are closely related in that servitude
of this nature can occur only after one has lost all of one's land. But that
being said, this section emphasizes not the loss of land but the consequences
of having all one's sources of income dry up.) Leviticus, however, refrains
from using the term slave (ʿebed) to describe this unfortunate person: "If
your kinsman under you continues in straits and must give himself over to
you, do not subject him to the treatment of a slave. He shall remain with you
as a *hired or bound laborer*" (25:39–40a). This impoverished person loses
his freedom and lives within the household of his creditor as a resident
hireling and receives proper wages for his efforts. But when the Jubilee year
arrives, he and his family are freed from this bondage and are allowed to
return to their ancestral holdings. The grounds for this treatment issue from
fact that God acquired Israel as *his* people when he liberated them from
Egypt: "For they are My [slaves], whom I freed from the land of Egypt; they
may not give themselves over into servitude" (v. 42).[5] The only condition in
which Israel can be addressed as a "slave" is with regard to her relationship
to God. Only YHWH can be her Lord.

The chapter closes with a consideration of what happens to a non-Israelite (vv. 44–46, 47–55). First, should a non-Israelite find himself in desperate financial straits, unlike the Israelite, he can be purchased as a debt-
slave (vv. 44–46). The law against slavery, one must recall, is grounded in
God's redemption of Israel in Egypt; those nations who were not acquired
in this fashion do not share the special status that falls to Israel. One might
imagine that the non-Israelite in turn could enslave an Israelite. But such is
not the case. God guarantees the special status of the Israelites no matter
who "owns" them (vv. 47–55). Should an Israelite fall into financial straits
and be forced to work for a non-Israelite, this "owner" has no more rights
over the impoverished family than would an Israelite owner. The Israelite
will live under the authority of this resident alien as a "hired laborer"
(v. 53).

The above discourse presents four discrete stages of falling into poverty:
the selling of a portion of one's land; selling all of one's land; becoming a
hired laborer within the household of another Israelite; and, finally, be-

coming a laborer within the household of a non-Israelite. How is this literary unit related to the earlier portions of the chapter? The answer is simple: the Jubilee year. For the Bible imagines that however badly the Israelite may fare, there are three options open to him. First, should his good fortunes be restored, he can earn enough income while serving under another family to redeem himself and his land. Second, should his own fortunes not be sufficient, a family member is always free to step into the breach and provide the redemption monies. This is the socioeconomic background of the institution of the redeemer. God, as Israel's redeemer, is imagined as a near kinsman whose help is called upon when Israel is similarly beleaguered. Finally, if there is no redeemer, the impoverished Israelite (or his offspring) is entitled to return to his land with the arrival of the Jubilee year. As the option of last resort, the Jubilee guarantees that God's initial bequest of land to particular families within the tribal structure of ancient Israel can never be undone. Why is this the case? Because Israel is the personal property of the God who redeemed her in the first place: "For it is to Me that the Israelites are [slaves]. They are My [slaves], whom I freed from the land of Egypt. I the LORD your God" (25:54b–55). Because of God's prior claim over Israel, all other claims to ownership must be provisional and temporary.

LEVITICUS 26

At first chapter 26 appears to have no special relationship to 25. As we shall see, there are grounds for reading this chapter as the fitting conclusion to *all* the laws that have been promulgated over the previous twenty-five chapters of Leviticus. The chapter divides neatly into two parts. In the first, God tells Israel what the consequences of fidelity to the commandments will be. Should she prove obedient, a life of blessing and prosperity shall ensue (vv. 3–13): rain will come in its season, the crops will flourish in the fields, peace will reign in the land, and great success will attend every military sortie. In brief, God will look with favor upon the people of Israel and his presence shall abide in their midst. In the second, God warns of what will come should Israel prove unfaithful to her charge. God will not let such infidelity pass unnoticed. He will issue four stern warnings, and should they all fail, Israel will be exiled from her land.[6]

First Warning (vv. 14–17): Disease and defeat by enemies
Second Warning (vv. 18–20): Severe drought
Third Warning (vv. 21–22): Loosing of wild beasts
Fourth Warning (vv. 23–26): Sword, pestilence, and famine

Final Punishment (vv. 27–33, 36–38): Utter devastation of the land and exile of its inhabitants

Many scholars have noted the parallels between Leviticus 26 and Deuteronomy 28. Both texts document the blessings that will attend the keeping of the divine commandments and the punishments that will ensue should Israel rebel. Also, both texts come at the end of their respective law codes. Yet despite such similarities it is important to note a significant difference. In Leviticus 26 the interventions that God makes in light of Israel's disobedience are not punishments in the true sense of the word. They would be more accurately described as disciplinary measures intended to get Israel's attention.

If all we had was the first warning, we might not notice this, because it looks like a punishment, pure and simple:

> [First Warning] But if you do not obey Me and do not observe all these commandments . . . I, in turn will do this to you: I will wreak misery upon you—consumption and fever, which cause the eyes to pine and the body to languish; you shall sow your seed to no purpose, for your enemies shall eat it. I will set My face against you: you shall be routed by your enemies, and your foes shall dominate you. You shall flee though none pursues. (26:14a, 16–17)

But as soon as we read the next verse, we discover the rationale for this divine intervention. The punishments that God visits upon Israel are best characterized as disciplinary measures:

> [Second Warning] And if, for all that, you do not obey Me, I will go on to discipline you sevenfold for your sins, and I will break your proud glory. I will make your skies like iron and your earth like copper, so that your strength shall be spent to no purpose. Your land shall not yield its produce, nor shall the trees of the land yield their fruit. (26:18–20)

The opening sentence says all one needs to know about how to contextualize the second punishment that God plans to deliver against Israel. It is not so much a punishment weighed out against a specific offense as a warning signal designed to get Israel's attention. Indeed, each of the succeeding sets of actions are prefaced in the same formulaic manner:

> [Third Warning] And if you remain hostile toward Me and refuse to obey Me, I will go on smiting you sevenfold for your sins. I will loose wild beasts against you. (26:21–22a)

[Fourth Warning] And if these things fail to discipline you for Me, and you remain hostile to Me, I too will remain hostile to you: I in turn will smite you sevenfold for your sins. I will bring a sword against you to wreak vengeance for the covenant.(26:23–25a)

If all four warnings fail to achieve their purpose, God will have no other choice but to bring Israel to the brink of destruction:

[Final Punishment] But if, despite this, you disobey Me and remain hostile to Me, I will act against you in wrathful hostility; I, for My part, will discipline you sevenfold for you sins. You shall eat the flesh of your sons. (26:27–29)

In the concluding section (vv. 27–38), the time for warnings has passed. There is no language about disciplining Israel (cf. vv. 18 and 23). Rather, God promises to destroy all of Israel's cities and sanctuaries, to leave the land in such desolation that even conquering armies will stand in horror, and to scatter the Israelites among the nations (vv. 31–33).

AN EDITORIAL ADDITION TO LEVITICUS 26

One might think that the picture drawn in this penultimate chapter of Leviticus is clear and straightforward. Blessings are promised in response to obedience (vv. 1–13), and warnings are issued should Israel rebel (vv. 14–26). After the fourth warning, God's patience will have reached an end and Israel will be exiled from her land (vv. 27–39). Yet the chapter contains one more section. After describing the price of not heeding divine warnings, it closes with the promise to restore Israel (vv. 40–45). Nearly all scholars agree that this final section constitutes a later editorial addition. In their minds, it is unlikely that the original author would have ended his composition on an upbeat note. To inject such optimism would spoil the rhetorical effect that had been building since the beginning. For some thirteen verses (vv. 14–26) the author provides a set of escalating warnings. The purpose of these warnings is to *persuade* Israel to reconsider her behavior before it is too late. Should Israel prove uncorrectable, one can assume that she will eventually exhaust God's patience will have to pay the ultimate price for her rebellious ways. At its earliest level of composition, the chapter would have ended like this:[7]

But if, despite this, you disobey Me and remain hostile to Me, I will act against you in wrathful hostility: I, for My part, will discipline you sevenfold for your sins. You shall eat the flesh of your sons and the flesh of your daughters. I will destroy your cult places and cut down your incense stands, and I will heap your carcasses upon your lifeless fetishes. I will spurn you. I will lay your cities in ruin and make your sanctuaries desolate, and I will not savor your pleasing odors. I will make the land desolate, so that your enemies who settle in it shall be appalled by it. And you I will scatter among the nations, and I will unsheath the sword against you. . . . You shall not be able to stand your ground before your enemies, but shall perish among the nations; and the land of your enemies shall consume you. (vv. 27–33a, 37b–38)

If this had been the original form of the chapter, the author would have put before his hearers a stern but persuasive message: Consider carefully how you will act, O Israel! But if the chapter ends with God reversing course and allowing Israel to return (vv. 33b-37a, 39–45), the threats he had issued would lose much of their rhetorical force. As H. L. Ginsberg explains, "[A] suzerain would be defeating his purpose of deterring a vassal from playing him false if he weakened at any point and intimated that his bark was worse than his bite and the vassal need never despair of being restored to grace even if he rebels and fails; and by the same token, a religious writer who wished to deter Israel from going the limit would be defeating his own ends if he assured Israel that YHWH was incurably indulgent after all."[8]

One may wish to venture an objection here. The logic Ginsberg employs may be suitable for ancient Near Eastern treaty texts that deal with earthly vassals and suzerains, but things could be different for the Holy One of Israel. He, after all, need not follow the political calculus of human potentates. In theory that is true, but if we look at other texts in the Bible, we see that when God warns Israel about the abuse of his covenant, the result for Israel is not always pretty. For example, among the oracles of the eighth-century prophet Amos we find a long diatribe against the rebellious ways of the citizens of the northern kingdom. After mocking their feigned religious observances (Amos 4:4–5), Amos declares that God will send a series of warnings in hopes that Israel might turn away from her disobedience. The first consists of a severe failure at harvest time:

> *[First Warning] I, on My part, have given you*
> *Cleanness of teeth in all your towns,*
> *And lack of food in all your settlements.*
> *Yet you did not turn back to Me*
> *—declares the Lord. (4:6)*

But this warning, like those we see in Leviticus 26, was evidently not sufficient to restore Israel to her senses. So this time God takes harsher measures and sends a drought that sorely affects both the food and water supplies:

> [Second Warning] I therefore withheld the rain from you
> Three months before harvest time:
> I would make it rain on one town
> And not on another;
> One field would be rained upon
> While another on which it did not rain would wither.
> So two or three towns would wander
> To a single town to drink water,
> But their thirst would not be slaked. (4:7-8)

Yet despite this second set of warnings, Israel does not heed the message. This warning ends exactly as did the first: "Yet you did not turn back to Me, —declares the LORD."

God then sends even more warnings upon Israel. The third (v. 9) consists of blight and mildew that destroy the gardens and vineyards. Locusts then follow, which devastate the fig and olive trees. And yet again, Israel does not turn back. God endures this patiently and tries once more to get Israel's attention (v. 10). This time he sends a pestilence like the one the Egyptians had endured, followed by the sword, leaving many slain. Yet Israel remains stubbornly unbowed. At this point, Amos declares, Israel's fate is sealed. The warnings have failed and God's patience has come to an end. Amos tells the citizens of Israel to "prepare to meet your God" (v. 12), which threatens an end to the existence of the northern kingdom. And, in fact, that end did come. In 721 BCE Assyrian armies invaded Israel from the north, destroyed the major urban centers of Israelite nation, and sent many of its leaders into exile (see II Kings 17).

A similar sort of logic informs the set of blessings and curses found in Deuteronomy 28. Like Leviticus 26, this text closes the Deuteronomic law code (chaps. 12–26). Second, both chapters can be divided into two sections: a set of blessings that will follow upon obedience and a set of curses should Israel commit apostasy. Although the punishments in Deuteronomy 28 are not a set of structured warnings like those in Leviticus, the overall rhetorical effect is similar. Should Israel brazenly resist being tutored in the ways of the Lord, her existence as his vassal will come to an abrupt termination. The chapter provides not even a scintilla of hope; the results of disobedience are catastrophic.[9]

Up to this point I have been examining the rhetorical shape of literary units within larger biblical books. The threatened total destruction of Israel holds true only if we keep our focus on a specific literary unit such as Amos 4:4–12 or Deuteronomy 28. If we step back, however, and cast our glance over the final form of a biblical book, the picture looks different. No biblical work, in its full canonical form, is content to describe Israel's destruction as a closed and final matter. Although God will for a time avert his face (*hester pānîm*, in rabbinic terminology), in the end he will "turn" (from the Hebrew root *šûb*) his glance back toward his people and restore them. Whatever Amos might have thought, the person who edited his oracles made room for the reconstitution of the people of Israel. The sections that speak of Israel's restoration, however, are found at some distance from the oracles that threaten her complete destruction. Indeed, one must wait until the last nine verses of the book (Amos 9:7–15) to find them. There, God declares that though he had to punish Israel for her unrepentant apostasy, he "will not wipe out the House of Jacob" (9:8). Indeed, the day will come when he shall restore "the fallen booth of David" and "restore [his] people of Israel" (vv. 11, 14). Similarly in the book of Deuteronomy one can find a promise of restoration (30:1–10), but it is located at some remove from the prophecy of Israel's utter destruction (28:58–68). In other words, the editors of Amos and Deuteronomy were willing to leave the threat of destruction untouched in its immediate literary environment. Only at a point somewhat removed from the oracle did the subsequent author-editor see fit to update the message to allow for the restoration of Israel.[10] What makes Leviticus 26 unique with respect to Amos and Deuteronomy is that the words of restoration have been incorporated into the very chapter that has spoken of the demise of Israel.[11]

KEEPING THE SABBATH

If we grant that H. L. Ginsberg and his many supporters are correct in hypothesizing that Leviticus 26 originally ended in the destruction of Israel, let us step back and take a look at the editorial additions at the conclusion of this chapter and how they are related to what comes before. I think we will see that the way the editor of Leviticus 26 has reshaped his material so as to hold out hope for Israel is as brilliant as it is creative.

In its final form, Leviticus 26 differs remarkably from the note of encouragement found at the close of Deuteronomy. The focus of the latter work is rather simple turn to the Lord in remorse over sin and make a genuine appeal for forgiveness: "When all these things befall you . . . and you take them to heart . . . and return to the LORD your God, . . . then the LORD your God will restore your fortunes and take you back in love" (30:1–3). The issue is slightly more complicated for the author of Leviticus. Contrition is certainly important, but just as important is satisfying the debt that both the land and the nation owe: "For the land shall be forsaken of them and will *repay the debt for its Sabbath years by being desolate of them, while they shall repay their debt*; for the abundant reason that they rejected My rules and spurned My laws. Yet, even then, when they are in the land of their enemies, I will not despise them or abhor them so as to destroy them, breaking My covenant with them: for I the LORD am their God. I will remember in their favor the covenant with the ancients, whom I freed from the land of Egypt in the sight of the nations to be their God: I, the LORD" (Lev 26: 43–45).[12]

I mentioned at the beginning of the chapter that the Sabbatical year was a deeper concept in ancient Israel than its modern agrarian parallel might suggest. It is not simply an ecological action that assures the ongoing fertility of the land. By leaving the land fallow every six years, one is keeping a divine command that instantiates the fact that land belongs not to human beings but to God. Just as the rest on the seventh day bespeaks a larger claim of God over the domain of time, so the setting to rest of the land in the seventh year testifies to the ownership of land by God.[13] Because this obligation is imposed on both Israel and the land,—both will be in violation of their duties should the commandment be flouted. And accordingly, both will be required to make amends. In the description of that compensation, it should be noted that the verb used to denote repayment is the same verbal root we saw in Second Isaiah, *rāṣâh*. Just as Second Isaiah declares that the exile has drawn to a close because the debt owed on Israel's sin had been repaid—*nirṣâ ʿăwōnâh*—so Leviticus 26 declares that Israel will remain in her current plight until such time as the land has "repa[id] the debt of its Sabbath years" and the Israelites have "repa[id] the debt accrued through their iniquity."[14] The only real difference, then, between Isaiah 40:2 and Leviticus 26:43–45 is that the former looks backward on a debt that has already been repaid, whereas the latter anticipates what sort of repayment will be required should Israel not respond to the warnings her God has issued.

Let us step back and look at Leviticus 26:43–45 in light of the overall structure of the chapter. First, the special significance accorded to the Sabbatical year is unexpected. The language of commandment keeping in this chapter has a generic quality and does not seem to privilege one commandment over another. Second, the introduction of the theme of repaying a debt through enduring the exile transforms in toto the force of the final punishment that God has imposed on Israel. As we noted, this chapter takes care to mark how God warns Israel as a means of provoking her to reconsider her sinful ways.

In its immediate literary environment (26:2–33a; 37b-38), the punishment appears total and final. But once we factor in the redactional additions to this chapter (26:33b–35, 39–45), God's final punishment takes on a new character. Devastation of the land is no longer just a punishment but a means of securing enough years of nonuse so that the land can pay back what it owes for the Sabbath years it has not observed. And the suffering Israel must undergo is not simply a measure-for-measure punishment but rather a process of restoration. Over her many years of willful violation of the Lord's statutes, Israel has amassed a grievous debt. Her only hope at this point is to endure the penalty she owes in a righteous manner and in so doing begin to repay the debt she owes.

Jacob Milgrom has noted that use of the verb *rāṣâh* in the sense of "to atone" (by repaying a debt) can be explained by the fact that Israel had no cultic modes of atonement available while she was in exile and the temple was in ruins.[15] Although there may be some truth to this observation, the reader should recall what we established in earlier chapters: in the exilic and postexilic periods the leading metaphor for sin becomes that of a debt, and atonement is construed as repaying on a debt. Given that fact, the appearance of this idiom in Leviticus 26 does not require the absence of the temple. Rather, it fits the historical development of the metaphors for sin we have been tracing. But in addition there is an important literary dimension. By describing Israel's sin as a debt to be repaid, our canonical editors were able to forge a crucial link between Leviticus 25 and 26. And we shall see in the next chapter on the book of Daniel that the influence of Leviticus 25–26 on Second Temple Judaism was enormous. Without the link between these two chapters, the book of Leviticus would be read very differently.

LINKING LEVITICUS 25 TO LEVITICUS 26

For most casual readers, there are few elements of commonality between Leviticus 25 and 26. Chapter 25 has as its main concerns the commandments of the Sabbatical and Jubilee years (25:1–24) and how they are related to laws for redemption (vv. 25–55). Chapter 26 can be divided into two parts: the blessings that accrue to Israel should she obey *all the commandments* she has received (26:3–14) and the consequences for persistent disobedience (15–45). In between these chapters stand two transitional verses: "You shall not make idols for yourselves, or set up for yourselves carved images or pillars, or place figured stones in your land to worship upon, for I the LORD am your God. You shall keep My sabbaths and venerate My sanctuary, Mine, the LORD's" (26:1–2). These verses are aptly labeled "the essence of God's commandments" in Milgrom's commentary, for the wording of these verses recalls the opening and closing of Leviticus 19:

> Do not turn to idols or make molten gods for yourselves: I am the LORD your God. (19:4)
> You shall keep My sabbaths and venerate My sanctuary: I am the LORD. (19:30)

In between these two verses (Lev 19:5–29) one finds the most diverse catalogue of commandments anywhere in the book of Leviticus. This selection of commandments is meant as a summary of *all* the commandments in the Torah. Leviticus 19, in other words, makes the claim that every commandment is of equal weight and that through keeping *any* of them, the Israelites have the opportunity of absorbing something of the holiness of God and becoming holy themselves.[16]

The generic quality of the commandments must be underscored. Although Leviticus 26 follows a chapter devoted to specific commandments (those having to do with land tenure), its scope is far broader. Minimally, Leviticus 26 is to be considered a conclusion to the book of Leviticus and, maximally, a summary of all the legislation that has been given at Mt. Sinai, beginning with the Decalogue in Exodus 20.[17] This generic dimension of the text is clear from the way both the blessing (vv. 2–13) and punishment (vv. 14–45) begin. There is no hint that any special consideration is to be given to the Sabbatical and Jubilee laws of Leviticus 25.

> If you follow My laws and faithfully observe My commandments, I will grant your rains in their season. (26:3–4a)
> But if you do not obey Me and do not observe all these commandments, if you reject My laws and spurn My rules, so that you do not observe all My commandments and you break My covenant, I in turn will do this to you: I will wreak misery upon you—consumption and fever. (26:14–16a)

The most natural way to hear these texts is to imagine them as a logical conclusion to all the commandments heard at Mt. Sinai.

Yet the canonical shapers of Leviticus have complicated the picture by giving signs that Leviticus 26 is tightly integrated to the laws of the previous chapter. This is well documented in the way traditional Jewish commentators have heard the opening verses of Leviticus 26.[18] They do not understand the references to idolatry in 26:1 as an allusion to Leviticus 19 and its generic tabulation of Israel's legal responsibility. Rather, they take their cue for interpreting this verse from the end of Leviticus 25. The last literary unit of that chapter outlined the status of the Israelite who became so poor that he had to turn himself over to a non-Israelite landowner. For Rashi (R. Shlomo Itshaqi), an eleventh century Jewish commentator from France, this was the ultimate travesty, for even the most pious Israelite would feel a certain social pressure to act as his neighbors acted. In his mind, this unfortunate Israelite would reason as follows: "Since my owner worships idols, so shall I; since my owner desecrates the Sabbath, so shall I."[19]

It should also be noted that Leviticus 26 opens with the command "to keep My sabbaths and venerate My sanctuary." As Milgrom concluded, this command in its original form—that is, prior to the linkage of chapter 26 to 25—referred only to the regular weekly Sabbath, as is clear from the parallel in Leviticus 19:30 ("You shall keep My sabbaths and venerate My Sanctuary"). But when this verse is put in dialogue with Leviticus 25, it takes on new significance. The plural form "Sabbaths" must include the Sabbatical year mentioned in Leviticus 25. Ibn Ezra (a twelfth-century Jewish commentator from Spain) says this explicitly in his commentary and adds that the command to revere the sanctuary includes the responsibility to keep the Jubilee year. That way *both* parts of Leviticus 26:2 refer back to Leviticus 25. Even Ibn Ezra, who normally is more circumspect than Rashi in his use of the midrash, felt a need to link 26:2 to the context established in chapter 25.

The question, then, is why do traditional commentators such as Rashi and Ibn Ezra see the need to establish links between Leviticus 25 and 26? The answer can be found in the peculiar literary structure of these two chapters. First, whenever the author of Leviticus wishes to open a new literary unit he begins with the following formula: "The LORD spoke to Moses [regarding the keeping of some commandment] saying . . ." This formula occurs some thirty-three times within the twenty-seven chapters of the book. But when we get past chapters 8 through 10, which document the beginnings of the public liturgy at the Tabernacle and in which the revelation of the commandments begins again, every chapter from 11 through 27 begins with this formula—except for chapter 26. That gives chapters 25 and 26 the appearance of being one continuous literary unit. This is shown in Hebrew biblical scrolls and reflected in medieval Hebrew manuscripts as well. These texts, which did not possess chapter numbers (they are a late, Christian addition to the text), mark literary breaks by leaving a blank space of a few letters' length. Yet they placed no such blank space at the close of chapter 25; the last verse of chapter 25 runs right into the first verse of chapter 26. Only in 26:3 do these Hebrew texts indicate the beginning of a new paragraph.

Finally, the closing formula of this long literary unit is somewhat unusual: "These are the laws, rules, and instructions that the LORD established, through Moses on Mount Sinai, between himself and the Israelite People" (26:46). If one had only this verse in view, one would have to conclude that it refers back to all the "laws, rules, and instructions" that had been given over the course of the book. And, no doubt, that is true in part. But there is an oddity to this formula. Moses is said to have received all these laws "at Mount Sinai."[20] Why does the writer want to emphasize that location at this point in the text? This odd feature is repeated at the opening of chapter 25: "The LORD spoke to Moses on Mount Sinai: Speak to the Israelite people and say to them . . ." (25:1). The formula that opens chapter 25 is found all through the book of Leviticus. Thirty-two occurrences of this formula read: "The LORD spoke to Moses." Only in Leviticus 25:1 do we find the addition "The LORD spoke to Moses *on Mount Sinai*." Clearly our final editor has tried to create a "frame" between the beginning of this literary unit (25:1) and its conclusion (26:46).[21]

What is the significance of the structural links between these two chapters? For one, they explain the appearance of the Sabbatical laws near the end of Leviticus 26. As outlined above, the chapter is intent on showing the consequence of Israel's obedience or disobedience to the entire Torah she has received. But the redactor of Leviticus 26 is not comfortable with this generic picture that makes no distinction among the commandments. To be sure, the redactor reasons, the violation of the commandments has warranted God's harshest form of punishment, but restoration will depend on both Israel's *and the land's* making up for what they owed (26:34–35, 40–45). To make that point clear, the chapter ends by stressing the importance of one commandment: keeping the Sabbatical years.

In the context of Leviticus, this should not be surprising, since the land is imagined as an autonomous agent. Consider the unique story of the conquest. There was no need for marauding armies to wipe out the entire

Canaanite population, as the book of Deuteronomy envisioned.[22] According to Leviticus, it was the *land* itself that spewed the Canaanites forth (18:25). The verb used here means literally "to vomit" and therefore implies a reflexive quality over which the agent (the land of Israel) has little or no control. Israel herself will have no special privileges on this score. If she acts according to the norms of the Canaanites, the land will spew her forth as well (Lev 18:28). But in Leviticus 18 the writer's focus is the Canaanites' sexual mores. Sexual purity seems to be of preeminent concern regarding one's tenure on this special piece of real estate. In Leviticus 26, on the other hand, the central issue is the Sabbatical year.

One might conclude that the Sabbatical year is so important in Leviticus 26 solely because of two factors. First is the link the writer is trying to establish between chapters 25 and 26; second is the personification of the land, as evidenced in Leviticus 18. But there is a third historical factor as well. As scholars have long noted, biblical texts from the exilic and postexilic periods have a strong tendency to accentuate the significance of keeping the Sabbath. In fact, one could argue that for many late biblical writers keeping the Sabbath was understood as one of the most important commandments. Milgrom observes, for example, that in the book of Ezekiel Sabbath keeping "achieves an importance equivalent to the rest of the commandments (e.g., Ezek 20:13, 21), alongside [the proscription of] idolatry (Ezek 20:16, 24), and in one verse (23:38) it is conjoined with the sanctuary, just as in [Lev] 26:2."[23] But it is not just Ezekiel who ascribes such importance to this particular commandment; one finds a similar emphasis in Jeremiah (17:19–27), Isaiah (56:2, 4, 6; 58:13), and Nehemiah (13:18).[24] To appreciate how novel this is, one must recall that there are almost no references to keeping the Sabbath anywhere in the First Temple period. In other words, for most biblical texts, it is a commandment that receives scant attention.

READING LEVITICUS 25 IN LIGHT OF LEVITICUS 26

There is one more detail worth mentioning. In Chapter 3 I noted that the author of 11QMelchizedek linked the release of debtors in the Jubilee year with the release of Israel from her sins. I concluded that this document from Qumran interpreted Deuteronomy 15 and Leviticus 25 as though these biblical texts spoke to Israel's sinful state. Such an interpretive move is not surprising in light of the larger shift we have been documenting in the Second Temple period, wherein sins stopped being weights and turned into debts. I observed that one could consult numerous commentaries on Deuteronomy 15 and Leviticus 25 and not find a single one that would interpret those chapters in a way that had anything to do with sin. But is this claim really true? Does Leviticus 25 have nothing to do with sin?

In answer, let us turn to traditional Jewish exegesis. Both the rabbis and the medieval Jewish commentators on the Bible were conscious of the link that the first two verses of chapter 26 provided between Leviticus 25 and 26 (though they would not have described them as redactional). But the issue goes deeper. A number of rabbinic texts posited that the entire structure of Leviticus 25 could be understood anew in light of the contents of Leviticus 26. To appreciate these rabbinic texts, let us recall the structure of Leviticus 25. It begins with the law for the Sabbatical year (vv. 2–7) and then turns to the Jubilee (vv. 8–24). The rest of the chapters (vv. 25–55) are devoted to various individuals who fall on hard times: (1) a man who must sell part of his land (vv. 25–28); (2) a man who must sell a home in a walled city (vv. 29–34); (3) a man who must sell all of his land (vv. 35–38); and, finally, a man who becomes a slave and must move into the household of either an Israelite master (vv. 39–46) or a foreigner (vv. 47–55).

In my initial reading, I suggest that the chapter intended to cover as many themes of impoverishment as possible owing to the sale of one's land. R. Samuel, son of Gedaliah, however, in a midrash we shall follow, understands the chapter differently.[25] In his mind the opening laws about the Sabbatical and Jubilee years are closely connected to the subsequent case laws regarding individuals who fall into poverty. He begins his interpretation by invoking an architectural metaphor, observing that just as every capital must rest on a pedestal, so must the structure of a legal unit such as Leviticus 25 rest on a solid base. The chapter opens by stating its central subject matter (its "capital"), in this case, the two laws about the Sabbatical and Jubilee years (25:1–12), and then follows this with case laws (vv. 13–55) related to that subject matter (the "pedestal").

What is striking, however, is R. Samuel's understanding of the individual cases. They are not a simple miscellany; rather, they are to be understood as graded warnings. Should Israel not keep the Sabbatical or Jubilee years, then a set of progressive punishments will follow. After each punishment—or perhaps better, warning—the offender is given the opportunity to repent. Should that option not be exploited, the next case—construed as another warning—follows. In the end, when all the warnings fail, the offender, as well as the entire nation, finds himself in exile:

Rabbi Samuel, the son of Gedaliah, said:

A   There is no literary unit in the Torah that does not express its general subject matter ("capital") first and then its content ("pedestal").

B   How is the general subject matter of Leviticus 25 expressed? "The LORD spoke to Moses on Mt. Sinai: Speak to the sons of Israel. . . . When you enter the land that I assign to you, the land shall observe a Sabbath of the LORD." (25:1–2)

C   And after the unit about the Sabbatical year comes the unit about the Jubilee: "You shall count off seven weeks of years." (v. 8–12)

And from this subject matter follow these cases:

D   If one does not observe the Sabbatical year and the Jubilee the result will be that he will have to sell his movable property. This is in accord with scripture: "Should you need to sell property to your neighbor . . ." (25:14)

E   If he repents of the misdeed, then things will be well; if not, then he will end up selling his field. For scripture says: "If your kinsmen falls into straits and is forced to sell some of his property . . ." (25:25–28)

F   If he repents of the misdeed, then things will be well; if not, then he will end up selling his home. For Scripture says: "If a man sells a dwelling house in a walled city . . ." (25:29–34)

G   If he repents of the misdeed, then things will be well; if not, then he will end up being forced to beg. For Scripture says: "If your kinsman, being in straits, [begs to] come under your authority, and you hold him as though [he were] a resident alien, let him live by your side." (25:35–38)

H   If he repents of the misdeed, then things will be well; if not, then he will end up selling himself into your hands. For Scripture says: "If your kinsman under you continues in straits and must give himself over to you . . ." (25:39–46)

I   If he repents of the misdeed, then things will be well; if not, then he will end up being sold into the hands of foreigners. For Scripture says: "If a resident alien among you has prospered, and our kinsman being in straits, comes under his authority and gives himself over to the resident alien among you, or to an offshoot of an alien's family . . ." (25:47–55)

J   And this will not be his penalty alone, but that of all Israel. For so you find it written that in the days of the prophet Jeremiah that because Israel profaned the Sabbatical year, they were sold into the hands of the foreign nations. For scripture says: God brought the king of the Chaldeans upon them. . . . All the vessels of the House of God and its treasures . . . were brought to Babylon. . . . [All this was to the end that] the land pay back its sabbaths." (II Chron 36:17–21)

The linkage this midrash makes between Leviticus 25 and 26 is extraordinary. But given how our canonical editors had structured chapter 26, it should not come as a surprise. We noted that the introduction of the Sabbatical law in chapter 26 gave the violation of that commandment special prominence in explaining why Israel was sent into exile. The Sabbatical law itself looks like something of an outlier in chapter 25—it certainly does not carry the weight that the Jubilee law does—but given its structural significance in 26 early interpreters of that chapter must have felt some pressure to make it central in 25 as well. The links the midrash establishes are so ingenious that Jacob Milgrom asserts that the author of Leviticus 25 intended this result.[26] That seems something of a stretch to me. The midrash works, I would argue, only if we allow Leviticus 26 to provide the basic lens through which chapter 25 is read. It does not explain the composition of chapter 25 on its own. But Milgrom may be correct if we speak not of the author of chapter 25 on his own but of the editor who saw fit to weld 25 and 26. As we have noted, the link of 26 to 25 is rather artificial. In terms of its basic content, 26 would function better as a concluding chapter to the book. What grounds the redactional linkage of the two is the singling out of the Sabbatical year as the focus of Israel's disobedience and the need for both the land and the nation to repay its debts. Once this theme of repaying a debt emerges—something that could have happened only in the Second Temple period—it was natural for a later redactor to provide the scribal cues that tie the two chapters together (i.e., deleting the introductory formula to Leviticus 26 and making the remark at the beginning of 25 and the close of 26 that the revelation took place "at Mount Sinai"). Once this redactional move had been made, the reading of Leviticus 25 that R. Samuel offers sounds very much in tune with its context.

As scholars have long noted, there is a close linguistic relationship between Isaiah 40:2 (Israel's sins have been repaid or "satisfied"—*rāṣâh*) and Leviticus 26:43 (both the land and the Israelites will repay or make satisfaction [*rāṣâh*] for their sins). These are among the first attestations we possess of texts written in Hebrew that depict the sins of Israel as debts that must be repaid or "satisfied" by means of the exile. Biblical scholars are nearly unanimous in dating these texts to the exilic or even postexilic period. My discussion of Leviticus 26 was more complicated than that of Isaiah 40 because of the editorial history of that chapter and its redactional relationship to chapter 25. Tracing the use of the verb *rāṣâh* in Leviticus 26:34–35 and 41–43 meant covering considerable textual ground. But the story does not end here. Leviticus 26 will continue to exert considerable influence throughout the Second Temple period.

6

lengthening the term of debt

With the other nations the Lord waits patiently, staying their punishment until
they reach the full measure of their sins. Quite otherwise is His decree for us,
in order that He should not have to punish us after we have come to the
complete measure of our sins.

—II Maccabees 6:14–15

Poring over the law codes of Leviticus 25 and 26 regarding the redemption of
land and persons may seem to have no relevance for contemporary life. But
ancient readers were drawn to these chapters because of their detailed accounts of why Israel had been sent into exile and what had to transpire before
redemption could occur. As we shall see, even though the exile came to closure in 538 BCE, when Cyrus the Persian announced that the Judean captives
were free to return to their homeland and to begin restoring Jerusalem and
its temple (see II Chron 36:22–23 and Ezra 1–3), it was felt that God had bigger plans for the restoration of his people throughout the Second Temple period. Surprisingly, Jewish writers often ignored the rebuilding of the temple
in retelling Israel's sacred history.[1] The reason for this was the widespread ac-
knowledgment that the building erected in the late sixth century did not meet
the grand expectations that had evolved during the exile.

As a result of these hopes, texts like Leviticus 26 continued to be stud-
ied with great devotion. If the exile was not completely over, then perhaps
the study of these laws held the key as to what lay ahead. But to appreciate
what happens to Leviticus 26 during the several centuries following its composition, we must turn to a seemingly unrelated text in the writings of the

prophet Jeremiah, for it was the combination of Leviticus and Jeremiah that set the tone for much of the soul-searching among the Judean population in the Second Temple period.

JEREMIAH'S PROPHECY OF AN EXILE OF SEVENTY YEARS

The prophet Jeremiah lived in the late sixth and early fifth centuries BCE, which were perhaps the most tragic years of the biblical era. It was during this time that the Babylonians invaded the land of Israel, destroyed the capital city of Jerusalem, plundered its temple, and took many of its leading citizens into exile. Jeremiah the person has long been known as a somber and somewhat morose figure; even a cursory glance at the book that bears his name will make clear why. This prophet had the task of telling Israel that her terrible fate had been sealed. God had given the nation of Israel many chances to turn herself around, but none had been heeded. In words that recall a similar account in the book of Kings (II Kings 17) concerning the fall of the northern kingdom of Israel about 150 years earlier (721 BCE), the book of Jeremiah provides a damning indictment: "Moreover, the LORD constantly sent all his servants the prophets to you, but you would not listen or incline your ears to hear when they said, 'turn back, everyone, from your evil ways and your wicked acts, that you may remain throughout the ages on the soil which the LORD gave to you and your fathers'" (25:4–5).[2] In spite of the incessant warning that God had delivered, the southern kingdom of Judea was utterly intransigent. "You would not listen to Me" (v. 7), Jeremiah reported in the name of the God of Israel who had sent him.

What was to be the result of such insolence? Jeremiah declared that God was going to send the peoples of the north—this meant the nation of Babylon—to wreak havoc on the land, with disastrous results: "I will exterminate them and make them a desolation, an object of hissing—ruins for all time" (25:9). But as horrible as this must have sounded to his audience, it was not the end of the story. Jeremiah imagined that once the day of judgment had come and gone, God's wrath would have run its course and the process of restoration would take root. Although the land would be a desolate ruin, the Judeans would be forced to serve the king of Babylon for a period of seventy years. When that time had passed, God would intervene again to punish the Babylonians for their disobedient behavior.

The similarities to Leviticus 26 should be obvious. First, there is a period in which Israel's disobedience is subject to divine warning. In Leviticus this came in the form of a structured set of punishments; in Jeremiah it is a series of prophetic admonitions. When these prove devoid of any effect, God intervenes dramatically to bring the nation to utter ruin. But the devastation that will be visited on the land is not the final word. God will restore Israel, but not before a prescribed interval of time has passed. In Leviticus, the amount of time required is never specified. But the text does say that the land will need to make up for the Sabbaths that it has missed. This would seem to imply that a specific number of such Sabbaths could be calculated if one knew how many had been missed. During this time of devastation, when the land was not being worked, the Sabbatical years that were owed would be paid off. In Jeremiah, the time is set by what seem to be other criteria. The length of time is clear to the prophet: Israel must wait seventy years. When that time has passed, God declares, "I will fulfill to you My promise of favor—to bring you back to this place. . . . I will be at hand for you—declares the LORD—and I will restore your fortunes. And I will gather you from all the nations and from all the places to which I have banished you" (29:10b, 14).

Readers of this oracle have long asked, why seventy years? The answer can be gleaned from contemporary texts that were written in Assyria.[3] From these one learns that the idea of a seventy-year period of destruction was something of a commonplace in the ancient Near East. Evidently Jeremiah borrowed this typological number when he framed his prophecy of divine judgment. Other scholars, however, have suggested that an additional motif may have been influenced the selection of this number. According to Psalm 90:10, the normal human life span was thought to be seventy years. Jeremiah may have found the number seventy appealing because it meant that an entire generation would have to pass away before there could be any hope for restoration. This idea has a long pedigree in the Bible, because it forms the structure for the condemnation of Israel in the wilderness during Moses' own lifetime. After Israel refused to advance to the Promised Land because of fear of the military prowess of its inhabitants, God condemned the nation to forty years of wandering (Num 14:26–35). The forty years corresponds both to the number of days scouts had spent reconnoitering the land (Num 13:25, 14:34) and to the life expectancy of the adults who participated in the rebellion (14:31–32). The result of the latter was that by the time Israel was poised to enter the land at the close of the book of Numbers, she would comprise an entirely new generation.[4]

JEREMIAH IN LIGHT OF LEVITICUS 26

The prediction of Jeremiah ended up being a significant element of his preaching, one remembered long after his death. Biblical writers do not often cite one another directly, but the prediction of Jeremiah is an excep-

tion. The prophet Zechariah, whose career began under the Persian kingdom of Darius I (522–486 BCE), begins his prophetic work with an expression of anxiety over the delay in the restoration of Jerusalem. To provide some punch to his complaints, Zechariah records that an angel he saw
in a mysterious night vision exclaimed: "O LORD of Hosts! How long will
You withhold pardon from Jerusalem and the towns of Judah, which You
placed under a curse *seventy years* ago?" (1:12). This oracle, which is data-
ble to 520 or 519 BCE, may assume that the seventy-year period began with
the destruction of Jerusalem in 587. If so, given that the temple was completed and dedicated in 516 or 515, the figure of seventy years ended up
being remarkably accurate.

A similar mathematical calculation is in play in II Chronicles 36, where
we learn of the fateful last days of the Judean state. Having told of the Babylonian invasion and the destruction of the city of Jerusalem and its temple,
the author of Chronicles turns to the subject of those who survived, as well
as to the matter of the restoration of the Judean kingdom: "Those who survived the sword he exiled to Babylon, and they became his and his sons' servants till the rise of the Persian kingdom, in fulfillment of the word of the
LORD spoken by Jeremiah, until the land paid back its Sabbaths; as long as
it lay desolate it kept Sabbath, till seventy years were completed" (36:21).
The only way to appreciate this text is to compare it synoptically to Leviticus 26.[5] For in spite of what the author claims, Jeremiah is not the sole
source of inspiration. Rather, the author of Chronicles has read the prophecy of Jeremiah through the lens of Leviticus 26:

Leviticus 26:34–35	2 Chronicles 36:19–21
	[The Chaldeans] burned the House of God and tore down the wall of Jerusalem. . . . Those who survived the sword he exiled to Babylon . . .
	in fulfillment of the word of the LORD spoken by Jeremiah, *until*
Then the land shall repay its Sabbaths as long as it lays desolate.	*the land has repaid its Sabbaths; as long as it lay desolate it kept its Sabbath,* until seventy years were completed.[6]
And you are in the land of your enemies; then shall the land rest	

and make up for its Sabbath
years. Throughout the time that it
is desolate, it shall observe the
rest that it did not observe in
your Sabbath years while you
were dwelling upon it.

By placing a nearly verbatim citation of Leviticus 26:34 into the citation of
Jeremiah, the Chronicler provides a theological grounding for the seventy
years of exile that was lacking in the book of Jeremiah. Seventy years is the
period required to make up the Sabbatical years that were not kept prior to
the exile. Given that the Sabbatical year was kept every seven years, one can
infer from Chronicles that Israel failed to honor this requirement for ten
successive cycles $(10 \times 7 = 70)$.[7]

At one level, everything seems clear. After seventy years, during which
the land will lie abandoned and fallow, the missed Sabbatical years will be
observed, and Israel will be free to return to her land. In fact, the Chronicler ends his work with this observation: "And in the first year of King Cyrus
of Persia, when the word of the LORD spoken by Jeremiah was fulfilled, the
LORD roused the spirit of King Cyrus of Persia to issue a proclamation
throughout his realm by word of mouth and in writing, as follows: 'Thus
said King Cyrus of Persia: The LORD God of Heaven has given me all the
kingdoms of the earth, and has charged me with building Him a House in
Jerusalem, which is in Judah. Any one of you of all His people, the LORD his
God be with him and let him go up'" (II Chron 36:22–23). It is clear that
the Chronicler viewed the exile as a brief hiatus in Israel's history. It would
have no long-term consequences on Israel's relationship to her land or
God.[8] The rebuilding of the temple that took place in the late sixth century
at the behest of King Cyrus, and with the support of the prophets Haggai
and Zechariah, brought the tragedy of the exile to a swift termination. The
restoration of the fallen kingdom of Judea was complete.

PROPHETIC VISIONS OF ISRAEL'S RESTORATION

But the historical record is rarely so simple. In this case, two theological issues arise. First, Israel's prophets provided a number of idealized portraits
of the glorious restoration to be achieved once the exilic suffering had
reached its end. Jeremiah, for example, believed that a new covenant was
in the offing, a covenant unlike the one God had made with the Israelites
when they departed Egypt. Because that covenant had depended on falli-

ble human beings to fulfill its terms, it was subject to the vagaries of individuals' decision making. In the restored community that Jeremiah envisions, God would refashion the character of his people so that the commandments would become second nature: "But such is the covenant I will make with the House of Israel after these days—declares the LORD: I will put My Teaching into their inmost being and inscribe it upon their hearts. Then I will be their God, and they shall be my people" (Jer 31:33). It is not the commandments that are the problem (they are truly the word of God); it is Israel's capacity and resolve to obey them. God recognizes that to preserve Israel from future catastrophe she must be restored from within. By inscribing his teaching directly upon their hearts, God will do away with the need for conventional instruction: "No longer will they need to teach one another and say to one another, 'Heed the LORD'; for all of them, from the least of them to the greatest shall heed Me—declares the LORD" (Jer 31:34).

Isaiah, on the other hand, stresses the greatness that shall accrue to the city of Jerusalem. In his view it will not be sufficient simply to restore the Davidic city. God has far greater ambitions. The rebuilding of Zion will mark the onset of a near Messianic transformation. God will make his presence felt within His temple; indeed his presence shall radiate like light from its center. So attractive will the city become that the nations of the world will come as pilgrims, bringing the children of the exiles on their shoulders along with magnificent gifts of tribute in their train:

> *Arise, shine, for your light has dawned;*
> *The Presence of the Lord has shone upon you!*
> *And thick clouds the peoples;*
> *But upon you the LORD will shine,*
> *And His Presence be seen over you.*
> *And nations shall walk by your light,*
> *Kings, by your shining radiance.*
>
> *Raise your eyes and look about:*
> *They have all gathered and come to you. Your sons shall be*
>   *brought from afar,*
> *Your daughters like babes on shoulders.*
> *As you behold, you will glow;*
> *Your heart will throb and thrill—*
> *For the wealth of the sea shall pass on to you,*
> *The riches of nations shall flow to you. (Isa 60:1–5)*

Needless to say, these grand visions of what the restored Israel was to become did not eventuate. The nations of the world did not stream to Jerusalem with Israelite children on their shoulders, nor did they humbly send their treasures to its temple to the glory of the God of Israel. This prophetic vision was to remain a future hope.[9]

Although Jeremiah foretold a hiatus of approximately seventy years between the devastation of 587 and the rebuilding of 515, this proved, in retrospect, to be too brief a time for the true restoration to take place. A city and temple had been refounded in the wake of the Persian conquest of Babylon, but the restoration this foreign magistrate funded was only a small token of what was to come. The glorious promises of Isaiah as to what would unfold in the holy city (see 60:1–5, above) did not come to pass. Indeed, one of the surprising features of much Second Temple literature is that it ignores the rebuilding of the Second Temple when it tells the story of Israel's sacred past.[10] The only way to explain this is to assume that for some segments of the Jewish population it was as though the exile was still in effect. The glorious promises of restoration were yet to come.

THE DEPTH OF ISRAEL'S SIN

There was a second theological problem with the overly optimistic account of Jeremiah's prophecy found in II Chronicles 36. The seventy years were understood as repaying the debt that had accrued during the period of Israel's covenantal disobedience. But if we ponder all the implications of this number, we find that II Chronicles 36 was optimistic not only about how quickly the exile would pass but also about how deep the sinfulness of Israel was. In this view, the sinfulness that caused the exile stretches back only one generation.[11] Yet Jeremiah was not so sanguine about Israel's past. In his indictment of the nation he remarks that not only had he himself spoken out persistently about the infidelity of Israel but that a long train of prophets had done the same: "Moreover, the LORD constantly sent all his servants the prophets to you, but you would not listen or incline your ears to hear [them]" (25:4). This text matches very closely a similar indictment made about the northern kingdom of Israel in II Kings 17 in light of its imminent destruction in 721 BCE. Because that text imagines Israel's infidelity as stretching back to the founding of the northern kingdom, Jeremiah may have had a similarly negative estimation about the kingdom in the south. Ezekiel, however, goes even further. Not only were the northern and southern kingdoms corrupt from their inception, but the nation Israel had already given evidence of her rebellious ways in the wilderness of Sinai (20:10–26). If we accept the assessment of Jeremiah and Ezekiel that Israel's rebelliousness extends far into her sacred past, the interpretation given of the seventy years in II Chronicles begins to look rather glib. Could it be that the exile was punishment for the sins of a single generation, even though the perfidy of Israel reached much further back?

By the time we get to the middle of the second century BCE, another complication arises. The Persian empire had been displaced in the Near East in 333 by the invasion of Alexander the Great. After the death of that great military ruler, the Greek empire was split into two domains: the Ptolemies took control of Egypt, and the Seleucids held power in Syria. Around 167 BCE the Seleucid ruler Antiochus IV Epiphanes invaded Jerusalem to restore order to the city. As part of his strategy to assert his authority over the area he decided to seize control of the temple and desecrate its precincts by committing various abominations, such as the sacrifice of pigs. This led to the Maccabean revolt. This national tragedy was important because it impelled Jewish thinkers to revisit the prophecy of Jeremiah anew. The most well-known example of this is found in the book of Daniel.

DANIEL'S PRAYER

The book of Daniel must be read on two planes: the historical and the fictive or narratival. Historically it is clear that the book was written in the wake of the Seleucid persecutions in the mid-second century BCE. But the story line would have us believe that the tale derives from a figure by the name of Daniel, who would have been a near contemporary of Jeremiah, having lived a bit later. That an author in the second century would choose a sixth-century exilic setting to tell his story about how Israel will be restored is significant. It confirms the fact that the exile was thought to be still in effect, despite the efforts of prophets such as Zechariah.

According to the narrative level of the work, Daniel was among the Jews taken into captivity by the Babylonians. He continued to live in Babylon into the Persian era. As a result, one would think that he saw himself perched on the very edge of the moment of restoration. And, in fact, during the reign of the Persian king Darius, he writes: "In the first year of Darius son of Ahasuerus, of Median descent, who was made king over the kingdom of the Chaldeans—in the first year of his reign, I Daniel, consulted the books concerning the number of years that, according to the word of the LORD that had come to Jeremiah the prophet, were to be the term of Jerusalem's desolation—seventy years" (9:1–2). But because we know that the book was written in the second century, we know that the author cannot possibly think that the exile came to closure in 520 BCE or so. Yet at this point, we are not sure how this prophecy of Jeremiah is going to be interpreted.

What follows this citation from Jeremiah is a long prayer for the restoration of Israel. Appropriately, it begins with a lengthy confession of the sins that had necessitated the punishment of exile in the first place: "O, LORD, great and awesome God, who stays faithful to His covenant with those who love Him and keep His commandments! We have sinned; we have gone astray; we have acted wickedly; we have been rebellious and have deviated from Your commandments and Your rules, and have not obeyed Your servants the prophets who spoke in Your name to our kings, our officers, our fathers, and all the people of the land" (9:4–6). Daniel continues his prayer by declaring that God was just in the decree he passed against the land and its inhabitants. All of Israel had blatantly violated the statutes they had been given. Having given an honest and impassioned account of the nation's sins, he concludes his prayer with a fervent plea for God's mercy: "O our God, hear now the prayer of Your servant and his plea, and show Your favor to Your desolate sanctuary, for the LORD's sake. Incline your ear, O my God, and hear; open Your eyes and see our desolation and the city to which Your name is attached. Not because of any merit of ours do we lay our plea before You but because of Your abundant mercies. O LORD, hear! O LORD, forgive! O LORD; listen, and act without delay for Your own sake, O my God; for Your name is attached to You city and Your people!" (9:17–19).

When Daniel's prayer ends, one might expect the God of Israel to grant this pious supplicant his wish. After all, the Israelites, through the mediation of Daniel, have expressed contrition for their misdeeds ("We have sinned; we have gone astray; we have acted wickedly"). It would seem fitting to bring the seventy years that Jeremiah had predicted to termination. But such was not the case. The exile was to stretch well beyond the sixth century. Israel's sins required a longer penance than some of the earlier prophets such as Zechariah had reckoned.

But if the author of the book of Daniel, who lived in the second century, thought that the restoration of Israel was yet to come, how was one to understand the rather straightforward prophecy of Jeremiah? The seventy-year period he had spoken of was long past. It is hard to imagine that the author believed Jeremiah, an inspired prophet of canonical standing, was wrong. The solution to that problem is to be found in the exegetical move we first saw in II Chronicles 36. That text, as we indicated, had tied the seventy years to the Sabbatical system: ten Sabbaticals of seven years each.

We noted, however, that this piece of early exegesis had some logical problems. The prophets of Israel had spoken about Israel's rebellious activity as having begun long before the crisis of the late seventh and early sixth centuries. If Israel had been in the habit of flouting divine law for centuries, then presumably she had done the same with respect to her Sabbatical obligations. But the model of the Sabbatical year taken from Leviticus 26 may provide some other paths upon which we can tread. As noted, the Chronicler correlated the seventy years with Leviticus 26 in an optimistic fashion: he took the seventy years as the fixed sum from which the resulting lost Sabbatical years could be derived mathematically (seventy divided by seven). But what if Jeremiah was read differently? What if Jeremiah's seventy years was not the sum of years to be spent in exile but, rather, the number of Sabbatical years that had been missed? Consider the math: to make up seventy missed Sabbaticals one would need to multiply seventy by the length of time each Sabbatical would take—seven years would need to elapse between every Sabbatical year. The result would be an exile lasting 490 years.[12]

It must be emphasized, of course, that this type of calculation was not the sense of Jeremiah's prediction. Sometimes seventy years means just that, seventy years. Nor was it the intention of the Chronicler when he inserted the text of Leviticus 26 into the middle of his citation of Jeremiah. For him, the seventy years of Jeremiah meant ten Sabbatical cycles. But once the Chronicler had made Leviticus 26 part of the equation, the mathematical correlation of Jeremiah's seventy years and the time required to make up the lost Sabbaticals was open to new exploration.

This radical transformation accomplished two goals. First, it pushed off the date that was expected for the restoration of the Judean kingdom. One need no longer think that God had fully restored that kingdom in the late sixth century, during the period of the prophets Haggai and Zechariah. Second, it provides a better framework for understanding the legacy of sin in the First Temple period. No longer is the exile just a brief fillip in the grand progression of salvation history; it has now become a major stumbling block. The deep legacy of Israel's sins that led up to the exile would take some time to undo. The "cost" incurred would necessitate a considerable amount of suffering in the days to come. This idea also provided a convenient theological explanation for the Maccabean crisis. The desecration of the temple by the invading Syrian armies was still part of the punishment that God was meting out as a result of Israel's pre-exilic rebellion. In II Chronicles 36, it had been assumed that the full price had been paid by the dawn of the Persian period; Daniel, on the other hand, made the cost of forgiveness far higher. A mere seventy years would not be sufficient to cover Israel's debt; 490 years would be more like it.

UNTIL THE MEASURE OF TRANSGRESSION IS FULFILLED

One more detail in Daniel 9 is worth careful attention. The chapter begins with Daniel recalling the prophecy of Jeremiah and then recounts his long and moving prayer of contrition. Daniel acknowledges that God was just in the harsh judgment he rendered; he had done nothing more than carry out what he had threatened many times in the past (9:12–13). Daniel also realizes that the community of Israel, because of its terrible unfaithfulness, has no merits of its own to stand on. When he prays for forgiveness, he freely acknowledges that if God restores Israel it will be solely because of his immeasurable mercies (9:18).

At the conclusion of Daniel's prayer, Gabriel informs him that his pleas have been heard, and a verdict rendered. Unfortunately for Daniel, the appointed day of deliverance is still far off. The first part of that oracle reads: "Seventy weeks have been decreed for your people and your holy city until the measure of transgression is filled and that of sin complete, until iniquity is expiated, and eternal righteousness ushered in; and the prophetic vision ratified and the Holy of Holies anointed" (9:24). The question to be asked here is, How are we to understand the 490 years? That is an extraordinary amount of time, especially by ancient standards. The only analogy in the Bible is God's declaration to Abraham that the Israelites will have to wait four hundred years in Egypt until the Amorites have committed enough sins to be driven out of the country (Gen 15:13, 16). But here the focus is on the accumulation of sins leading to a punishment rather than on paying the bill for sin. To return to Daniel, the text in question explains that the punishment must continue until the "measure of transgression is filled and that of sin complete." When that has occurred, "iniquity is expiated and eternal righteousness is ushered in." These expressions have puzzled scholars for some time because it is not clear what is entailed. John Collins, for example, argues that the emphasis of these lines is not on the punishment of Israel but on the idea that "evil must run its course until the appointed time."[13]

There is good reason to adopt Collins's reading. If we can agree, however, that Leviticus 26 has been instrumental in how Daniel views both the onset of the exile and the means by which the exile will come to closure, then another way of reading these lines emerges. In light of Leviticus, the exile will come to closure only when Israel has done two things: repented of her sins (26:40) and paid the debt for the sins she has committed (26:41). When that moment has been reached, the restoration will be at hand. Although the Chronicler thought that it would take just seventy years to pay off those debts, Daniel has pushed the length of time far into the future. If the land "owed" seventy individual Sabbatical years, that would mean Israel had neglected this tremendously significant commandment for some 490 years. In addition, one might assume that if Israel was neglecting that commandment, she was also neglecting many others. And her debt for those other commandments, one might extrapolate, must have been adding up as well. This is the type of logic, I am suggesting, that Leviticus 26 would seem to demand. If that were the case, then Israel's restoration would have been put on hold until all that was owed was repaid.

This framework, I believe, explains what Daniel means when he says that at the end of "seventy weeks," Israel's debt for her sins will be "filled" and "complete." It is worth noting that in both cases the verbs used—to fill and to complete—can be used in financial contexts to denote the close of a payment. In fact, the idiom of "completing a sin" in the sense of paying off what was owed through some term of suffering is found in the book of Lamentations. When Zion's term of punishment has come to an end, the biblical author writes, "Your iniquity, Fair Zion, has been completed *(tam)*; He will exile you no longer" (4:22). As Adele Berlin has noted, this text should be compared to Isaiah 40:2, since both speak to the issue of the completion of a penalty paid for one's sins.[14] In light of this comparison, we should probably translate the text from Lamentations thus: "The debt accrued by your iniquity, Fair Zion, has been paid in full; He will exile you no longer."

But a problem with my analysis will surface if we compare Daniel 9:24 with a similar text found one chapter earlier. In Daniel 8 the subject is not the redemption of Israel but the rise and fall of the various kingdoms that have held Israel in check. The chapter begins with Daniel's vision of a ram that possessed two horns (8:1–3). The horns, we are told, represent the Medes and the Persians (20). In the far west appears a he-goat with a conspicuous horn on its head. This animal represents Alexander the Great (21), and, accordingly, it defeats the two-horned ram (5–7). Although the he-goat grows greatly in size—as did the empire of Alexander—eventually the horn on its head is broken and four other horns appear in its place (8–12). These are the four kingdoms that assumed power in the wake of Alexander's death (22). It is here that the text meets the contemporary world of Daniel, for one of those four horns symbolizes none other than Antiochus IV

Epiphanes. In describing the demise of these kingdoms, Daniel 8 uses an idiom that is almost identical to that in Daniel 9. In 8:23 he remarks that the turning point will be reached when "their sins have been completed"; this matches 9:24 almost exactly: "[Israel must remain in exile so as] to fill up [the measure of their] sins and to complete the [debt owed on their] transgression."[15] But how can Daniel 9 use this expression to refer to the conclusion of a payment for the debt of sin and Daniel 8 use it to entail the completion of a sufficient number of sins such that God can step in and punish the offenders? Collins's suggestion that Daniel 9 refers to the time needed for evil to run its course seems a more sensible interpretation in that it can account for the meaning of this phrase in both chapters.

The solution to this problem begins with the basic building blocks of the metaphor. Recall that we ran into a similar problem with the idiom "to bear a sin." In some circumstances this Hebrew idiom means "to be forgiven"; in others it expresses "to be guilty." How could a single verb convey two diametrically opposite meanings? This baffled biblical scholars until Baruch Schwartz pointed out that the same double meaning existed for the verb *nāśā᾽*, "to bear," in nonmetaphoric contexts. Because this verb can refer both to the act of picking up a weight that rests upon the back of another and to the act of ongoing porterage of a burden, its particular usage will have an enormous impact on how it is translated. When Joseph's brothers beg for forgiveness, they ask their brother to bear away the burden of their sin (Gen 50:17). But when Moses declares that the blasphemer "shall bear the weight of his sin" (Lev 24:15), he is using the idiom of the ongoing porterage to describe a continuous state of culpability.

A similar examination of the metaphor of debt is required to make sense of Daniel 8 and 9. In this case everything depends on which end of the commercial exchange we wish to reflect: the creditor's or the debtor's. For the creditor, the issue will be how long the debts will mount up before he steps in and takes decisive action. An excellent example of this is God's aforementioned conversation with Abraham regarding the promise of the land. After Abraham has solemnized the covenant by cutting an animal into two pieces and walking between them (Gen 15:7–11), evening falls upon the land and God appears to Abraham in a vision. God informs him that his offspring are to be strangers in a land that is not theirs and will be enslaved and oppressed for some four hundred years. But afterward God will step forward to execute judgment on the nation that Israel was forced to serve and will lead them forth. The reason the children of Abraham must suffer so long is that the time is not yet proper for granting the Israelites the land of Canaan, for "the iniquity of the Amorites is not yet complete *[šālēm]*" (Gen 15:16). This text provides the only unambiguous example of the conception of sin as a debt in the First Temple period (though some would date this later). But note that God is conceived of as a great bookkeeper in heaven, and though he promises to give the land of Canaan to Abraham's offspring, he cannot do so until the sins of the Amorites have risen to a sufficient level that he is justly warranted to drive them from the land. As any creditor knows, there is a limit to one's patience when the bills begin to add up; eventually one must step in and repossess the property.

We find the same usage of this verb at Qumran. The Apocryphon of Jeremiah, a text that assumes the same 490-year exile we saw in Daniel 9, reads: "Therefore I will hide my face [from Israel] until they have brought [the debts of] their sin to completion *[yašlîmû]*. This will be the sign that they have brought [the debts of] their sins to completion: I will abandon the land."[16] Yet we can find the root *š-l-m* used to indicate the completion of an obligation in both biblical and postbiblical Hebrew. Thus in the very same Apocryphon of Jeremiah the verbal root *šālēm* is used to refer to the completion of the cycle of 490 years. This root is used regularly to refer to the payment of an agreed sum.[17] The same holds true for verbal roots that are nearly identical in meaning such as *t-m-m* in biblical Hebrew and *g-m-r* in postbiblical Hebrew and Aramaic. Both can be used to refer to the completion of an obligation.

Everything, I would suggest, depends on context. If payments are not made, then the holder of the credit waits until a certain tipping point is reached *(šālēm)*, after which he steps in to punish. On the other hand, if a payment cycle has been established and the debtor has completed his obligation over the set period, his obligation is complete *(šālēm, tam,* or *gamār)* and the creditor can demand no more.

This dynamic explains the conundrum we encountered in the book of Daniel. In chapter 8, where the context is the elimination of an oppressive foreign king, the idiom "to complete their sin" means to bring to their debts to a predetermined tipping point; once it is reached God is entitled to intervene and remove the king from power, just as he was able to remove the Amorites from the land of Canaan once their sins had added up to a certain number. In chapter 9 the context is completely different. When Daniel declares that "seventy weeks" have been decreed so the "measure of sin might be fulfilled and sin brought to completion" he is referring to the price Israel must pay to discharge her debt. Although the idiom looks similar to that of Daniel 8, the context has altered the meaning considerably. The "completion of sins" in chapter 8 leads to divine judgment, whereas the identical phrase in chapter 9 leads to absolution.

WEIGHTS AND MEASURES IN ANTIQUITY

The idea of sin reaching a tipping point calls to mind a set of scales. In the marketplaces of antiquity one measured the value of goods by putting them in a pan on one side of a scale and then adding weights on the other side until a balance was achieved. This image of the scale created a host of metaphors. The verb *(le-hakrî'a)*, for example, used in rabbinic Hebrew to express the idea of rendering judgment, means literally "to push down [on a scale]." In a law court, unlike the marketplace, one strives not for perfect balance between the two pans but for the ability to discern which argument is "more weighty." The verb for "rendering a judgment" thus means finding evidence that is sufficient to push a particular pan down on a set of scales. Although two contesting opinions may initially look evenly balanced (a case of "he said, she said"), an investigation is required to reveal whose account is more sound. A discerning judge will distinguish even the finest level of difference. Sometimes, as in the weighing of souls, only a divine eye can do such.[18] Because weights and measures were a ubiquitous item in the ancient world for any kind of commercial activity, they frequently found their way into discussions of sin and debt. Rashi, the great medieval Jewish interpreter, for example, glosses "the iniquity of the Amorites was not yet complete" thus: "The Holy One—blessed be He!—does not extract payment from a nation until the measure [literally, *seah,* a dry measure] of its sin is filled." The metaphor of sin "adding up" is inherently commercial, and Rashi brings this to a point by comparing the sins of the Amorites to the filling of a bushel basket or sack in order to put it up for sale. This brings to mind Paul in his letter to the Thessalonians: "For, brothers and sisters, become imitators of the churches of God in Christ Jesus that are in Judea, for you suffered the same things from your own compatriots as they did from the Jews, who killed both the Lord Jesus and the prophets, and drove us out; they displease God and oppose everyone by hindering us from speaking to the Gentiles so that they may be saved. *Thus they have constantly been filling up the measure of their sins; but God's wrath has overtaken them at last*" (I Thess 2:14–16). In this text, Paul may have in mind a set of scales in which a certain measure of goods must be accumulated on one side in order for the transaction to be finished. When the "goods" have reached sufficient weight [scales] or measure [a sack size], God can extract his payment *(nipra',* if we translate the Greek into rabbinic Hebrew), that is, punishment (*pûr'ānût*). This is possibly what Paul means by the "wages of sin are death" (Rom 6:23), in that misdeeds "add up" (in the commercial sense) to a penalty that can be repaid only by death.[19]

One may harbor worries about this image of sin as debt. Is the hand of God woodenly tied to a set of financial obligations? Must we unfailingly pay for every cent of debt we accumulate? To be sure, the texts we explored in Leviticus and Daniel seem content to describe the matter in this fashion.[20] But these texts must be balanced against others that speak to God's ineffable mercy.

The book of II Maccabees is aware of this problem. Indeed, the author of this text is faced with what appears to be a terrible theological contradiction. It is an accepted truth in the Bible that God has a special affection for Israel and has chosen the Israelites as his special possession. Yet in the wake of the persecutions of Antiochus IV Epiphanes, it seems as though Israel receives more punishment than the nations around her. The author's burden in this text is to describe why God punishes Israel so readily while allowing the unrighteous nations of the world to continue their evil ways. This is a classic question of theodicy: How can one affirm the existence of a just God when the affairs of this world stand in such a striking contradiction? The ancient author writes:

> I beg the readers of my book not to be disheartened by the calamities but to bear in mind that chastisements come not in order to destroy our race but in order to teach it. If the ungodly among us are not left long to themselves but speedily incur punishment, it is a sign of God's great goodness to us. *With the other nations the Lord waits patiently, staying their punishment until they reach the full measure of their sins. Quite otherwise is His decree for us, in order that He should not have to punish us after we have come to the complete measure of our sins.* Consequently, God never lets His mercy depart from us. Rather, though He teaches us by calamity, He never deserts His people. Let this be enough as a reminder to my readers. Now we must quickly return to our story. (II Macc 6:12–17)[21]

The answer this author provides is ingenious. God does not punish the Israelites unfairly and avert his glance from their pagan neighbors. Rather, God treats the other nations as he did the Amorites; he stands patiently to the side so that their sins can mount up until the requisite tipping point has been reached. At that point, he can step in and wipe them out. This is, I have argued, the very picture found in Daniel 8:23; when the transgression is "completed," judgment follows. But God does not act in this way toward Israel. God never allows her sins to reach a level wherein he would be forced to disown her. Instead, he frequently intervenes and extracts payment from the chosen nation so that such a tipping point will never be reached. In other words, the unequal standards that caused one to question God's justice now affirm it! Israel suffers more visibly because God wants to make sure that her register of debits never rises too high.

In other texts, we find that undergoing a punishment that is believed to have been justly imposed becomes the basis for an impassioned appeal that God intervene and show mercy. Let us consider, in this vein, one prayer from a set of daily prayers for the seven days of the week, known as *Divre Ha-Me'orot,* the Words of the Luminaries. Although this text was found at Qumran, Esther Chazon has made a good case for seeing the prayers as being non-Qumranic in origin.[22] By this she means that they once circulated in a circle much wider than just the sect residing in the northwest corner of the Dead Sea. The portion of the text I wish to examine is simply a pastiche of Leviticus 26:40–44; virtually every word has been recycled from some place in this text: "And now, at this day, when our hearts have been humbled (Lev 26:41) we have paid off our sins and those of our fathers (26:40, 41) that accrued when we erred and walked in rebellion. We have not rejected your trials (26:43), nor did we loath your affliction of our bodies (26:43) such that we broke your covenant during our time of trial (26:44)."[23] But one should not be fooled by the close dependence this text shows on Leviticus 26. There is one exception that stands out very prominently. The biblical text, as we saw in the previous chapter, ascribed the punishment of Israel in the past (587 BCE) to her having "rejected My laws and loathed My statutes" (26:43). But in this prayer, the author uses the same vocabulary, but to express a different point: "we have not rejected your trials nor loathed your affliction of our bodies."

In effect, the verse from Leviticus has been radically transformed. The text from Leviticus,

> Israel shall repay the debt of her sins on account of the fact that they have rejected My laws and loathed My statutes,

becomes in our prayer:

> [We have repaid the debt in that] we have not rejected the trials you have imposed nor loathed the bodily afflictions you have visited upon us.

What had been a prediction of punishment in Leviticus now becomes a prescription for restoration in this prayer. Israel has repaid her debts by willingly assuming the cost of her actions. There could be no better proof that the debt of Israel's sins must be paid down by suffering. Furthermore, the supplicant recognizes that Israel's present suffering is part of the ongoing duty to repay the accrued debt that was called due in 587.

By acknowledging that Israel does not despise the trials that have come her way, the author of this prayer provides the grounds for a fervent appeal that God act in accordance with his mercy and bring this penitential cycle to closure: "O Lord, I pray you, as you have done wonders from age to age, may your anger and wrath turn from us. See our affliction, our toil and oppression and deliver your people Israel from all the lands both near and far to which you have scattered them." This appeal would not possess nearly the rhetorical power it has were it not for the confession just a few lines above about how sincerely Israel has undergone the various punishments for her grave offenses. The implied logic can be summarized thus: given that we have willingly endured the suffering due upon our transgressions, take note of our affliction and deliver us from our present oppressors. Although this prayer shares much in common with Daniel 9—both see the need to pay the price for the exile—this prayer grounds an appeal for divine mercy on that fact that the price has indeed been paid. The force of this appeal is to place some subtle pressure on God to act in accordance with his name.

I cannot close without mentioning a text that takes an even stronger stance with respect to how mercifully God treats those who stand in his debt. Let us consider the rabbinic commentary on the book of Leviticus known as the *Sifra* (literally, "*the* book," such was the significance of Leviticus in rabbinic thought). In this commentary we find the following gloss on the verse "and they shall pay the debt of their sin" (26:43): "Did I collect [*pāraʿ*] from them the full amount for full amount? Rather I collected only one hundredth of their sins before me!" What better way to indicate divine graciousness than to indicate that God collected far less than he was due. The *Sifra* was written several centuries after the Maccabean persecution and therefore represents a different political and theological climate. Israel in the third century CE is not suffering from such overt oppression. It is not surprising, then, that the rabbis can look back on the exile from a position of greater equanimity. Unlike human creditors, God need not demand his "pound of flesh."[24]

In this chapter I have shown the extensive influence of Leviticus 26 in the Second Temple period. We have seen how Leviticus 26 was picked up

by the Chronicler to provide a startling new reading of Jeremiah's prophecy of the seventy years. This hermeneutical move was further extended
in the book of Daniel. There Israel would require 490 years of exile to
make up the debt she owed. The influence of Leviticus 26, however, continued into the Dead Sea Scrolls as well. The "completion of sins" became
important parts of the Apocryphon of Jeremiah and the Words of the Luminaries.

In Daniel 8 and 9 we saw a single idiom used in service of two different
ends, a problem that had long perplexed commentators. The answer, I suggested, was not that different from the one proposed by Schwartz for the
two meanings of "to bear a sin [as a burden] *[nāśāʾ ʿăwōn]*." We distinguished two points of view:

(1)   The creditor who waits for the debts of his client to rise to a certain tip-
      ping point before taking punitive action. In the case of the Amorites
      who resided in Canaan (Gen 15:16), this led to the repossession of
      land, and in Daniel 8, to repossession of the right to rule as king (al-
      ways a divine prerogative).

(2)   The debtor who has faithfully made his payments and awaits release
      from further obligation. This is the sense of "satisfaction" *(rāṣāh)* in
      Second Isaiah and Leviticus 26 and "completion [of iniquity]" *(tam)* in
      Lamentations 4:22. It is also, I have argued, the sense of "to fulfill [the
      measure of sin]" *(le-kalleh)* and "to bring to completion" *(le-hātēm)*
      the sin in Daniel 9:24. The seventy weeks of years are over, and the Is-
      raelites await word that their debt has been satisfied.

Finally, I raised the issue of weights and measures as a means to illu-
minate a number of Second Temple texts that speak to the culpability for
sin. I noted that the metaphor that sin is a debt is not used in a univocal
manner. God need not always demand full payment on what is owed. In
II Maccabees, God intervenes regularly in Israel's life such that she is never
faced with the extreme penalty that is meted out on the unchosen. Discipline is a sign of love. This is just the other side of the coin of that famous
line from Amos that God expects more from those he has chosen and that
is why God says:

> *You alone have I singled out*
> *Of all the families of the earth—*
> *That is why I will call you to account*
> *For all your iniquities. (Amos 3:2)*

The author of II Maccabees, we might say, has done nothing more than interpret this truism from Amos in terms of the dominant metaphor of his day.

In the Words of the Luminaries, the text of Leviticus 26 was turned somewhat on its head. Whereas Leviticus 26 foretold the punishment that would come upon Israel because of her disregard for God's commandments, the voice of the supplicant in the prayer confesses that the punishments are fitting and have been willingly assumed by the nation. But the prayer goes even further. Its closing lines beg God for a redemption that has been delayed. Evidently the people feel they are on the verge of paying more than their sins deserved.

What must be borne in mind about these various pictures is that the metaphor of sin as a debt is subtle and adaptable to a variety of contexts. In the wake of the Seleucid persecutions, it serves to underscore the rationality of what Israel is currently experiencing (hence Daniel 9 and II Maccabees, each in its own way). After the close of that persecution, the metaphor can be used in an earnest appeal that God act in accordance with the piety of his supplicants (the Words of the Luminaries) or even as a complete exoneration of the merciful ways of God *(Sifra)*. As in much of religious life, theological language is rarely univocal; much depends on context.

7

loans and the rabbinic sages

"To you, O LORD, belongs a charitable inclination *[ḥesed]; you indeed repay each individual according to his deeds" [Ps 62:13]. Yet if one lacks [sufficient merit], God will provide some of his own.

—Jerusalem Talmud

God acts mercifully not by doing anything contrary to His justice, but by doing something that goes beyond His justice. In the same way, if one gives 200 denarii of his own money to someone who is owed 100 denarii, then he is acting generously or mercifully and not contrary to justice. The same thing holds if someone forgives an offense committed against himself. For in forgiving this debt, he is in a certain sense making a gift of it; hence, in Ephesians 4:32 the Apostle calls forgiveness a "gift": "Make a gift to one another, just as Christ has made a gift to you."

—Thomas Aquinas, *Summa Theologica*

Up to this point I have examined how the metaphor of sin as a debt functioned in late biblical material and some early postbiblical texts. These texts adapted the classical Hebrew vocabulary to fit a radical new way of thinking about sin. But to get the best perspective on this metaphor, I turn to the two living languages of first-century Palestine, the era of Jesus of Nazareth and the early rabbinic sages: they are Mishnaic Hebrew and the Palestinian and Babylonian dialects of Aramaic. Mishnaic Hebrew, in its limited sense, refers to the Hebrew of the Mishnah itself, a relatively early rabbinic work (redacted around 200 CE, though a good percentage of the work originated much earlier) that codified six legal collections thought to both supplement and complete the legal codes of the Hebrew Bible. But when we speak of the dialect of Mishnaic Hebrew, we are talking about the living Hebrew language of the first couple of centuries of the Common Era, in other words, the language of Jesus himself.[1]

What we see in rabbinic literature, whether of Hebrew or Aramaic origin, is an almost complete overlap between the vocabulary for commerce and that of sin and forgiveness. No longer must we tease out the idea of "satisfaction [of a debt]" from a verb such as *rāṣâh* (hence Isa 40:2 and Lev 26:34–35, 41 and 43) or from texts such as 11QMelchizedek, which utilize laws of debt release in the Bible to speak to the issue of the forgiveness of sins. In rabbinic literature, the movement between commercial terminology and religious application is altogether organic and harmonious. (But recall that even the authors of the Dead Sea Scrolls use Mishnaic idioms to speak about sin and forgiveness.)[2] Every dictionary of rabbinic Hebrew provides explicit testimony to it. Eliezer Diamond summarizes this well: "A market place model was . . . used by the sages to portray the calculation of one's spiritual merits and debits. The word generally used by the sages for reward, *sākhār,* has the primary meaning of wages or payment. *Pûrʿānût,* a common rabbinic term for punishment (literally: retribution), derives from the root *prʿ*, 'to pay off a debt.' The notion of *pûrʿānût* is connected to viewing one who sins as having incurred a *ḥôbâ,* an obligation towards God. As George Foot Moore puts it, 'Man owes God obedience, and every sin, whether of commission or of omission, is a defaulted obligation, a debt.' That obligation is satisfied through God's retribution; God allows one to pay off one's debt by undergoing punishment." The significance of this system, Diamond argues, is to assure that there be "some degree of proportionality between righteousness and sinfulness on the one hand and reward and punishment on the other." It is not the case, however, that "God is obligated a priori to reward the righteous nor does God need for his own sake to punish the wicked." Rather, God "has created a system of debits, credits, rewards and punishments" and has chosen, for the most part, to operate within its confines.[3] As the two epigraphs indicate, God's capacity to show mercy does not always follow the rules of a strict monetary accounting.

BONDS OF INDEBTEDNESS

In our own day one cannot take out a bank loan without signing official documents, and so it was in antiquity. Indeed some of the oldest written documents from the ancient Near East are loan dockets. We have so many of these texts (some of which are over four thousand years old) because of the special care taken to preserve them. Just as we deposit such papers in safe-deposit boxes or fireproof safes, citizens of the ancient Near East also put loan documents away for safekeeping.

In classical Mesopotamia terms of a loan were recorded on a clay tablet (ṭuppu), which the person or institution making the loan would retain as an official record.[4] Should the borrower be in a position where repayment became difficult, the issuer of the funds could produce the tablet in a court of law as a means of demanding reparation. To forestall the possibility that a person might deny the terms of the loan, the tablet would constitute legal proof of the obligation. Upon repayment of the loan, the tablet would be broken (ṭuppam ḥepû) as a sign of its invalidity.

In Second Temple Judaism, as well as in the latter Talmudic period, loan notes were executed not on clay tablets but on documents of one form or another. Such notes were referred to as bonds (šṭar, šṭārôt in the plural).[5] A šṭar-ḥôb was literally a bond of indebtedness that the debtor was obligated (ḥayyāb) to repay (pāraʿ) within a given unit of time, sometimes with the addition of a predetermined rate of interest (rabbît).[6] The person who issued the loan became the holder or owner of the note (baʿal šṭar in Hebrew, mārēʾ šṭārâʾ in Aramaic, "lord," or better, "possessor of the bond"), and as long as one held the bond, one was entitled to collect (gābâh) its repayment. As in Mesopotamia, these bonds of indebtedness were legally binding texts, and money lenders were in the habit of depositing them at a public archive for safekeeping. During the first Jewish revolt (66 to 70 CE), the rebels stormed the urban archives to burn the debt records stored there.[7] The zeal to destroy these documents reflects the wide-spread anxiety about the level of indebtedness among the general population. Babylonian kings, cognizant of this fact, would often declare a release (andurārum, Hebrew dĕrôr) from indebtedness upon ascending the throne. This act of royal largesse served a political end: it solidified support for the new king.

LAMECH'S BOAST

All the terms I have underscored above reappear time and again in early Jewish texts about sin and forgiveness. An example is Genesis Rabbah, a fifth- or even sixth-century anthology of midrashic traditions on the book of Genesis. The text in question concerns the figure of Lamech. In the original Genesis narrative, Lamech was a brazen sinner who happened to be the seventh and final individual in the fated line of Cain, who had brutally murdered his brother, Abel. After Cain was banished from the presence of the

Lord and settled in the land of Nod, just east of Eden, we read: "Cain knew his wife, and she conceived and bore Enoch. And he then founded a city, and named the city after his son Enoch. To Enoch was born Irad, and Irad begot Mehujael, and Mehujael begot Methusael, and Methusael begot Lamech. Lamech took to himself two wives, the name of the one was Adah, and the name of the other was Zillah. . . ."

> *And Lamech said to his wives,*
> *"Adah and Zillah, hear my voice;*
> *O wives of Lamech, give ear to my speech.*
> *I have slain a man for wounding me,*
> *And a lad for bruising me.*
> *If Cain is avenged sevenfold,*
> *Then Lamech seventy-seven fold." (Gen 4:17–19, 23–24)*

The biblical writer has clearly placed Lamech at the close of Cain's line to demonstrate how wicked the human race has become and to prepare the reader for the cataclysm about to be unleashed: the flood that only Noah and his immediate family will survive. Lamech's address to his wives, in which he demands their attention, puzzled rabbinic readers. They solved this problem by presuming that his wives had resisted his request for sexual relations. His demand, they felt, was ridiculous in light of the oncoming flood. Why create more humans who would be doomed to drown? Lamech, the rabbis infer, did not answer his wives with a simple declarative sentence, as the Bible assumes ("I have slain a man for wounding me"). Rather, the rabbis frame Lamech's remarks as a rhetorical question: "Have I slain a man for wounding me?" The result was a new way of understanding the biblical story. "In commenting on this verse ['Hear my voice; O wives of Lamech . . .'], R. Yose b. Hanina said that [Lamech] had demanded sexual intercourse of his wives. But they said to him, 'Tomorrow the flood shall come upon us—should we hearken to your voice? Should we produce children for a curse?' Lamech responded, 'Have I slain a man for wounding me so that wounds come upon me?' 'Or a lad for bruising me so that bruises would come upon me?—By no means! Yet consider the example of Cain—he murdered [Abel], and his punishment was suspended for seven generations. [So would it not be logical that] for me, who did not murder, that punishment would be suspended for seventy-seven generations?' " (Gen 4:24). Lamech's point is that if the punishment for Cain's crime could be put off for seven generations, then his own sins, which were so much lighter, would not be punished until much later. At this point, there is a brief interruption in the argument and an additional observation is made: "This speech of Lamech is a logical inference of darkness. For if what he says is true, when would the Holy One (Blessed be He!) be able to collect [gābâh] the debt that is owed on his bond [šṭar ḥôb]?"[8] The logic of Lamech, the rabbis conclude, is faulty. If this was how the historical process worked, then when could God ever collect (gābâh) what is owed him? The punishment of Cain—or any other criminal for that matter—could be endlessly deferred. According to the metaphor used here, it is assumed that a bond had been written in heaven the moment that Cain murdered his brother and that it was fully within God's right as holder of that bond (baʿal šṭar) to collect (gābâh) repayment. If he chose to postpone it for seven generations, he would collect at that time; it would not be endlessly deferred.

AS LONG AS THE BOND CAN BE FOUND

The story of Joseph provides another example of how the rabbis inserted the notion of a bond into the plotline of a biblical story in order to make sense of human culpability. At the beginning of Genesis 37 Joseph is described as the darling of his father, a position of favor he exploits, to the chagrin of his brothers. In anger over Joseph's arrogance, the brothers decide to do away with him, though they must find a way to conceal their crime. Fooling their father turns out to be rather simple: they kill an animal, dip Joseph's coat in its blood, and show the coat to their father. Upon seeing it, he exclaims: "My son's tunic! A savage beast devoured him! Joseph was torn by a beast!" (37:33). The chapter closes with the brothers attempting to assuage the grief of their father. But the father refuses any such comfort: "No," he cries out, "I will go down mourning to my son in Sheol" (37:35).

Immediately following this tragic scene, we learn that Joseph has been sold into slavery in Egypt to Potiphar, the chief steward of Pharaoh (37:36). This detail is picked up again at the beginning of Genesis 39, the chapter that recounts the story of Joseph in Potiphar's home. Curiously, stuck in between these two references to Joseph's descent into Egypt (37:36, 39:1), is a story of Judah's departure from his siblings (chap. 38). Evidently, after having behaved so despicably toward his younger sibling, Judah decides to leave home and take up residence in the vicinity of a certain Adullamite by the name of Hirah. There he falls in love with Hirah's daughter Shua, whom he marries and with whom he has three children. Biblical scholars have long puzzled over the placement of this episode. Because it interrupts the story of Joseph's descent into Egypt—a tale that begins in chapter 37 and is resumed in 39 —it has been understood as an interpolation of a later redactor. Rabbinic readers also puzzled over this seeming textual interruption. But given that the rabbis believed that Moses had written the entire Pentateuch, they would never explain a textual irregularity like this by recourse to a redactor. Instead, this odd detail about Judah's abrupt departure from his brothers impelled them to examine the narrative of the previous chapter in search of some clue that might explain it.

The rabbis assumed that the brothers of Joseph knew they were guilty of a crime against their father and God. They had ingeniously avoided coming under the suspicion of their father, but could they escape the hand of God? According to the rabbis, the brothers gathered together and said: "Come let's disperse ourselves, for as long as we are together the bond can be *found* and God can collect *(gābâh)* what he is owed."[9] The story of Judah's departure from his brothers then is quite logical. While the brothers live apart, the bond is lost and God will not be able to collect what is owed him.

But in the world of rabbinic thinking, matters can never be so simple. God will not be party to such a foolish scheme. "The Holy One (Blessed be He!) said: 'If ten men are found guilty for a theft, can't one be taken for all of them?' And so [later in the story, when to the brothers' consternation Joseph's cup is found in Benjamin's bag and it appears that Jacob's favorite son will be doomed to permanent slavery in Egypt as the price for this crime] the brothers said, 'God has *found* the sin of your servants!' (Gen 44:16).[10] R. Isaac said the possessor of the loan note *[baʿal ḥôb]* has *found* the opportunity to collect *[gābâh]* on his bond of indebtedness *[šṭar ḥôb]*."[11] In the eyes of the brothers, the crime accrued to the accounts of each one of them. For God to be fair, he must punish them together. The brothers reason that if they disperse, it will be as if God has lost the bond; without the bond, God will not be able to collect what is due. But God, the midrash assumes, cannot be captured by such wooden logic. Although all the brothers are culpable, God is free to exact repayment from any one of them ("Can't one be taken for all of them?").

At this point the midrash makes a striking move. As the biblical story develops, Joseph devises a test to see whether his brothers' attitude toward him has changed. Because Joseph was hated as the favored son of his father, it is probable that in his absence the same sort of favoritism would be shown to Benjamin, in that Joseph and Benjamin were the only sons born to Jacob's favorite wife, Rachel. During the brothers' sojourn in Egypt to secure grain, Joseph instructs a servant to place his favorite divining cup in Benjamin's bag (Gen 44:2), making it appear that Benjamin has stolen it. Upon discovering the cup, Joseph threatens to enslave the boy in Egypt while letting the other brothers return to their father. In other words, Joseph provides the brothers with an opportunity to divest themselves of a favored sibling just as they had divested themselves of him earlier. It is all the more impressive then, in this midrashic retelling, that when the brothers see that Benjamin has been taken they say, "God has *found* the sin of your servants!" (Gen 44:16). For God has chosen to punish not just any one among the brothers but the son who was beloved of his father—a son who was innocent of the crime of selling Joseph in the first place, given that he was still at home with his father when the event transpired.

According to the logic of R. Isaac, God's act of finding the sin of his servants does not mean that the bond had been forgotten or lost as the brothers had reasoned. Rather, R. Isaac argues, God has found the most fitting moment to collect on the debt. It is only when Joseph's alter ego, Benjamin, appears on the verge of succumbing to the same fate as Joseph's that the brothers realize their scheme has been discovered—God has found the propitious time to collect on the debt owed him.

In this brilliant piece of midrash, God chooses to collect payment from an innocent, for Benjamin had nothing to do with the sale of Joseph into slavery. Moreover, Benjamin assumed the role that Joseph once enjoyed: he became the beloved son of his father, Jacob.[12] As a sign of the other brothers' dramatic maturation, they now react to Benjamin—a stand-in for Joseph—in a charitable fashion. They now find it horrifying that Jacob's beloved son is to be taken from him. As a result Judah steps forward and requests from Joseph, the vizier of Egypt, that he bear the price of Benjamin's crime. Because the brothers have come to grips with the affection that Jacob has for Benjamin, God will not have to collect on his bond after all. The brothers tearfully reconcile, and the midrash makes no further mention of the bond. We can assume that the bond drawn up when the brothers sold Joseph into slavery has been voided. The pedagogical ordeal the brothers have been through has provided sufficient payment for what was owed.

YOUR OFFSPRING SHALL BE OPPRESSED
FOR FOUR HUNDRED YEARS

According to the book of Genesis, the relationship between Jacob and Esau is fraught with arbitrary favoritism, jealousy, and rage. The problems are evident even when these twin brothers are in the womb. As the children struggle, Rebekah turns to the Lord to ask what this means. She is told,

Two nations are in your womb,
Two separate peoples shall issue from your body;
One people shall be mightier than the other,
And the older shall serve the younger. (Gen 25:23)

The last line proves crucial. In contrast to societal convention, Jacob usurps the blessing that was destined for the firstborn, and, in anger over this slight, Esau seeks to murder him. Jacob then hastens to leave the land of Canaan and settle in Aramea, where he meets the women he will marry, Rachel and Leah. After many years, Jacob returns home with his family, hoping that the anger of his brother has abated. As fortune would have it, Esau is no longer enraged and, in a moving scene, runs to greet Jacob; they embrace and weep in each other's arms (33:3-4). Jacob offers Esau a considerable portion of his property as a gift, presumably an attempt to make amends for the blessing that Jacob had stolen earlier. At first Esau is unwilling to accept this gift; he needs no such strategy of appeasement. Only after persistent urging is the gift conveyed (33:8–11).

Given this reconciliation, one might think that Jacob and Esau would settle near each other and that the family once divided would now live together in harmony. To the surprise of the reader, however, the brothers separate. Although the tale of this separation has been told earlier (Gen 33:16–17), we shall now look at how it is treated a few chapters later. In Genesis 36:6 we read: "And Esau took his wives, his sons and daughters, and all the members of his household, his cattle, and all his livestock, and all the property that he had acquired in the land of Canaan and went to [another] land because of his brother Jacob." I have put the modifier "another" in brackets because the Hebrew original lacks this important word. As the text currently stands, it seems that Esau has beat a hasty retreat to an undisclosed location (literally "a land," perhaps in the sense of "*any* land") on account of his brother. But how could this be? He and his brother had just tearfully reconciled after years of painful, near murderous enmity. R. Eleazar (late first to early second century CE) solves the enigma by declaring that Esau departed from his brother "on account of the bond."[13]

What would have been the bond that Esau owed? If a bond had been inscribed as a result of his murderous intentions, surely his reconciliation with Jacob would have cancelled its terms. This is, after all, how the bond against Joseph's brothers was rendered null and void. What, then, is this *šṭar ḥôb*? Evidently the original editors of *Genesis Rabbah* believed that the motif was sufficiently well known so as to require no explanation. Later copyists felt otherwise, however, and provided helpful glosses. One reads: "[Esau separated from Jacob] because of the bond of indebtedness of exile that Esau did not wish to be included in, [namely the bond whose terms were told to Abraham: 'know well] that your offspring shall be strangers [in a land not theirs and they shall be enslaved and oppressed four hundred years (Gen 15:13)].'"[14] According to this explanation, the bond has nothing to do with the sins of Esau; rather, it was drawn up a couple of generations earlier. It seems Abraham had committed a sin so grave that it necessitated a bond being written in heaven that would doom his offspring to spend some four hundred years in abject slavery in Egypt. The punishment that the Israelites were to suffer there would generate the needed currency to pay off the bond.

It is not difficult to see why a tradition arose regarding a bond that Abraham or his offspring would have to repay. The text of Genesis 15 provides a strange codicil to the promise God made to Abraham. Several chapters back, when Abraham is first called by God to make his way from Mesopotamia to the land of Canaan, everything is described in rosy terms:

> The LORD said to Abram, "Go forth from your native land and from your father's house to the land that I will show you.
>
> *I will make of you a great nation,*
> *And I will bless you;*
> *I will make your name great,*
> *And you shall be a blessing.*
> *I will bless those who bless you*
> *And curse him that curses you;*
> *And all the families of the earth*
> *Shall bless themselves by you." (Gen 12:1–3)*

There is not a hint of any dark side to the promise. Abraham and his posterity are to be the subject of a great, unmerited blessing. And this optimism accompanies a subsequent iteration of the promise in Genesis 13:14–17. Yet in Genesis 15 everything changes. When God enters into a covenant with Abraham—which is solemnized by cutting several animals in two and passing between them—chilling new terms enter into the bargain: "As the sun was about to set, a deep sleep fell upon Abram, and a great dark dread descended upon him. And He said to Abram, 'Know well that your offspring shall be strangers in a land not theirs, *and they shall be enslaved and oppressed four hundred years;* but I will execute judgment on the nation they shall serve, and in the end they shall go free with great wealth'" (Gen 15:13–14). Why was this horrendous codicil of slavery lasting four hundred years appended to the glorious promise? Four hundred years was nearly an eternity in biblical times. Although the text does not say so explicitly, rabbinic readers discerned that Abraham had sinned earlier in the narrative. And earlier in the same chapter we do see Abraham express grave doubts about God's ability to make good on his promise to him.[15] As a result, the midrash assumes that a bond was "written" in heaven and all the descendants of Abraham would now be obligated *(ḥayyāb)* to pay it off through bodily suffering. Because both Esau and Jacob were among the descendants of Abraham, both of them would fall under this onerous obligation. But Esau, it seems, found some wiggle room within the contract. Since Jacob and his sons constituted the chosen lineage, it could be supposed that the terms of this bond had to involve them. If Esau was not present when this happened, the terms of the bond would be paid in full by his favored brother. It was altogether logical, then, that he hastened to "a land" (perhaps, in his desperation, to "*any* land," as the Hebrew puts it) so as to leave his brother to pay the bond on his own.

This is not the only midrashic source to use the sin of Abraham and its effect on Jacob and Esau to its advantage. The next time we hear of Esau's descendants is when Moses and the Israelites are marching toward the land of Israel. As they approach the border of the land of Edom, the territory in which the descendants of Esau took up residence, Moses shows deference to his near kinsfolk and politely asks permission to cross through their territory: "And Moses sent messengers from Kadesh to the king of Edom. 'Thus says your brother Israel. You know all the hardships that have befallen us; that our ancestors went down to Egypt, that we dwelt in Egypt a long time, and that the Egyptians dealt harshly with us and our ancestors. We dwelt in Egypt for a long time and the Egyptians were cruel to us and our fathers. We cried to the LORD and he heard our plea. . . . Allow us, then, to cross your country'" (Num 20:14–17). The rabbis were struck by two matters in this text. First, Moses identifies his people as "your *brother* Israel." Why would Moses need to remind the Edomites that both they and Israel descend from a common father? Second, Moses emphasizes the cruel treatment that Israel suffered while in Egypt. Why did Moses highlight that part of their experience? For the midrash, the answer to both questions was obvious: Moses was making it clear to the Edomites that the suffering Israel had undergone was necessary so as to pay the bond owed by both the Edomites and the Israelites. In effect, Israel had suffered on behalf of Edom. As a result of this overwhelming act of generosity, it would be most fitting for the Edomites to show Israel the favor of granting her safe passage through Edom.

The midrash to the book of Numbers interprets the unstated logic of Moses' request in the form of a parable: "We can compare this situation to two brothers against whom a bond of indebtedness was issued on account of their grandfather. One of the two paid that bond. After some time he asked his brother to loan him a certain item. He said to him, 'You know that I was the one who paid that bond which was the responsibility of the two of us. So don't turn down my request to borrow said item from you.'"[16] The parable aptly summarizes the strategy that Moses has employed. A bond had been issued against Abraham, the grandfather of Jacob and Esau. Because the sons of Jacob had taken it upon themselves to pay off the entire bond, it was fitting for their relatives to return the favor.

CHRISTIAN CRITIQUE OF RABBINIC RELIGION

The Jewish concept of sin has been the subject of some rather heated polemics from Christian readers. In particular, scholars of the New Testament who have been heavily influenced by a Protestant concept of law have tended to draw an unflattering picture of rabbinic Judaism. The metaphor of sin as a debt seems to conjure the notion that God sits in heaven with his account books open and scrutinizes every human action with an eye toward properly recording it as either a debit or credit. There is little room for the merciful side of the Godhead to emerge. One need not study theology to understand this exacting or even punitive side of God; a degree in accounting may do just as well.

One of the principal sources of this sort of critical assessment is the multivolume commentary on the New Testament produced by Hermann Strack and Paul Billerbeck.[17] These two German scholars of the early twentieth century went through the New Testament line by line with a view toward comparing those writings with parallels from the rabbinic corpus. This magisterial work, which continues to inform the work of countless New Testament scholars, frequently cites only rabbinic texts that illustrate the larger theological program of the authors. Scholars were once ignorant of the prejudicial *Tendenz* of this work and used it as though it were an unbiased record of rabbinic thinking. All of this changed in 1977, when E. P. Sanders rocked the world of New Testament studies with a devastating critique of this approach in his much acclaimed book *Paul and Palestinian Judaism.*[18] In this work Sanders presented a summary of how Strack and Billerbeck conceived the theological world of rabbinic Judaism:

God gave Israel the Torah so that they would have the opportunity to earn merit and reward. Individuals have the capability of choosing the good and the entire system of "Pharisaic soteriology" stands or falls with man's capability to fulfill the law. Every fulfillment of a commandment earns for the Israelite a merit (zekût) while every transgression earns a debt or guilt (ḥôbâh). God keeps a record of both merits and demerits. When a man's merits are more numerous he is considered righteous, but when transgressions outnumber merits he is considered wicked. If the two are balanced, he is an intermediate. Man does not know how his reckoning with God stands; consequently he has no security on earth. The balance of his account may alter at any moment. At the end his destiny is decided on the basis of the account. One with more fulfillments goes to the [Garden of] Eden, one with more transgressions to Gehinnom, while for one in the intermediate position God removes a transgression from the scale so that his fulfillments will weigh more heavily.[19]

This ledgerlike approach to theology is presented as both the beginning and the end of rabbinic thought. As Billerbeck himself put it, "The old Jewish religion is thus a religion of the most complete self-redemption [Selbsterlösung]; it has no room for a redeemer saviour who dies for the sins of the world."[20] The texts I have cited from Genesis Rabbah would seem to support this. In response to the arrogance of Lamech, God expressed his freedom to collect on the bond he held; the sin of Abraham left so many demerits that not only he but his children and the children of his children would be required to pay it off.

At the same time, these same texts reveal that God does not administer his ledger in a mechanical fashion. God found sufficient reason, for example, to suspend payment in the case of Cain for a full seven generations, as Lamech himself observed. In the case of Joseph, the bond was rescinded altogether when the brothers made amends. Yet in other texts (which I shall consider shortly), God treated the heavenly account books with more abandon. Rather than playing "by the book" and adjusting each debit to the credit, God was willing to overlook various financial obligations in order to save his people. Although in the world of finance such creative accounting can have catastrophic effects, within the spiritual realm different rules are in play. God is not adverse to "cooking the books" if the end result falls to the favor of the nation Israel he loved so dearly. Indeed, in some midrashic narratives the element of fairness disappears altogether. In its place appears the virtue of grace, that is, the receipt of un-merited benefits from God. Strikingly, Strack and Billerbeck do not at-tend to examples like this.

DAY OF ATONEMENT

To illustrate this other side of rabbinic thinking, I wish to discuss a text from *Pesikta Rabbati,* a relatively late collection of rabbinic homilies dedicated to the various festivals of the Jewish liturgical year. The forty-fifth chapter of this work contains a homily dedicated to the Day of Atonement. Ac-cording to rabbinic thought, God judges the sins of Israel on this day and determines the fate of every sinner for the following year. If God were per-ceived as a fastidious banker dealing out just punishment for each person, one would expect God to gather the various bonds in his possession and begin to demand payment so as to balance his books at the close of the year. Israelites who stood in considerable arrears because of their sins would have reason to tremble in fright. But such expectations are radically overturned by the rabbinic interpretation of Psalm 32:1–2.

> "An instruction of David. Happy is the one whose wrongdoing is car-ried away [*něśûy pešaʿ*], whose sin is covered over [*kěsûy ḥaṭṭāʾt*]" [Ps 32:1]. This is what David means: you have carried away the sins [*nāśāʾ ʿăwōn*] of your people, all their sins you have covered up.
>
> Once, on the Day of Atonement, Satan came to accuse Israel. He detailed her sins and said, "Lord of the Universe, as there are adulterers among the nations of the world so there are in Israel. As there are thieves among the nations of the world, so there are in Israel." The Holy One, blessed be He, itemized the merits [*zěkûyôt*] of Israel. Then what did he do? He took a scale and balanced the sins against the merits. They were weighed together and the scales were equally balanced. Then Satan went to load on further sin and to make that scale sink lower.
>
> What did the Holy One, blessed be He, do? While Satan was look-ing for sins, the Holy One, blessed be He, took the sins from the scale and hid them under his purple royal robe. When Satan returned, he found no sin as it is written, "The sin of Israel was searched for, but it is no longer" [Jer 50:20]. When Satan saw this he spoke before the Holy One, blessed be He, "Lord of the World, 'you have borne away the wrongdoing of your people and covered over all their sin'" [Ps 85:3]. When David saw this, he said, "Happy is the one whose wrongdoing is borne away, whose sin is covered over" [Ps 32:1].

It is important to note that Satan is not the personification of evil we might expect. Instead he is a cipher for the principle of justice. His claim is that Israel does not deserve forgiveness; her debits outweigh her credits. But God will not allow strict accounting procedures to govern his heart. Even if Satan is correct, he cannot win. God amends the situation by "bearing away" the sin of Israel. In this case, God removes not a weight from someone's shoulders, as the biblical expression would require, but a bond.[21] With those bonds removed from the scales, the credits of Israel now have the upper hand, and God can "justly" forgive his people.

The theme of angelic ire at the generosity of God is hardly rare in rabbinic literature, and a massive catalogue of examples could be compiled to demonstrate this.[22] In some stories the angels are punished; in others they are deceived. But the crucial point is that in the end, God's accounting for human sin is not according to the pattern that Strack and Billerbeck laid out. Although God is just, he is also generous. In the epigraph to this chapter Thomas Aquinas remarked that such generosity does not offend against justice. Just as the person who owes one hundred dollars is free to pay two hundred, so the person who is owed a hundred dollars can refuse to collect anything. In forgiving a debt, the creditor is in a sense making a gift of it— and God is always free to make a gift. Of course there are many rabbinic stories about sinners who are punished for their wrongdoing. But to give a proper accounting of rabbinic theology, these stories must be balanced with narratives that show God altering the rules so that mercy can win. Since all debt is ultimately owed to God, it is his right to rescind from collecting it. He does not act unjustly when he offers the debtor such a gift.

One might protest that the story from the late medieval collection *Pesikta Rabbati* is too recent to cast light on how the rabbis construed the matter of debits and credits. Perhaps, one might suggest, this is a newer and more generous corrective to a much more stern and uncompromising picture that prevailed in an earlier time. Yet the story as we find it in *Pesikta Rabbati* has a close counterpart in the much earlier Jerusalem Talmud (fifth century CE). In tractate *Peah* of the Jerusalem Talmud, the observation is made that one who has a preponderance of merits will inherit paradise, whereas the one who has a preponderance of transgressions will be heir to the fires of Gehenna. But what about the person whose merits and debits are of the same weight?

> Said R. Yose b. Hanina, "Consider the description of God's attributes [in Exod 34:6–7]. 'Who takes hold of transgression*s* [plural] so as to

remove them' is not written. But rather, 'Who takes away [a] transgression [singular]'. This means that the Holy One (Blessed be He!) will snatch away one bond, so that his good deeds will predominate."

R. Eleazar cited the verse, "To you, O Lord, belongs a charitable inclination [ḥesed]: you indeed repay each individual according to his deeds" [Ps 62:13]. Yet if one lacks [sufficient merit], God will provide some of his! This is in accord with the thought of R. Eleazar for he has [also] said in respect to the verse, "God is abounding in charity [rab ḥesed]" [Exod 34:6], that God inclines the scales of justice towards a charitable decision. (JT Peah 5a)

In the first statement we can see that R. Yose has taken the biblical text in an overly literal way. The noun "transgression" in the verse "who forgives transgression" is singular, though the sense of the Hebrew is clearly plural. Nevertheless, that "transgression" was stated in the singular struck R. Yose as peculiar. Why would a verse that purports to describe God's mercy say that he will take away only a single transgression? The answer R. Yose provides is that the biblical text has in mind a person whose scales are evenly balanced. In this case, God shows mercy by taking away a single bond so that the debits of the individual cannot predominate.

R. Eleazar arrives at a similar conclusion but from a different starting point. Psalm 62:13 says clearly that each person is repaid according to his deeds, but it qualifies this affirmation by saying, "To You, O Lord, belongs a charitable inclination." What might this mean? In the mind of R. Eleazar it means that it is God's right to mete out justice in accordance with human deeds, but that this general affirmation should not be taken as an iron-clad rule. Since God is defined by the principle of charity, he is free to bestow his infinite merit on those who are lacking. Eleazar reaffirms this principle through a citation of one of the merciful attributes of God (Exod 34:6). The fact that God is one who is "abounding in charity" means that God puts his thumb on the scale so that the balance tilts in favor of the person he deeply loves. Because the obligation is to him, he is free to overlook it should he wish.

As we saw in the discussion of Paul Ricoeur, there is no way to approach the notion of sin apart from the metaphors embedded in a given language. Ricoeur did not mean that those metaphors rigidly determined the types of stories to be told. Rather, metaphors provided the raw material that religious traditions could shape in various ways. The mistake of Strack and

Billerbeck, and a generation of New Testament scholars that followed, was to assume that Jewish thinking about the forgiveness of sins was determined by rules of strict financial propriety. As we have seen in this chapter the use of the motif was complex and subtle. To be sure, God could be depicted as an imperious lending officer who would demand every penny he had coming. But he could just as easily be portrayed as a soft-hearted aunt who was prone to forget the money she had lent a favorite nephew. Everything depends on the literary context in which we find the metaphor. To spur on moral attentiveness, it is appropriate to describe the divine tribunal as committed to a strict accounting of human sin. Here the image of being audited by the IRS comes to mind. But on Yom Kippur, the holiest day of the year, when God judges the entire world, we notice that the metaphor assumes a different texture. God in these stories is ever ready to bend the rules so that Israel can emerge from this trial forgiven. If the preservation of Israel— God's beloved son—was the bottom line, any form of creative accounting could be justified.

8

early christian thinking on the atonement

But I am of the flesh, sold into slavery under sin.

—Romans 7:14

Christ erased the bond of indebtedness that stood against us.

—Colossians 2:14

As New Testament scholars have long noted, reading about Jesus of Nazareth in Greek is problematic. Although this text represents our most ancient witness to his life and teaching, it is one step removed from the historical person. There can be no question that Jesus addressed his disciples and the larger circle of his fellow Jews in their own tongue, either Hebrew or Aramaic (or most likely, some combination of the two). Evidence of the underlying Semitic flavor of Jesus's teaching comes through from time to time in the form of the Greek we presently possess. As I have noted previously, the words of the Our Father, "forgive us our debts as we have forgiven our debtors," would have sounded somewhat odd for a native speaker of Greek in the first century, for sins were not customarily thought of in financial terms.[1] But if we retrovert the Greek to Aramaic or Hebrew, the resulting idiom would have fit in perfectly in the Palestine of Jesus's day. Indeed the form of the Our Father found in the Peshitta—the Syriac or Christian Aramaic Bible—is probably a close approximation of what Jesus might have said: *šbûq lān ḥawbayn*, where the verbal imperative *šbûq* means "to waive one's right [to collect]" on the "debt"*(ḥawbayn)* that we owe.

Another narrative that betrays a Semitic ambience would be the story of Jesus's forgiveness of the sinful woman in Luke 7:36–50. In this narrative, a Pharisee by the name of Simon invites Jesus to a meal at his home, but to the host's surprise a woman in town, who has the reputation of being a sinner, shows up at the door at the same time. Simon, for reasons that are left unstated, does not bother to bathe Jesus's feet or anoint him upon entry, as would have been the social convention of the day. Instead, the woman does this in a moving manner. The text records that she "bathed his feet with her tears and dried them with her hair" and anointed them with oil. Simon becomes increasingly annoyed as he watches this spectacle and wonders why Jesus does not take the occasion to upbraid her for her sins. Jesus, however, knows what he was thinking and rebukes him with a parable. I provide the Syriac of the key financial terminology: "A certain creditor [*mārēʾ ḥawbâ*] had two debtors [*ḥayyābē*]; one owed [*ḥayyāb*] five hundred denarii, and the other fifty. When they could not pay [*praʿ*], he canceled [*šbaq*] the debts for both of them" (7:41–42).

In this brief story almost all the terms we have seen in Jewish material reappear. The creditor is described as a possessor of a bond (*mārēʾ ḥawbâ*) that the debtor is obligated (*ḥayyāb*) to repay (*praʿ*). Should they find themselves unable to make good on what they owe, the creditor—provided he is a gracious man—can cancel or waive his right to repayment (*šbaq*). The verb for waiving or canceling is also the verb normally used to describe forgiveness in the New Testament. Once Jesus has finished this parable, he addresses Simon directly: "Now which of [the two debtors] will love [their creditor] more?" And Simon answers wisely, "I suppose the one for whom he cancelled the greater debt" (7:42–43).

The narrative sounds more conventional and less contrived in a Semitic idiom, and so it is perhaps worthwhile to hear the interpretation of an early Syriac-speaking theologian. Syriac tradition represents a vibrant form of early Christianity in which all of its theological ideas are expressed in the Semitic idiom. Most persons usually think of the early Christian movement as divisible into two basic groups: those in the West who spoke Latin (and lauded Augustine as their principal theologian) and those in the East who spoke Greek (and reserved a special place for the three thinkers known as the Cappadocians: St. Basil, St. Gregory Nazianzus, and Gregory of Nyssa). But it is more accurate, I believe, to divide the early church into three sectors: the Latin West, the Greek center, and the Syriac (and ultimately Armenian) East. The most towering figure of the early Syriac church was St. Ephrem (d. 373), who lived just prior to the terrible doctrinal divisions of the early fifth century. I turn to his writings because the story of the sinful woman and Simon the Pharisee (Luke 7:36–50) was basic to his whole theology of atonement.[2]

Ephrem was so fascinated by this story that he provided at least three commentaries on it.[3] For him, the key to Jesus's charitable behavior toward the sinful woman was the love she displayed. Although Simon, as the owner of the home, was the one who was obligated, or "indebted" (ḥayyāb), to provide for the washing of his guest's feet, this responsibility was discharged instead by the sinful woman. Although only a simple act of washing was involved, the woman showed her moral virtuosity by using her own tears and hair to complete the task. It was this deep display of love—toward both the host and Jesus—that spurred Jesus to forgive her sins. In Ephrem's words, "The one who invited Jesus to the great meal was rebuked because of the meagerness of his love. But that woman wiped away with her few tears the *great bond* that had accrued to her sins."[4]

ERASING THE BOND THAT STOOD AGAINST US

The reference to the bond brings to mind the theme explored in the previous chapter. It should not be a surprise that Ephrem, who wrote in the Aramaic idiom, would employ the same terms we find in contemporary Jewish texts. Ephrem's home was in the northern rim of what was once called classical Mesopotamia, and he spoke the same language as his rabbinic brethren, many of whom also lived in the near vicinity. Christians of this period had frequent opportunities to interact with Jews. Although some of Ephrem's theological terminology can be traced back to Second Temple Jewish writings, one can presume that Ephrem and the rabbis used the same terminology for sin and forgiveness simply because it was their shared native vocabulary. Indeed, in our own day both Jewish and Christian writers describe the sinful state of humanity using the vocabulary of alienation, anomie, and so forth that derives from existentialist philosophy. They are not necessarily borrowing from one another but, rather, drawing on a common philosophical lexicon.

But Ephrem had additional grounds for invoking a bond to describe the sinful plight of humanity. On the one hand, his choice of words is thoroughly natural to the literary context, for what could Luke mean by a "possessor of a debt" (Syriac mārē' ḥawbâ) other than a person who has in his possession a physical document (šṭar ḥawbâ)? Ephrem was referring to an economic custom that was alive and well in his time. On the other hand, the reference to a bond also had a significant scriptural source: Ephrem's words allude to the atonement as described in Colossians 2:14. In this verse, Christ's act of forgiveness is described as "the erasure of the bond of indebtedness."

This text was central to early Christianity and may be the most cited New Testament passage on the subject of the atonement.[5] It reads: "And when you were dead in trespasses and the uncircumcision of your flesh, God made you alive together with him, when he *cancelled [charizo] the debt of all our trespasses, erasing the bond of indebtedness [cheirographon]* that stood against us with its legal demands. He set this aside, nailing it to the cross. He disarmed the rulers and authorities and made a public example of them, triumphing over them in it" (Col 2:13–15). The key phrases here are "cancelled the debt of all our trespasses" and "erasing the bond of [our] indebtedness." The first uses a verb *(charizo)* whose basic meaning is "to give freely and generously." It is the same verb used earlier in the story of Simon the Pharisee ("A certain creditor had two debtors; one owed five hundred denarii, and the other fifty. When they could not pay, he canceled *[charizo]* the debts for both of them"). As such it is an excellent verb for denoting the cancellation of a debt, for the creditor has graciously converted a loan into an outright gift.[6]

The second, and far more important, phrase, "erasing the bond of indebtedness," places us right in the Jewish milieu we have been tracing. The Greek term that is used here is *cheirographon*. (In the Syriac New Testament the term is rendered *šṭar ḥawbâ,* which is the Aramaic equivalent of Hebrew *šṭar ḥôb.*) The term literally means "a hand-written document" (from *cheiro,* "hand," and *graphon,* "written item") and probably refers to a process wherein a borrower would sign such a bond in his own hand before witnesses. This public ceremony would make the bond legally binding. In contemporary Greek papyri, the term is regularly used to refer to a bond of indebtedness.[7]

These papyri have proved important for New Testament scholars because they provide a close parallel to word usage in Colossians. Unlike some of them, however, I do not think they alone provide us the entire context from which Colossians 2:14 is to be understood. To use these papyri thus is to claim that the Greco-Roman world offers a better context for understanding the growth of early Christianity than does contemporary Judaism. Yet, despite their relevance, they are deficient in one important area: the term *cheirographon* is almost always found in the context of loan dockets and the like; there is no evidence of widespread use of the term as a metaphor for sin.[8] For this context, the diction of Colossians has a more natural home in the Hebrew and Aramaic of Second Temple Judaism. Although none of the rabbinic texts we have discussed dates earlier than the fourth century, this does not mean that Jewish usage did not begin earlier.[9] Indeed, it may just be that Colossians provides the earliest evidence of such Jewish usage.

BONDS OF INDEBTEDNESS IN EARLY JUDAISM

The term *cheirographon* first occurs in the Greek Bible in the book of Tobit, though in a somewhat different sense. Although the book dates to the second or third century BCE and was written in either Hebrew or Aramaic, it is not part of the Jewish Bible. It can be found, however, in the Catholic Bible (though some Protestant Bibles print the book as part of the Apocrypha). The book tells the story of a deeply religious man named Tobit, who is scrupulous about the command to be generous toward the poor. Early in his life he is exiled to Mesopotamia where he quickly rises through the ranks as a skilled merchant in the royal court. During one of his business ventures into Media, he leaves a considerable amount of money on deposit with a man named Gabael (1:14). In the Greek version, Tobit secures this deposit by drafting a *cheirographon* (see 1:14, 5:3, and 9:2).[10] Although this is not technically a loan, the obligation imposed upon Gabael is similar: like a borrower he is entrusted with funds that he is obligated to return at some future date. The bond serves as Tobit's receipt for said transaction and later in the story proves invaluable when Tobit sends his son Tobias to recover the money.

Curiously, in the Latin translation of St. Jerome (early fifth century CE), this financial exchange is described differently. To appreciate the difference I have assembled the Greek and Latin verses dealing with the loan and its return. Note that the Vulgate transformed what was originally an act of leaving money on deposit in the Greek into making a loan to an indigent man. Although both required trust, issuing a loan was certainly the riskier of the two. Perhaps because of this, the Vulgate makes more frequent reference to the note of indebtedness (*chirografum*) that Tobit holds, because that document (1) represents his legal rights to collect what is owed him and (2) must be turned over to the debtor once the sum has been paid in order to clear him of any future obligation toward his creditor. I have included the two sections where this *chirografum* is mentioned: at the beginning of the book, when Tobit leaves his money with Gabael, and in the middle of the book, when Tobit sends his son Tobias to collect the money.

Latin Vulgate

1:16. And when he was come to Rages, a city of the Medes, and had ten talents of silver of that with which he had been honored by the king 17. and when amongst a great multitude of his kindred he saw Gabelus in want, who was one of his tribe, taking a note of his hand [*chirografum*], he gave him the aforesaid sum of money.

4:21. "I tell thee also, my son, that I *lent* ten talents of silver, while thou wast yet a child, to Gabelus, in Rages a city of the Medes, and I have a note of his hand [*chirografum*] with me:
22. Now therefore inquire how thou mayst go to him, and receive of him the foresaid sum of money, and restore to him the note of his hand [*chirografum*].
23. Fear not, my son: we lead indeed a poor life, but we shall have many good things if we fear God, and depart from all sin, and do that which is good."
5:1 Then Tobias answered his Father . . .

2. "But how I shall get this money, I cannot tell. . . . What token shall I give him?"
3. Then his father answered him, and said: "I have a note of his hand [*chirografum*] with me, which when thou shalt shew him, he will presently pay it."[11]

Greek

1:14. So I used to go into Media, and once at Rages in Media

I left ten talents of silver in trust with Gabael, the brother of Gabrias.

4:20. "And now let me explain to you about the ten talents of silver which I *left in trust* with Gabael the son of Gabrias at Rages in Media.

21. Do not be afraid, my son, because we have become poor. You have great wealth if you fear God and refrain from every sin and do what is pleasing in his sight."
5:1. Then Tobias answered him, "Father, I will do everything that you have commanded me,
2. but how can I obtain the money when I do not know the man?"

3. Then Tobit gave him the receipt, and said to him, "Find a man to go with you and I will pay him wages as long as I live; and go and get the money."

Although the Greek version is the more ancient, Jerome's text is still of considerable value. Jerome himself indicated that in doing his Latin translation he was helped by an Aramaic version of the story put at his disposal by a Jewish colleague.[12] If this was the case, we can presume that some later Jewish scribe altered the original story line so that Tobit's deposit to Gabael became a loan. The literary advantage of such a change is that now Tobit is making a loan to an impoverished person, which is perceived as a charitable act, for the odds of recovering one's money in such a situation are very low.[13] This means that Tobit must have considerable faith in God's providential care to assume such a large financial risk. In the end, Gabael's business ventures take a turn for the better, and he is able to repay Tobit's kindness.

In changing the tale in this fashion, the scribe also had to alter the details to reflect the convention governing loans in Palestine in the first few centuries of the Common Era. To secure the loan, Gabael must have a bond drawn up and signed, indicating his pledge to repay the sum in full. The bond is then turned over to Tobit, who becomes the *mārē' šṭārâ*, or "possessor of the bond." The possession guarantees his rights to collect what is his due.[14] Once repayment was made, the bond holder returns the bond to the borrower who disposes of it as he pleases.

The *Testament of Job* provides another perspective on the custom of drawing up a bond. This text, which most scholars believe to be of Jewish origin, dates from between 100 BCE and 200 CE. This tale, like other texts of the Testamentary genre, is constructed around a bedside address to the family shortly before death. In this apocryphal retelling, Job emphasizes his extraordinary generosity to the poor. At one point he recounts that a number of persons wished to assist him in his generosity but were too poor to have anything to give away. "We beg you," they implored him, "may we also engage in this service. We own nothing, however. Show mercy on us and lend us money so we may leave for distant cities on business and be able to do the poor a service. And afterward we shall repay what is yours." Job responds with joy to their request and allows them to take what they need. "I would give them as much as they wished, taking no security from them except a *written note*. So they would go out at my expense. Sometimes they would succeed in business and give to the poor. But at other times, they would be robbed. And they would come and entreat me saying, 'We beg you, be patient with us. Let us find how we might be able to repay you.' Without delay I would bring before them the note and read it before them. Then I would *rip it up* and set them free from their debt saying: 'Since I trusted you for the benefit of the poor, I will take nothing back from you. Nor would I take anything that was owed to me'" (11:2–4, 7–12). As in Jerome's version of Tobit, the creditor becomes the holder of the signed bond. Because the bond is in his possession, he has the right to claim the specified sum. In Job's case, he would read the note out loud, but instead of promptly demanding repayment, he would rip up the bond. This was not some momentary whim or fancy but a legal action that voided the rights of the holder. By doing this Job had magnanimously set the borrower free from any future obligation.

SOME UNANSWERED QUESTIONS ABOUT THE BOND

The texts I have explored in the Gospel of Luke, Tobit, and the *Testament of Job* provide a fairly complete narrative of what went into drawing up a bond and canceling it. In the text from Colossians ("[God erased] the bond of indebtedness that stood against us with its legal demands"), the basic idea is clear, but many of the details are not. Who actually signed the bond and who possessed it when God erased it? Because the text is unclear on these matters, these questions were subject to a variety of hypothetical solutions. The hundreds of commentaries that have been written on Colossians over the centuries attest to the challenge these verses present. The author offers only a passing glance at the atoning work of Christ and does not spell out the specific theological context of this metaphor.

If we assume that both the writer and the earliest readers of the letter to the Colossians were aware of the other Pauline letters, we can shed more light on the ambiguities by turning to that corpus of work.[15] In his letter to the Romans, for example, Paul is clear that our sinful state is like that of a *slave*.[16] Christ's act of salvation redeems us from that woeful condition. But redemption means literally to buy back a slave, that is, to repay the debt that led to the slavery in the first place. On this view, our sinful state is imagined as akin to a debt-slave. The debt of our sins has put us in arrears with God, and so we have been sold into spiritual slavery.

But how did humankind fall into such debt? Paul, in his epistle to the Romans, sees the origination of human sin in Adam's disobedience in Eden (Rom 5:12–14). If we stay within the bounds of the Pauline corpus and read Colossians in light of Romans, we can answer that question: Adam and Eve were the ones who signed a bond that enslaved humankind.

Given the obvious correlation of Romans and Colossians, it should not surprise us that one of the earliest patristic thinkers, Irenaeus of Lyons (second century CE), draws this same conclusion. He declares that humanity became "God's debtors" in Eden when Adam and Eve ate the forbidden fruit.[17] The remission of that debt, Irenaeus continues, is grounded in the Crucifixion, for scripture declares clearly that "[Jesus] destroyed the hand-writing of our debt and fastened it to the cross" (Col 2:14). This particular choice was fitting because just as "by means of a tree [in the Garden of Eden] we were made debtors, [so also] by means of a tree [i.e., the cross] we may obtain the remission of our debt."

Although Irenaeus states plainly where this bond originates (with Adam), he does not say who holds that bond. The work of Jacob of Serug, a renowned Syriac theologian writing in the fifth century, holds a few more pieces of the puzzle. In commenting on the words from the Our Father, "forgive us our debts," he assumes the voice of Adam lamenting the condition of his fall:

> I have been sold, O my Lord, how can I return to Freedom?
>   By my own will I came among those of this Evil Lord.
> The devious serpent took my pen and wrote;
>   He and Eve wrote a bond [šṭārâ] of servitude and enslaved me.
> I consented and I who was once free became a slave.
>   The Enemy, who purchased me, bound me for naught.[18]

These few lines elucidate what was left unstated in the Pauline epistles. Adam imagines himself as a miserable debtor who has been sold into slavery to make up his losses. Even though it was God who issued the command that Adam violated, somehow Satan ends up holding the bond. There are strong narratological and theological reasons for why Jacob of Serug and many other early Christian thinkers would tell the story in this fashion. Because the life of Christ is a tale of God's defeat of the power of death, it makes sense that this very power (a.k.a. Satan) should hold some advantage over humanity from which Christ can save them. This manner of depicting salvation, which was widespread in the early church, was nicknamed "Christus Victor" in the oft-cited book of Gustav Aulén.[19]

HOW WAS THE BOND DISCHARGED?

If the picture of humanity's plight emerges from Paul's writings with a certain degree of uniformity, the question of *how* Christ delivers humanity from this bond of indebtedness is much less clear. The Nicene Creed reveals that the church spent considerable time and effort clarifying the nature of

Christ's personhood but showed no similar interest in defining how the atonement actually worked. Compare the number of lines devoted to the person of Christ:

We believe in one Lord, Jesus Christ,
the only Son of God,
eternally begotten of the Father,
God from God, Light from Light,
true God from true God,
begotten, not made,
of one Being with the Father.
Through him all things were made.

with the number of lines devoted to his salvific work:

For our sake he was crucified under Pontius Pilate;
he suffered death and was buried.

As a result of this laconic expression—"For our sake he was crucified"—a variety of explanations for the narrative contours of the atonement arose.

In the Syrian tradition one finds two distinctive accounts for how the bond with Satan was overturned. One derives from Narsai (d. 503), the leading theologian of what is known as the Church of the East (located in eastern Iraq and Persia); the other is from the work of Jacob of Serug, who represents the Syrian Orthodox Church in the West (located in Lebanon and Syria).

I have chosen these Syriac thinkers for several reasons. First, from a historical perspective, it is important to note that the early Christian movement spread in two directions, to the Greek and Latin West and to the Syriac-speaking East. It is a little known fact that until the rise of Islam in the seventh and eighth centuries the number of Christians who lived in the East was comparable to those in the West. And Christians in the East continued to outnumber Muslims several centuries after the Arab conquest. Syriac-speaking Christians may sound exotic to modern ears—they can still be found in various pockets of the Middle East and in diaspora communities in Western Europe and the United States—but in the first several centuries of the Common Era, Syriac Christianity constituted a major wing of the nascent Christian Church. The second reason for picking Syriac theologians is that they wrote in a Semitic idiom, indeed an idiom that was nearly identical with that of their Jewish confreres. By following debt imagery in Syriac theological writings, we will see how the various Semitic idioms of the

New Testament were received and elaborated upon in their native environment. Although it would be an exaggeration to say that these Syriac writers retained the original sense of early Christian ideas, they do provide a check on the common tendency of scholars to assimilate them into their Greco-Roman counterparts.

NARSAI: SATAN OVERREACHES THE TERMS OF THE BOND

Narsai, like Jacob of Serug, locates the drama of undoing the bond in the context of the death and resurrection of Jesus. Yet, in his homily on the Passion of Christ, he does not begin with the events of the final week of his life as one might expect. Instead, Narsai begins with a brief flashback to the moment of Christ's temptation in the desert, an event that inaugurates the public ministry of Jesus.[20] In Matthew and Luke, there are three temptations, but it is the first that will be the most important: "Jesus, full of the Holy Spirit, returned from the Jordan and was led by the Spirit into the wilderness, where for forty days he was tempted by the devil. He ate nothing at all during those days, and when they were over, he was famished. The devil said to him, 'If you are the Son of God, command this stone to become a loaf of bread.' Jesus answered him, 'It is written, "One does not live by bread alone"'"(Luke 4:1–4).

The connection of this temptation to the story of the Passion may surprise modern readers, but it certainly would not have appeared unusual to Narsai's audience. In the patristic tradition, the conflict with Satan was imagined to have two principal staging grounds: the first was the temptation in the desert and the second was the Passion.[21] Early Christian readers had two strong exegetical reasons for linking these events. First, Luke tells us that once "the devil had finished every test, he departed from him until an *opportune time.*"[22] There can be no doubt that this refers to the Passion, because during the last week of Jesus's life, we read: "Satan entered into Judas called Iscariot, who was one of the twelve" (Luke 22:3). Having succumbed to the devil's wiles, Judas made his way to the Jewish authorities to find a means of turning Jesus over to them (22:4–6). During the agonizing prayer in the Garden of Gethsamene (22:39–46), Jesus was tempted for a second time to abort his divine mission but consented wholeheartedly to do his Father's bidding. "Father," Jesus cried out, "if you are willing, remove this cup from me; yet, not my will but yours be done" (22:42).

The second reason the fathers of the church linked the temptation in the desert to the Passion stems from a widespread notion in the early church that the encounter with Satan in the desert was a resumption of the temptation of Adam.[23] This typological interpretation was prompted by the fact that in Eden Adam succumbed to the offer of food, whereas in the desert the Second Adam did not. The desire for food is the common factor that Satan attempts to use to his advantage. Because Christ undid the rueful effects of Adam's sin on the cross, there was a natural tendency among early Christian thinkers to link the victory in the desert with the victory on the cross—both served to overturn the woeful legacy of Adam's sin.

Narsai opens his homily with some remarks about the incarnation. Christ has assumed a body so that he can go forth to restore humankind, whom Satan ("the Evil One") has taken captive.

[The human] race was captive to the Evil One and Death, those [two] tyrants who rebelled;
[So Christ] took up the struggle on behalf of his people.
He went forth to the desert to battle the Evil One, and having conquered him,
He prepared himself for a struggle against Death, the Insatiable One. (ll. 23–26)[24]

Although Christ is visibly indistinguishable from the other captives (humanity at large), he differs from them in that he has been armed with the hidden power of the Spirit through which he can overcome the temptations that beset the body.

Satan had attempted to overpower Christ through the temptation to turn stones in the desert into bread. But whereas in Eden, when the weakness of Adam's corporeal nature succumbed to the blandishments of the "Spiritual One," in the desert, the reverse was true:

The Spiritual One was defeated [hāb] by the Corporeal One through spiritual power.
The body [of Christ] that trampled down the passions overcame the Prince of the Air.
The body that was contemptible derided and mocked the Strong One,
And removed the weaponry lest he use it to wage war on mortals. (ll. 29–32)

The first round in this struggle has drawn to a close. The incarnate Christ, the "Corporeal One," had overcome the "Spiritual One." But this first skirmish should not be confused with a final victory. The "Prince of the Air" survived to fight another day.

Knowing that Satan had more in store, Christ used his initial success to taunt his opponent. He urged Satan to prepare better weaponry for his next engagement. This time Satan would seek the assistance of his comrade in arms, Death.

Be gone, Evil One, to your counterpart, [Christ] said to him.
Be gone, prepare other weaponry for Death.
Be gone, prepare deadly nets with the help of mortals
For your power is too weak on its own for the struggle. (ll. 33–36)

Merely repeating the temptation of Adam and Eve has proved insufficient. Christ suggests that his opponents make use of the "deadly nets" (l. 35) that only mortals can provide. What are those deadly nets? Christ goes on to specify:

Be gone, gather the children you have begotten by your stratagems.
Arm them with slander as you are accustomed.
Summon lying comrades to assist you
for you are a liar and through lies you are accustomed to conquer. (ll. 37–40)

Christ has urged Satan to gather the Jews and to "arm them with slander," as he is accustomed to do. This is an apt stratagem because Satan was known as the father of lies (John 8:44). So it was "through lies that [he was] accustomed to conquer." Here we have in view the work of Judas as well as the false witnesses who will testify against Jesus when he appears before the High Priest (cf. Mark 14:53–65 and parallels).

At this point Narsai skips directly to the moment when Christ dies on the cross and descends to the abode of the dead. Narsai must continue his story without scriptural aid, for the Gospels are silent as to what happens to Christ once he breathes his last breath. The fathers of the church, however, found hints that a larger cosmic struggle was going on against the backdrop of the more mundane, historical events that Scripture narrates. In the Gospel of John, for example, when Jesus begins to speak in detail of his death, he remarks, "Now is the judgment of the world; *now the ruler of this world will be driven out. And I, when I am lifted up from the earth, will draw all peoples to me*" (12:31–32). For Narsai and other patristic readers this reference to the defeat of Satan indicated that the events of the Passion would take place on both a historical and a suprahistorical plane. What happened on earth somehow mirrored what was transpiring elsewhere. That the Jewish High Priest used false witnesses to find a way to condemn Christ to death suggested that Satan would pursue a similar course when Christ appeared in the realm of the dead a day later.

Satan begins his accusation by stating how he acquired his rights over humankind in the first place. He presents before Christ the bond of indebtedness that is in his possession. This bond was the guarantee that all humanity had become enslaved to him through the act of eating the forbidden fruit in Eden (ll. 47–48). As if in a court of law, Satan steps forward and presents his evidence:

The signature of Eve and Adam he showed him.
Look! Your forefathers signed and handed this over. Read it carefully.
The bond *[šṭārâ']* that Adam wrote for me in Eden when he succumbed to
    sin *[ḥāb]*.
Because he did not repay it, he pledged his sons as interest. (ll. 49-52)

Satan is no amateur at this sort of gamesmanship. He knows that such a bond could be falsified in two rather obvious ways: first, if the bond had been signed in private and without witnesses, and second, if the bond had been forced upon the signees against their will. Satan takes care to note that "it was not in secret that they wrote this bond" (l. 54), nor did they sign it by dint of force. Through their misplaced affections (for fruit rather than the word of God) "they *willingly* became slaves" (l. 56).[25] Moreover, it was not just Adam and his immediate generation that had become bound by mortality, Satan argues, but rather *all* those who are of a corporeal nature. So Satan closes his case with a question that he believes will seal the fate of his opponent. Because Christ possesses a body, he must also be bound by its disordered passions. And if he is so bound, then he falls within the ambit of Satan's power:

If you are corporeal and share the [disordered] passions of the body
Then examine your nature; know that you are bound by the bond of my
    lordship.
There is no corporeal being, a possessor of limbs, that is not mortal
And if he is mortal, he is a slave to me and Death. (ll. 59–62)

Satan makes a grave mistake, however, when he presumes that every corporeal nature necessarily suffers from the legacy of Adam's sin. Although this would be true for everyone directly descended from Adam, it would not be the case if God himself put on a body and made it his own. As Narsai observes in another portion of his homily:

[Because] our mortal nature was too imperfect to serve as its own redeemer
The Self-Subsistent One put on our nature and thereby freed our race. (ll.
    659–60)

It is this gracious act of incarnation on the part of God that will prove the undoing of Satan. Because he does not understand the ontological nature of the God-Man who stands before him, Satan overreaches the legal rights that God had once ceded him. After the Fall, God had given Satan the right to take all of those descendants of Adam who were sinful—their "desire for fruit" being the physical sign or "guarantee" that they belonged to him. But Satan had no rights over a person for whom this desire had been vanquished. Satan could have learned that during the temptation in the desert, because there Christ did not succumb as Adam had. Despite his ignorance about the true nature of Christ's being, he continues to press his case. He shows Christ the bond that Adam and Eve had signed (ll. 49–50) and presumes that Christ is one of the descendants of Adam who has become his debt-slave (l. 55). "Pay back [by your death]," Satan will go on to say, "just as the others do who are legally obligated [ḥayyāb]" (l. 82).

Christ, surprisingly, does not contest the account that Satan has given. He acts before his spiritual accuser just as he acts before his human accuser, Caiaphas: he keeps his peace:

In silence, I conceal my majesty from him
until he completes his treachery of putting me to death. (ll. 91–92)

The silence has a role. For Christ to achieve salvation for humanity, Satan must overreach his rights. Only on this condition can God redeem humankind from his control. It should be recalled that Satan's lordship over creation was allowed by God as a consequence of the Fall. God had threatened Adam and Eve with death should they sin, and it would have been unjust to go back on his word. Yet God was in no way obligated to cede to Satan *permanent* rights over humankind. If he could induce Satan to overreach, his rights would come to an ignominious end.

And so, for this reason, Christ remains silent and lets Satan pursue his misguided thinking to its logical conclusion. Christ, Satan concludes, must belong to him because by nature of his human body and the passions it exerts he falls under the "bond" that Satan holds. Once the testimony of Satan has concluded, Christ lays out his case in a soliloquy that remains just out of earshot of Satan.

If mortals are obligated to repay because they have sinned
then I, who am clean of all such stain, who could enter a suit with me?
If Adam fell into debt and was taken in pledge because he took his advice—
Then how could he enter a suit with me, whom he could not overpower at
  all? (ll. 95–98)

Christ is shocked at the audacity of Satan. Having defeated him during the temptation in the wilderness, what gives Satan the right to think he falls under the bond *[šṭārâ']* of Adam and Eve?

If Adam's bond is guaranteed by an ongoing desire for forbidden fruit, Christ clearly cannot fall within its bounds if he is "clean of all such stain" (l. 96). If Satan puts to death an innocent man, he will be guilty of an egregious act of overreaching the legal rights that were given him with his "bond of indebtedness" *(šṭar ḥawbâ,* cf. Col. 2:14).

By death he sealed the bonds of indebtedness *[šṭar ḥawbê]* of the human
    race,
But through [my] death on top of a cross I shall rip it in two.
In the eyes of both angels and humanity I will void it,
That legal verdict which he boasts about as if he were a victor.
I will demonstrate for those on heaven and earth
The redemption of the living and their renewal which is fulfilled in me. (ll.
    109–14)

By putting Christ to death on the cross, the originating terms of this bond are voided. Christ can declare that on the cross he has ripped this bond in two (l. 110), by which he means it is null and void owing to misuse. The whole salvific event has been witnessed by both heaven and earth (ll. 111–12), and the promise of Christ therefore rests on far surer ground than the bond Satan had held, which could not claim such reliable witnesses.[26] The authority of sin and death has been broken. Since Satan and Death have lost the battle *(ḥābû),* Christ the victor *(zākyâ)* is free to share the spoils of his victory with his companions in faith.[27]

JACOB OF SERUG: CHRIST REPAYS THE BOND

Jacob of Serug provides a very different account of how Satan's bond was undone through the events of the Passion. He begins with the account of the baptism, just as Narsai did. That is because he also sees the salvific action of Christ as a two-stage event: the process begins with the temptation in the desert and concludes with the Passion and Resurrection. Because eating forbidden fruit caused the fall of humanity, the penalty for that sin could only be paid by abstaining from such a choice. Fasting was the fit remedy for the human predicament: "Fasting is the first remedy that was set up to heal the first lesion of the flesh.[28] Through eating came the fall and from fasting came the rising again. The first commandment was, 'do not eat.' That one who did not obey and ate was swallowed up by Death. And because he was defeated, became a debtor [*ḥāb*], and stumbled so as to fall, it became necessary that his debt be repaid [*p-r-ʿ*] by fasting and his stumbling be corrected so that he could rise from his fall."[29]

But the repayment of the debt (*p-r-ʿ* + *ḥāwbâʾ*) was not by any means brought to a close during the period of fasting in the desert. It was simply the first act in a two-act play. The full terms of Adam's debt could not be brought to completion until the Passion. Given that the word for physical punishment in Syriac (*pûrʿānût*) derives from a verbal root (*p-r-ʿ*) that means "to repay a debt," it was logical to understand the suffering of Christ in terms of the "currency" needed to pay off the debt of Adam.

And this is precisely what happens. For Jacob, the entire reason that Christ must suffer the Passion is to repay the debt bequeathed to humanity by Adam. Jacob begins by identifying Christ as "the heir." He probably derives this title from the Epistle to the Hebrews, wherein we read that God appointed Christ "heir of all things" (1:2).[30] In Jacob's mind, Christ is the heir in the sense that he is the one who shall redeem the lot of humankind by "repaying the debt" that they had inherited from Adam. Jacob has Christ confess: "The inheritance of these ruins has come upon me. I shall rebuild the house of Adam; as the heir, I shall repay. On account of this, my father had sent me: I shall be the heir to Adam. For He saw that there was no other heir who could repay his debts [*pāraʿ ḥāwbātâʾ*]. I shall rebuild his ruins. I will not let our image be ruined in Sheol. I will not forsake our likeness nor allow them to be trodden under foot in the mire by the champions of perdition. I am the heir. All which Adam owes [*ḥayyāb*], I myself will repay."[31] Jacob's emphasis on the necessity for Christ to repay the debt puts his soteriological schema in a different category than that of Narsai. For the latter, the bond was voided by Satan's act of overreaching. As a result Narsai takes almost no interest in the actual suffering of Christ during the Passion. Jacob, on the other hand, is not interested in the theme of a legal suit. The bond of indebtedness in his view "was onerous and justice was fierce. That which was demanded [of the human race] was great." The love of God is exemplified in Christ's willingness to suffer on behalf of humankind and by doing so to pay off the bond. Only when the bond was fully repaid could it be ripped in two.

For Jacob, this point is made clear during the trial before Pilate, when Barabbas and Christ are placed before the people (Matt 27:15–23 and parallels). According to the biblical narrative, at the festival of Passover Romans practiced the custom of releasing a prisoner to the worshipers. Pilate fulfills this responsibility by bringing forward two individuals to the throng.

The one, of course, is Jesus of Nazareth; the other is a notorious criminal by the name of Barabbas. The crowd, spurred on by the chief priests and elders, urges Pilate to release Barabbas. Pilate then asks them, "Then what should I do with Jesus who is called the Messiah?" And the people respond in unison: "Let him be crucified." Pilate, in evident surprise, asks: "Why, what evil has he done?" But he gets no answer. The people simply shout in an even louder voice: "Let him be crucified."

Jacob takes the kernel of this story—the fact that Jesus is put to death in place of Barabbas—and teases out the entire redemptive purpose of Christ's life, death, and resurrection. The key to his interpretation is the name of the man that the crowd picks, Barabbas. In Aramaic the name would be rendered Bar Abba, meaning "son of the Father." For Jacob this could not be accidental, because the name pointed back to the figure of Adam, who was also a son of the Divine Father. Because Adam was the progenitor of all humankind, Barabbas becomes, in this reading, a cipher for everyone. And so, Jacob concludes, when the people cry for the release of Bar Abba, they were really demanding their own freedom.

This interpretation creates an ironic effect. Just as Adam had sinned, so Bar Abba had rebelled. Just as Adam was legitimately bound as a prisoner in the depths of Sheol, so Bar Abba was paying justly for his crime as a prisoner of the state. Just as the entire purpose of the incarnation was the release of Adam—and so all humanity that derives from him—from the powers of sin and death (Rom 5:12–21), so the people do God's bidding by requesting the release of Bar Abba, while at the same time demanding the death of Christ. In asking for the release of Bar Abba, the people were unwittingly aiding a providential end. Jacobs tells the story thus:

> It was a wicked desire [on the part of the crowd] but a beautiful clamor ["crucify him"]. Jesus was bound and Bar Abba was freed. The innocent one was declared guilty while the one who was guilty was declared innocent. The strong man was bound; the sinner went free. Our Lord was scourged while Adam was spared the scourgings. The Sun took hold of the pillar and the flame was scourged with lashes. The champion bore the weight of the world and removed the ills of sinners by his sufferings. The rich one paid the debts of the sinners and tore up the bond that all generations had not the resources to repay. The crucified one renewed creation by his sufferings and reestablished the world without corruption by his afflictions. For this reason the church cries out in a loud voice, "Let it not be that I should boast except in the cross of our

Lord Jesus, the Messiah" to whom be glory in all times and for ever and ever. Amen.[32]

The providential plan of God the Father required that the Second Adam repay the debt of the sins of the first. And the crowd played its role to perfection. The people of Jerusalem did the bidding of the Father by releasing the First Adam and putting the second to death. "It was a wicked desire," Jacob writes, "but a beautiful clamor."

The events of the Passion, then, were to be read on two levels. As simple historical fact, we see a brigand and an innocent man. The brigand has committed crimes whose repayment will require considerable bodily suffering. Yet the crowd cries for his release. In his place, an innocent man will be forced to suffer. At the cosmic level, this brigand is none other than Adam himself. The punishment he owes has become our own tragic patrimony. Yet because of divine grace, Adam does not have to pay the full price. The Second Adam will stand in his place and undergo the scourge that was his and our due. Christ, "the rich one," steps forward and repays "the debts of the sinners and [tears] up the bond (Col 2:14) which all [previous] generations had not the resources to repay."

As I mentioned at the beginning of my discussion of Narsai and Serug, the church, in its creeds, has not outlined a prescription for how to understand the atonement. That Jesus saves from sin is affirmed, but how this happens is left unanswered. (And note that Robert Jenson makes the church's nonanswer of this question, after some two millennia, a matter of systematic reflection itself.)[33] In spite of their many differences, Narsai and Jacob still share a striking number of assumptions: the indebtedness of humankind begins with Adam and Eve. They signed a bond in Eden that put all of us in their debt. Because this is a real bond, someone must be the holder of it. For both Narsai and Serug the natural candidate is Satan. He is the accuser par excellence in Scripture, and as we saw in Narsai, his accusations during the course of the Passion are grounded in the bond he holds. To this figure, God had ceded certain rights over humankind as a result of their violation of his law. But as Athanasius argued, God could not keep silent in the face of the destruction of the human beings he had himself fashioned.[34] Something had to be done to void the bond that Satan held (cf. Col 2:14).

Here is where the story lines begin to diverge. For Narsai, the voiding of the bond requires that Satan overreach the legal terms that he had been given. Since it would be unjust of God simply to take them away by force, he must trick Satan into thinking that Christ falls under the terms of the bond he holds. When Satan determines that Christ is truly a man and then decides to have him executed, his legal rights over humankind evaporate. Christ reveals himself as the Son of God and rips up the bond in front of all the assembled host of heaven. In this view, Christ must suffer, but solely as a means of showing himself as an innocent victim whom Satan has wrongly accused. His suffering does not provide any "currency" with which to repay the bond.

Jacob, on the other hand, believes there is a real price to be paid and that the bond can be abrogated only by Christ's fulfilling its terms. Everything turns, in his view, on the exchange of Christ for Bar Abba. The latter is a stand-in for the First Adam. When Pilate presents these two figures before the crowd on the Friday of Holy Week, the choice is between a criminal who justly deserves punishment (Adam and his legacy) and an innocent victim (Jesus, the Second Adam). It is the death of the innocent one that generates the necessary currency, a currency that was beyond the reach of any other son of Adam: "The rich one paid the debts of sinners and tore up the bond which all generations had not the resources to repay." The unique ability of the Second Adam to generate such an infinite store of merit (and as a result, receive the title "the rich one") is not fully worked out in this homily of Jacob (for this we must await the work of St. Anselm). In any event, what is crucial in Jacob of Serug's thought is that Christ makes good on the bond and as a result is entitled to void it by ripping it in two.

The advantage of choosing Narsai and Serug is that we see two native Syriac speakers working out a doctrine of the atonement in a Semitic idiom that stretches back to the dawn of the Second Temple period. The Christus Victor model they embody has often been criticized as wholly mythical in orientation, and unbiblical to boot, but such is certainly not the entire truth.[35] The story line we find in Narsai and Jacob clearly goes beyond the laconic accounts in Scripture, but it is hardly a full-scale invention of the imagination. Its roots lie deep within the idiom for sin that took shape in Second Temple Judaism. That so many ideas are shared by Jewish and Syriac writers is testimony to the power of Second Temple materials to reach beyond the limits of their historical origins.

AUGUSTINE AND THE LATIN WEST

In this chapter I have traced how two Syriac theologians engaged the problem of how Christ was able "to void the bond that stood against us." The reader may assume that the legacy of the metaphor of sin as a debt was particular to Syriac Christianity. After all, we have seen that the intrusion of debt vocabulary into the Greek New Testament was not natural. Indeed, a number of scholars have suggested that the Matthean form of the Our Father was altered in the Gospel of Luke ("forgive us our trespasses") so as to make the prayer more intelligible to a Greek audience.

Contrary to what one might have expected, however, the idiom for sin as debt was not suppressed or altered when it moved into the Greek- and Latin-speaking world. Indeed, the image of a bond of indebtedness became an important symbol among both Greek and Latin theologians.[36] If one were to do a computer model of which texts in the New Testament were most cited in the patristic period, I am confident that Colossians 2:14 would be near the top of that list. One cannot always trust concordances for finding these references, because the words of this biblical text (erase, annul, or tear up the bond of indebtedness) have become part of the contemporary theological idiom. Frequently editors of patristic texts leave allusions to this text unnoted. What we see is the slow but steady penetration of the metaphor of sin as a debt into every aspect of Greek- and Latin-speaking Christianity.

As an example, let us consider how St. Augustine addresses the issue of his mother Monica's death in his *Confessions*.[37] In a moving scene he lays out for us his deep affection for his mother and his longing that she attain the kingdom of the blessed in the world to come. Two things are striking as he considers how that might happen. First, he recognizes that though her sins had been forgiven through her baptism, she continued to sin afterward. In his prayer that those subsequent sins also be forgiven, he points out her propensity toward acts of mercy to those around her. Employing the vocabulary of the Our Father, Augustine implores God to forgive her debts just as she forgave her debtors their debts.

But rather than dwelling solely on Monica's acts of virtue, Augustine also recalls her tremendous faith in God. Monica, Augustine relates, was an altogether humble woman. She did not give special instructions for her burial, nor did she desire a special monument to mark her grave. "All that she desired," Augustine writes, "was that she should be remembered at your altar, which she had served without ever missing a single day, and from which she knew was dispensed that holy sacrifice by which 'the handwriting that is against us is blotted out' [Col 2:14], by which the enemy was triumphed over, who reckoning up our sins and seeking what there was to lay to our charge, 'found nothing in Him' [John 14:30–31], in whom we conquer."[38] In one sentence, Augustine summarizes the type of thinking traced in this chapter. We could paraphrase Augustine in this fashion: the devil who held a bond of indebtedness against all of humanity sought to find grounds for exacting its price, death. Although no sin worthy of death could be found in Christ, the devil put him to death anyway. The result of this overreaching was the blotting out of the bond the devil once possessed. The victory that Christ achieved during his Passion and Resurrection was a one-time historical event, but its benefits were made perpetually available through the sacrifice of the Mass. Monica demonstrated her faith in Christ's saving act by attending that sacrifice on a daily basis. And so Augustine can conclude that just as the debts of her youth were dispensed with at baptism, her continual acts of mercy and reliance on the sacrifice of the Mass would take care of later debts.

Clearly the theology of Augustine shows strong affinities with the portrait Narsai drew. There is, of course, much more to Augustine's theology of the cross than we can examine here, but this brief selection from his *Confessions* is sufficient to show that the theme of a bond of indebtedness held by the devil took deep root outside the immediate sphere of Syriac Christianity.

part three:
balancing debts with virtue

9

redeem your sins with alms

Almost as soon as the idea of sin as a debt appears on the scene, so does its financial counterpart, credit. These two ideas are a natural pair in the commercial world, and they continue to be such in religious thinking. In this respect the idiom of sin as a debt represents a *novum*, or new idea, in biblical thought, since previous idioms for sin such as stain or weight did not produce such obvious counterparts. Although it is theoretically possible to imagine a virtuous person such as a Mr. Clean, who could have scoured away the blot of sin upon Israel's body, or a St. Atlas, who was sufficiently strong to bear up under the weight of the nation's sin, no such images exist in scripture.

In the lexicon of rabbinic Hebrew, one finds both a logical and lexical opposition between the terms for debt *(ḥôb)* and credit *(zĕkût)*. From an etymological point of view, the use of these verbal stems in Syriac is natural, because in that dialect of Aramaic the verb *ḥāb* means "to lose," and *zākâ*' "to win." The primary contexts in which the winning and losing occur are the battlefield and the courtroom (though in the courtroom the terms have a slightly different nuance, for there losing implies "guilt," and winning "innocence"). It is easy to see how one gets from losing in battle or the courtroom to owing a debt, for losers in either realm are almost always saddled with some form of payment. Losers in war become bearers of tribute (ancient art frequently depicts the vanquished as bringing their booty in tow in homage to the victor), whereas losers in the courtroom must pay damages or a fine.

Baruch Schwartz has shown how neatly the latter works in rabbinic law, wherein the sinner is obligated *(ḥayyāb)* to pay a price to clear the slate of what he owes. In some cases he owes a goat as a sin offering or a lamb as a reparation offering. For more serious offenses he must "pay" by being lashed (see the Mishnah tractate *Makkot*, "Lashes") or even by extirpation *(karet)*. These graded penalties served to raise sufficient currency to satisfy the debt owed.[1] As the apostle Paul, himself a good Second Temple Jew, put it, "the wages of sin is death" (Rom 6:23). For every sin there was a cost.

Within this setting, one who is defeated or declared guilty is shackled with an obligation to pay a price. From there it is only a short distance to locate this semantic root in the domain of money lending, for the person who borrows is also one who owes *(ḥayyāb)* and what he owes comes to be called a debt *(ḥôb)*.

The etymology of *zĕkût* is a bit harder to trace. From Syriac, we learn that the basic sense of the verbal root is "to win." The nominal form in Syriac means "victory" (in battle) and "innocence" or "acquittal" (in the courtroom). But how do we get from there to the concept of "merit"? One possible explanation comes from the battlefield: to the victors go the spoils. In a court of law, on the other hand, the winner frequently receives payment in the form of compensatory damages.[2] Yet the problem with this sort of semantic development is that in Hebrew and Jewish Aramaic—the only languages with the nominal form *zĕkût*—the verbal root *z-k-y* only rarely means "to win." In Syriac, that verbal meaning does exist, but the correlative noun does not have the sense of "a merit." In Jewish material, it is likely that the verbal root originally meant "to be clean, pure." In legal and commercial contexts, it acquired the secondary meaning of being "quit from all claims."[3] From there it was a small step to the meaning "to acquire, purchase" and, hence the nominal sense of "the thing acquired" or, more simply, "a merit, credit."

Whatever the etymology of *zekût*, there is a natural semantic affinity in Jewish Aramaic and Syriac between *ḥôb*, "debt," and *zĕkût*, "credit." The rabbis, for example, were fond of telling stories in which a person's credits *(zĕkûyôt)* were weighed against debits, as though the heavenly courts were outfitted with a set of scales. When God needed to determine the future fate of a person, he would put the accumulated bonds of indebtedness in one pan of the scale and the credits in the other. If the debits were heavier, one would be required to make up the difference.

But the God of Israel was not always so exacting in his standard of justice. R. Yose ben Hanina taught in the late first century that when the scales of judgment were evenly balanced between debts and acts of merit, God would snatch away one of the bonds so that he could forgive the sinner.[4] In a more striking midrashic narrative, Moses was able to avert the hand of God that was bent on destroying Israel after she venerated the golden calf by recalling the merits that had accrued to the patriarchs (zĕkût ʾābôt), the most important being Isaac's willingness to offer himself as a sacrifice (Gen 22).[5] In his consent to being sacrificed, Isaac had done a work of supererogation that yielded an immeasurable outpouring of merit. And so, the midrash reasoned, it was logical for Moses to ask God to draw from this "treasury of merits" so as to pay down Israel's debt.[6]

The parallels between Judaism and Christianity regarding a treasury of merits are patent. Just as Isaac's self-sacrifice generates a credit upon which Israel can subsequently draw, so Ephrem prays that he might benefit from the victory of Christ who, as possessor of a bond, can demand his wages and distribute them as he pleases. Ephrem describes Christ as a creditor who is free at any time to demand payment from his debtors. All sinners need do is plead that Christ, who is also the font of all mercies, provide remission to "cover the note of debt" that is owed.[7] The underlying concept of a treasury of merits is deeply embedded in the language and culture of Second Temple Judaism and two of its natural heirs, rabbinic Judaism and early Christianity.

One might suppose that although the idea of sin as a debt emerged in biblical times, the idea of virtuous activity as a merit came only after the close of the scriptural canon. But such is not the case. As we shall see, the idea of conceiving virtuous activity in the form of a merit has an ancient pedigree as well. In the Old Testament, the book of Daniel contains the first fruits of an idea that will come to full harvest in latter rabbinic and patristic thought. Indeed, much of both Jews' and Christians' understanding of the forgiveness of sins will follow from that text.

KING NEBUCHADNEZZAR'S "DEBT"

In the fourth chapter of the book of Daniel, King Nebuchadnezzar has a terrifying dream and summons Daniel to his court to lay bare its meaning. At the beginning, the king sees a tree of great stature whose top reaches the heavens. Underneath its vast foliage, the animals of the field congregate to enjoy its shade and to consume its abundant fruit. Then the scene changes abruptly as an angel descends from heaven and orders that the tree be cut down, its foliage stripped, and its fruit scattered. The stump, however, is to be left in the ground. The curious image of the tree transforms itself into the person of the king.

But leave the stump with its roots in the ground.
In fetters of iron and bronze
In the grass of the field,
Let him [Nebuchadnezzar] be drenched with the dew of heaven
And share earth's verdure with the beasts.
Let his mind be altered from that of a man
And let him be given the mind of a beast
And let seven seasons pass over him. (4:12–13)

The dream concludes with the observation that this sentence has been decreed by the angelic host so that all creatures shall come to know that it is God Most High who "is sovereign over the realm of man and he gives it to whom he wishes; and he may set over it even the lowest of men" (4:14).

Daniel realizes the ominous future this dream portends and hesitates to reveal its meaning. But Nebuchadnezzar presses him, so Daniel must declare that it is the king himself who is the gigantic tree that will be cut down and stripped of foliage and fruit. Because of the king's arrogance, he will be reduced to a near animal state until he learns that his grandeur comes solely from God.

There is a certain family resemblance between the king's dream and those of Pharaoh in the book of Genesis (Gen 41:1–24). Both dreams warn of terrible days ahead (seven consecutive years of severe famine; eviction from the throne), and both require a righteous Israelite (Joseph; Daniel) to interpret them. But Pharaoh's dreams curiously occurred as a *pair*. In one dream he saw seven gaunt and sickly cows emerge from the Nile and consume seven sleek and fat ones (Gen 41:2–4). In a second, he saw seven thin shafts of grain blighted by the hot east wind swallow up seven ripe and plump shafts (41:5–7). Each dream foretold a dreadful famine, Joseph concluded. That Pharaoh had two dreams with the same meaning meant that "the matter had been [firmly] determined by God, and that God will soon carry it out" (Gen 41:32).

Unlike Pharaoh, Nebuchadnezzar had just one dream, which led Daniel to conclude that this dream could not possess the same degree of certainty as to its fulfillment. In other words, there must be a way to avert or at least ameliorate what was coming. So Daniel concludes his interpretation of the dream with a short piece of advice. "Therefore, O King, may my advice be acceptable to you: Redeem your sins by almsgiving (*ṣidqâʾ*) and your iniquities by generosity to the poor (*miḥan ʿănāyîn*); then your serenity may be extended" (Dan 4:24, 27 in the English).[8]

WHENCE THE IDEA OF ALMSGIVING?

For a long while, however, many interpreters were not convinced that *ṣidqâ'* in Daniel 4:24 meant "almsgiving." Although it is certain that the word developed this meaning in rabbinic literature, what proof is there that it already had this meaning in Daniel? One argument in its favor is the Greek translation of Daniel, which renders *ṣidqâ'* with *eleēmosynē*, the normal Greek rendering for "almsgiving."[9] The Dead Sea Scrolls also confirm that the root *ṣdq* could mean almsgiving in this period.[10] One might still wish to claim that though the possibility of rendering *ṣidqâ'* as almsgiving was real, the author of Daniel was innocent of such a usage. To rebut this position, I turn to Franz Rosenthal's landmark article on the problem, in which he notes that the key to translating this verse properly lies in the parallelism of its structure.[11] The command to "redeem your sins through *ṣidqâ'*" is balanced by the phrase "and be generous (*miḥan*) to the poor." To appreciate the meaning of *ṣidqâ'*, we must look at the second half of the verse, for the development of the verbal noun *miḥan* parallels almost exactly the development of *ṣidqâ'*.

The noun *miḥan* comes from the root *ḥnn*. This verbal root originally had the general sense of "to show favor" or "to be generous"; it was not associated with a specific act of generosity to the poor. Rosenthal found it significant, however, that twice in the Psalms *ḥnn* is used in exactly this sense:

> *The wicked man borrows and does not repay;*
> *The righteous give generously* [ḥônēn wĕ-nôtēn]. *(Ps 37:21)*[12]

> *[The righteous person] is gracious* [ḥanûn], *compassionate, and*
>   *beneficent;*
> *all goes well with him who lends generously* [ḥônēn û-malveh].
>   *(Ps 112:4–5)*

In these two texts the verbal phrases *ḥônēn wĕ-nôtēn* and *ḥônēn û-malveh* clearly mean "to give *generously.*"[13] The most likely recipients of such largesse would be disadvantaged persons in need of charity. What Rosenthal is suggesting, then, is that in later biblical texts both the roots *ṣdq* and *ḥnn* acquire the extended sense of giving charitably to the poor.

The preceding examples do not stand alone.[14] This special meaning is attested in six other texts, two additional instances in wisdom psalms and four wisdom sayings from the book of Proverbs.[15] Let us begin with a consideration of the selections from Proverbs.

He who despises his fellow commits a sin;
But happy is the one who gives generously to the poor [mĕḥônēn
  ʿănāyîn]. *(Prov 14:21)*

He who withholds what is due to the poor affronts his maker;
He who is generous (ḥônēn) to the poor honors him. (Prov 14:31)

He who is generous to the downtrodden [ḥônēn dal] *makes a loan to*
  the LORD;
He will repay him his due. (Prov 19:17)

He who increases his wealth by loans at a discount or interest
Amasses it for one who is generous to the poor [ḥônēn dallîm].
  (Prov 28:8)

In each of these texts, being generous to the poor means providing them
with material goods. Proverbs 14:31 and 19:17 make the point that the poor
person can be a direct conduit to God. In the former, giving a gift to the
poor is described as honoring God.[16] Even more striking is Proverbs 19:17,
which declares that a donation to the poor is like "making a loan to God."
In the Babylonian Talmud, R. Yohanan expresses his shock at its theological implications: "Had it not been written in scripture, it would have been
impossible to say it! It is as though the borrower becomes a slave to the
one who offers the loan [Prov 22:7]."[17] The Peshitta, the second- or third-
century Syriac version of the Bible, does R. Yohanan one better by translating the verse in such a way that the idea of making a loan to God disappears
completely.[18]

The point is clear: what one does toward the poor registers directly with
God. It is as though the poor person was some sort of ancient automatic
teller machine through which one could make a deposit directly to one's
heavenly account. Just as an altar was a direct conduit of sacrifices to the
heavenly realm, so was the hand of the impoverished soul seeking charity.

The texts from the book of Psalms strike a similar note. For instance, in
Psalms 37:21 and 112:4–5, quoted above, *ḥnn* also refers to a gracious gift
to the needy. We note two further examples:

[The righteous man] is a generous lender [ḥônēn ûmalweh]
and his children are held blessed. (Ps 37:26)

May no one show him mercy;
May none be generous [ḥônēn] *to his orphans. (Ps 109:12)*

In all eight of the texts we have read, the object of generosity is not humankind in general but the poor, the downtrodden, and orphans, which proves that these texts are not talking about the display of a congenial disposition; the matter at hand is providing material support for the poor.

If a select group of late-wisdom Psalms and the book of Proverbs use the root ḥnn to mark specific acts of generosity to the poor, we might wish to examine whether the same would be true for the root ṣdq in these texts. In both Psalms 37:21, 26 and 112:4–5, it is the righteous one (ṣaddîq) who is described as being generous (ḥônēn) with his wealth toward the downtrodden. In these psalms, the root ṣdq is linked with ḥnn just as it is in Daniel ("Redeem your sins by almsgiving [ṣdq] and your iniquities by generosity [ḥnn] to the poor"). Both terms, in the latter strata of the Bible, have acquired a new meaning—that of showing charity to the poor.

JUSTICE, JUDGMENT, AND THE JUBILEE

I have provided strong arguments for why Daniel 4:24 should be understood as one of the earliest biblical texts to commend almsgiving as a practice.[19] Many, however, have found it surprising that the word for *righteousness* would come to be the standard designation for almsgiving. Righteousness, after all, is a term that conveys the sense of a just and equitable distribution of goods. Justice is usually considered blind; it is not a respecter of persons, be they rich or poor. The Bible gives elegant testimony to this fact: "Don't act iniquitously when you render judgment; don't show preference toward the poor or undue honor toward the well to do" (Lev 19:15).[20] So how could the Hebrew noun ṣĕdāqâh come to mark an act of gracious benevolence toward the poor?

The answer lies in the cultural world of the ancient Near East. As scholars have long noted, it was not uncommon for a Mesopotamian king to declare a period of liberation when he ascended the throne.[21] This proclamation entailed the lifting of the obligation to repay one's debts. The political purpose of such a move is simple: by lifting such an obligation, the king sought to rectify extreme disparities between the rich and the poor that would, in time, threaten the stability of the kingdom. This act of royal generosity was termed the "establishment of release."[22]

Furthermore, it cannot be accidental that the Akkadian term for release, *andurārum*, has an almost exact Hebrew cognate, *dĕrôr*, because Israelite culture no doubt experienced similar problems with disparities between the rich and the poor. In the Bible, however, it was not the human king who declared a year of release but God himself. Every forty-nine years, the Israelites were commanded to inaugurate a Jubilee year by means of a trumpet blast on the Day of Atonement.[23] On that day a "release," or *děrôr* (Lev 25:10), was proclaimed, and every Israelite who had lost his land because of personal debt was freed from the obligation to repay and allowed to return to his ancestral patrimony. Because God owned all the land ("But the land must not be sold beyond reclaim, for the land is mine; you are but strangers resident with me" [Lev 25:23]), it was fully within his rights to redistribute it according to his will.

It is important to note that this edict of liberation—which was an extraordinary boon to the poor and underprivileged—was also termed in Akkadian the "establishment of *righteousness*" (*mîšaram šakānum*; cf. the Hebrew cognate *mîšôr/mêšar*).[24] Righteousness does not mean a blind application of equity toward all but, rather, the specific act of *redressing economic injustice*. For this reason Isaiah 11:4, a text about the coming of an ideal Davidic ruler, links the justice of the king with his compassion for the poor. "Thus he shall judge the poor with equity *[bě-ṣedeq]*; And decide with justice *[bě-mîšôr]* for the lowly of the land."

As Weinfeld documents at considerable length, it is difficult to understand the prophetic pleas that Israel's ruling elites act justly without recourse to this larger concern of restoring equity to the poor and marginalized. From this perspective, then, we can understand why the root *ṣědāqâh* acquired the secondary meaning of "acting charitably toward the poor." Just as a king might demonstrate his righteousness by releasing the poor from debt, so ordinary citizens could do their part through more personal acts of benevolence. Such acts of liberation on the part of a private citizen were appropriately termed *ṣědāqâh*, "[deeds of] righteousness."

REDEMPTION THROUGH ALMSGIVING

The one final element we need to consider is the theological logic that informs the thinking of the biblical prophet when he says: "Redeem your sins by almsgiving and your iniquities by generosity to the poor." Daniel assumes that almsgiving is a suitable way to secure forgiveness for sin. But how would that work?

First, it is important to see that Daniel understands forgiveness in terms of redemption, a notion that accords nicely with the debt imagery we have been tracing. King Nebuchadnezzar is treated as though his sins have put him in terrible arrears. To be forgiven he must redeem himself by purchasing his way out of debt. The rabbis caught the sense of this passage exactly.

In the *Mekhilta Ishmael* we read: "Ishmael says: 'Come and see how merciful He, by whose word the world came into being, is to flesh and blood. For a man can redeem himself from the heavenly judgment by paying money, as it is said . . . "therefore, O king, may my advice be acceptable to you: Redeem your sins by almsgiving"'" (Dan 4:24).[25] The underlying logic to Daniel's proposal is almost exactly the same as what we saw in Isaiah 40 and Leviticus 26. The commission of sin puts one in terrible debt, and the only remedy is to find some way to make payments on what one owes.

But the linkages to Leviticus are even deeper, for the Aramaic verb that is used for "redeem" is *praq*.[26] This is the term that normally translates the Hebrew verb *gāʾal* when it refers to redeeming a person who has been reduced to slavery by his creditors. In Leviticus 25, a chapter dedicated largely to the topic of debt slavery, we encounter a situation that is analogous to King Nebuchadnezzar's. "If a resident alien among you has prospered and your kinsman, being in financial hardship, comes under his authority . . . he shall retain his right to be redeemed even after he has been sold (into slavery). One of his kinsmen shall redeem him . . . or, if he prospers, he may redeem himself" (Lev 25:47–49).[27] In the original Hebrew, each of the words for "redeem" has been rendered by the root *gaʾāl*. All the Aramaic translations use the root *praq*—the same root used in Daniel.[28] In Levitical law, when a family member falls into terrible debt and is sold into slavery, one of two things can happen.[29] A family member can intervene and redeem him (*gaʾāl, praq*) by paying off his debt. Alternately, the debtor himself, should he prosper and raise the necessary funds, can redeem himself. If we understand King Nebuchadnezzar's plight according to the analogy of Leviticus 25, we would say that his sins have left him in considerable arrears. As Israel was once sold into slavery in Babylon, Nebuchadnezzar is about to be sold as a slave so that he can begin repaying his debt through the currency of bodily suffering.[30] But as in the case of the Israelite debt-slave, he can purchase his way out of this state if his fortune changes and he prospers.

How is Nebuchadnezzar supposed to raise the currency that will allow him to buy his way out of this predicament? The prophet Isaiah had assumed that the debt caused by one's sins could be repaid only by suffering the consequences of the misdeed. Daniel's advice is quite different; he urges the king to redeem his sins by almsgiving. In rabbinic Judaism and early Christianity, Daniel's advice will become a commonplace. Repentance without the giving of alms, in some sources, is unimaginable.[31] Somehow the act of giving goods to the poor allows one to raise a form of "spiritual currency" that will alleviate the debt of sin. But there is a considerable paradox here: the act of giving away money allows one to turn a considerable profit. How are we to understand this?

EARTHLY AND HEAVENLY TREASURIES

In the same group of Proverbs we examined earlier, we find that the noun *ṣĕdāqâh* is used in parallel to expressions about financial capital. It is as though *ṣĕdāqâh* referred to a way of handling one's monetary resources. Consider, for example, these similar maxims in the book of Proverbs:

> *The treasuries of the wicked are of no avail,*
> *But* ṣĕdāqâh *saves from death. (Prov 10:2)*[32]

> *Financial capital is of no avail on the day of wrath,*
> *But* ṣĕdāqâh *saves from death. (Prov 11:4)*

Both sayings contrast the way the wicked acquire goods with the way of the righteous. The point is that wealth, which is often accumulated as a hedge against the future, will have no value if improperly valued.[33]

But what does the proverb mean when it says that "righteousness [*ṣĕdāqâh*] saves from death" (Prov 11:4)? It seems unlikely that this proverb is referring to the general behavior of a person. Proverbs are not in the habit of trading in vague banalities. More likely is the supposition that the author wants to contrast a righteous attitude toward the accumulation of wealth with a wicked one. It would seem that wickedness is defined not so much by how one acquires the wealth but by what one expects from it. Why else would the proverb use the term *treasuries* (Prov 10:2)? This word choice suggests the activity of *hoarding* one's money. So whatever would be the opposite of hoarding is most likely the type of righteousness that delivers from death. Righteousness, therefore, most likely refers to a generous distribution of one's wealth. This would fit well with the other trope we encountered —that the righteous man is a generous lender (e.g., Ps 37:26, among others). As we shall see, this was the way most readers of the Second Temple period interpreted this verse.

The book of Tobit reveals how Jews in the Second Temple period understood this proverb. Tobit was written in the third or second century BCE and is thus a close contemporary of the book of Daniel.[34] The tale begins with Tobit exiled from the land of Israel to Assyria, where he embarks on a life of extraordinary generosity toward those around him. Among his many virtuous traits is the habit of almsgiving. In Mesopotamia, however, things do not turn out so well. Eventually he goes blind and is unable to work. In despair he pleads that God take his life and begins to make preparations for his death.

In chapter 4, Tobit gives what he believes is his last address to his son prior to his imminent death. In this last will and testament, he condenses the large corpus of Torah instruction that would have been at his fingertips to three main categories: tending to one's parents, giving alms, and selecting a proper wife. In terms of the larger structure of the book, the command to give alms is supreme. In regard to that theme, Tobit says: "Remember the Lord our God all your days, my son, and refuse to sin or to transgress his commandments. Live uprightly all the days of your life, and do not walk in the ways of wrongdoing. For if you do what is true, your ways will prosper through your deeds. Give alms from your possessions to all who live uprightly, and do not let your eye begrudge the gift when you make it. Do not turn your face away from any poor man, and the face of God will not be turned away from you. If you have many possessions, make your gift from them in proportion; if few, do not be afraid to give according to the little you have. So you will be laying up a good treasure for yourself against the day of necessity. For almsgiving delivers from death and keeps you from entering the darkness; and for all who practice it, almsgiving is an excellent offering in the presence of the Most High" (4:5–11). There are many important ideas about almsgiving in this text, but what concerns us are the final three sentences (9–11). Having urged his son to give alms in proportion to what wealth he has, Tobit declares that by doing so he will "be laying up good treasure for [him]self against the day of necessity. For almsgiving delivers from death and keeps [one] from entering the darkness." Clearly the clause "almsgiving delivers from death" is a verbatim citation of the second half of Proverbs 10:2 and 11:4. But I would claim that the reference to a "good treasure" in Tobit also derives from the two proverbs. Because the words for the wicked and the righteous are frequently paired in the Bible, one could expect that the treasuries of the wicked would be counterbalanced by the treasuries of the righteous. And since it is in the very nature of good poetry to be elliptical, an astute reader of the Bible in the Second Temple period could gloss both proverbs in the following manner:

> The treasuries of the wicked provide no benefit,
> but the treasuries gained by almsgiving save from death. (Prov 10:2)

> Financial capital provides no benefit on the day of wrath,
> But the capital gained by almsgiving saves from death. (Prov 11:4)

If we fill out the logic of our poetic couplets in this fashion, we arrive at the text in Tobit. What the author of Tobit has done is to interweave these two proverbs to achieve his own unique formulation: "One should store up a good treasure [in heaven by giving alms] against a day of wrath. For [it is] almsgiving [that] delivers one from death [and not hoarding one's money]."

In summary, the book of Tobit, I would contend, provides an important puzzle piece for my larger argument. In the book of Daniel we are told that King Nebuchadnezzar is likened to a debt-slave who must redeem himself. To alleviate that problem Daniel advises the king to give alms. But what is the logic behind this advice? The book of Daniel assumes that money given to the poor can pay down a debt that has accrued in heaven, but it does not explain how. In the book of Tobit we can put our finger on the solution. According to this work, one of the surprising features of giving alms is that it directly funds a treasury in heaven. For Tobit, this treasury will be needed to save the family from future trials. In the book of Daniel, the treasury is needed to clear King Nebuchadnezzar's account of the sins he has accrued.

But the idea of giving to the poor and funding a treasury in heaven is by no means limited to the books of Daniel and Tobit. The concept that the poor person serves as a unique link to the heavenly treasuries becomes a commonplace in nearly every genre of literature one can find in early Judaism and Christianity.

In the Gospels one thinks of Jesus's teaching: "Do not store up for yourselves treasures on earth, where moth and rust consume and where thieves break in and steal; but store up for yourselves treasure in heaven" (Matt 6:19–20). And there is also the story of the rich young man who desires eternal life. In response to his question as to what he must do, Jesus advises him to give his riches to the poor so as to acquire a treasury in heaven (Matt 19:16–30 and parallels). Perhaps the best example would be the story of the rich man who believes that the abundant yield he has enjoyed from his crops will secure him years of comfort: "Soul, you have ample goods laid up for many years: relax, eat, drink, be merry" (Luke 12:19). To this, God responds: "You fool! This very night your life is being demanded of you. And the things that you have prepared, whose will they be?" Jesus then concludes: "So it is with those who store up treasures [on earth] for themselves but are not rich toward God [in alms]" (12:20-21). But Jesus's teaching on the security of a heavenly treasury was already foreshadowed by an earlier Jewish sage, Ben Sira, writing in the early second century BCE:

Help a poor man for the commandment's sake,
and because of his need do not send him away empty.
Lose your silver for the sake of a brother or a friend,
and do not let it rust under a stone and be lost.
Lay up your treasure according to the commandments of the Most High,
and it will profit you more than gold.
Store up almsgiving in your treasury,
and it will rescue you from all affliction;
more than a mighty shield and more than a heavy spear,
it will fight on your behalf against your enemy. (Sir 29:9–13)

Ben Sira anticipates the teaching of Jesus by advising his pupils not to let their silver come to ruin; rather, they should lay up a proper treasure in heaven. But Ben Sira also repeats the teaching of Tobit when he declares that such a treasury will rescue from affliction better than any weapon made for battle.

The instructions of both Jesus of Nazareth and Ben Sira imply that coins put in the hands of a poor person do double duty. They help alleviate the pain of poverty, but they are also directly transferred to the heavenly realm to the benefit of the donor. This double benefit is neatly summed up in a much later rabbinic teaching of the fifth century CE: "Rabbi Ze'ira observed: Even the ordinary conversation of the people of the Land of Israel is a matter of Torah. How might this be? A [poor] person on occasion will say to his neighbor: '*zĕkî bî*,' or '*izdakkî bî*,' by which he means: 'acquire a merit [for yourself] through me.'"[35] This text is remarkable for a couple of reasons. First, we see that the act of giving alms to a needy person is thought to be tantamount to depositing money directly in a heavenly treasury. Mere mammon becomes a heavenly merit (*zĕkût*). This also recalls Sir 29:10–11: "Lose your silver for . . . a friend. . . . Lay up your treasure [in heaven]." Second, the saying is significant for it shows how deeply into the popular imagination this notion of heavenly merits has penetrated.[36] This is not simply a learned trope that circulated among the sages; it was the idiom of casual conversation on the streets of Israel. And no doubt this colloquial expression—precisely because it was a commonplace—must have been older than its occurrence in this particular text. Indeed, I would argue that the same logic that informed the semantic development of the root *zākâh* (and so the verbal forms, *zĕkî*/*izdakkî*, "acquire a merit," and the nominal form *zĕkût*, "merit") also informed the logic of Daniel's advice to King Nebuchadnezzar. Almsgiving funds a treasury in heaven.

ALMS AND SACRIFICE

There is one more line worth attending to in Tobit's speech. At the very close of his address Tobit adds: "Almsgiving is a *good gift [dōron]* in the sight of the Most High for all who give it." To call almsgiving a *gift* in the sight of God calls to mind an offering or sacrifice that one might bring to the temple. Indeed, the Greek term *dōron* regularly translates the Hebrew term for a donation to the altar, *qōrbān*. And the reason one brings a *qōrbān*, according to the book of Leviticus, is to put it on the altar in the presence of God. In other words, Tobit is suggesting that placing coins in the hand of a beggar is like putting a sacrifice on the altar—for both the hand and the altar provide direct access to God.

This idea is also present earlier in the book if one attends to the structure of its opening chapter. The narrative opens with a reference to the many acts of charity Tobit has performed over the course of his life (1:3). As soon as Tobit arrives in Mesopotamia, we see him acting on this principle (1:16). Sandwiched in between is an account of Tobit's religious fervor while he resides in Israel. There he is distinguished by his zeal to bring sacrifices to the temple (1:5–9). The point seems to be that almsgiving in the diaspora (1:3, 1:16) replaces revenue for the temple in Israel (1:5–9).[37]

Ben Sira sheds ample light on this. In one section of his work, he considers a theme that is dear to the wisdom tradition: the fear of—or perhaps better, reverence for—the Lord. One of the most exemplary ways of displaying such reverence is through a gift.

> *With all your soul fear the Lord,*
> *and revere his priests.*
> *With all your might love your Maker,*
> *and do not forsake his ministers.*
> *Fear the Lord and honor the priest,*
> *and give him his portion, as you have been commanded:*
> *the first fruits, the guilt offering, the gift of the shoulders,*
> *the sacrifice of sanctification, and the first fruits of the holy things.*
>
> *Stretch forth your hand to the poor,*
> *so that your blessing may be complete.*
> *Give graciously to all the living,*
> *Do not withhold kindness even from the dead.*

Do not avoid those who weep,
*   but mourn with those who mourn.*
Do not hesitate to visit the sick,
*   because for such deeds you will be loved.*
In all you do, remember the end of your life,
*   and then you will never sin. (Sir 7:29–36)*

This important text juxtaposes two classes of people through whom one can demonstrate one's reverence for God: the priests and the poor. Fearing the Lord means both revering his priests—that is, providing the priests with the requisite temple donations—and stretching forth one's hand to the poor.

The comparison of almsgiving to an offering appears frequently in the book of Ben Sira and is rather basic to his religious worldview. Ben Sira 35:1–2, for example, states:

He who keeps the law makes many offerings;
*   he who heeds the commandments sacrifices a peace offering.*
He who returns a kindness offers fine flour,
*   and he who gives alms sacrifices a thank offering.*[38]

It is worth noting that a thank offering is simply a special type of peace offering and that fine flour, because it is the most inexpensive of the sacrificial objects one can bring, is something that can be brought *many* times. Ben Sira's famous exhortation to honor father and mother concludes with these words:

For kindness to a father will not be forgotten,
*   and will be credited to you against your sins;*
in the day of your affliction it will be remembered in your favor;
*   like frost in fair weather, your sins will melt away. (Sir 3:14–15)*[39]

This text is close to the theological world of Daniel 4, for here we learn that acting charitably toward one's father can serve in place of a sin offering. As in Tobit, this kindness will be remembered to one's favor on a day of affliction.

REDEMPTIVE GIVING

In a world that viewed sin as a debt and the poor person as a direct conduit to heaven, what more logical way to balance one's bank account than to put a plentiful deposit in the hands of the needy? According to the logic of the texts I have been tracing, the money deposited in heaven in this fashion could be used to pay down what one owed on one's sins.

Daniel's advice to King Nebuchadnezzar to give alms is not an isolated event in the history of Jewish and Christian thinking about the forgiveness of sins. To the contrary, almsgiving becomes the most important means of securing divine favor. Consider this ancient tradition attributed to Rabbis Meir and Akiba (second century CE): "It has been taught: R. Meir used to say: The critic [of Judaism] may bring against you the argument, 'If your God loves the poor, why does he not support them?' If so, answer him, 'So that through them we may be saved from the punishment of Gehinnom.' This question was actually put by Turnus Rufus (Roman Governor of Judea) to Rabbi Akiba: 'If your God loves the poor, why does He not support them?' He replied, 'So that we may be saved through them from the punishment of Gehinnom.'"[40] We find similar judgments being made by Christian writers of the time. As an example, in *2 Clement,* an epistle written in the mid-second century, we read: "Almsgiving is therefore good as repentance from sin. Fasting is better than prayer, but almsgiving is better than both. Love covers a multitude of sins but prayer from a good conscience rescues from death. Blessed is every man who is found full of these things for almsgiving lightens sin."[41] The *Didache,* a very early Christian text, which some date to the first half of the first century CE, adds: "Do not be one who stretches out his hands to receive, but shuts them when it comes to giving. Of whatever you have gained by your hands, you shall give the redemption-price for your sins."[42] For Clement almsgiving is better than prayer for the forgiveness of sin. In the *Didache* we find language that directly echoes that of Daniel—almsgiving provides the redemption monies for what one owes. Note that the Greek term translated as "redemption-price" is *lytrōsis* and is derived from the same root used to translate the Aramaic term *praq,* "redeem." For the *Didache,* as in Daniel, almsgiving provides a currency that will cover one's sins.

Rabbinic texts show clearly that the idea of sin as a debt and virtuous activity as a credit are linked both semantically and theologically. As I have shown, however, this link is by no means limited to this corpus of writing. In fact, the idea of virtuous activity as a credit appears at almost the same time as sin as a debt, and the relationship between the two concepts is already assumed in the book of Daniel. Because Nebuchadnezzar's sins have put him in arrears, he requires a means of paying down his heavenly debts. Daniel suggests that he redeem himself—that is, buy his way out of slavery—by giving alms to the poor. His moral virtuosity will cover what he owes.

This "balancing of the books" approach to the forgiveness of sins led in-exorably to a second issue. Why is it that almsgiving, of all possible virtu-ous acts, was so exalted? Why was it uniquely constituted so as to assist in the process of redemption? The most striking text to address serving the poor and serving God is Proverbs 19:17: "He who is *generous* to the down-trodden [ḥônēn dal] makes a loan to the LORD; He will repay him his due." This idea of the poor person as a direct conduit to God is turned to a new end in the book of Tobit, where we learn that giving alms to the poor will fund a treasury for oneself in heaven, an idea found throughout Second Temple Judaism. We followed traces of that idea in Ben Sira and the Gospels. Strikingly, the idea is not limited to learned theological circles. Rabbinic texts show that the imagery of the heavenly treasury had become part of everyday speech in Palestine by the fifth century (and probably much ear-lier). Poor persons would greet their benefactors with the words "acquire a merit through me," by which they meant, make a deposit to your heavenly treasure by giving alms to me. The relevance of this to Daniel's advice to King Nebuchadnezzar is clear. The king had fallen into terrible arrears as a result of his arrogant behavior. To clear his name he needed to make an im-mediate payment on his debt; in brief, he needed to make an electronic transfer of funds to his heavenly treasury. What better way to do this than to give alms to the poor?

The story does not end there, however. If alms given to the poor were thought to register directly in heaven, then the hand of the poor person be-gins to resemble the altar that stood in front of the temple. Many Second Temple Jewish texts make much of this analogy. After 70 CE, when the tem-ple in Jerusalem had been destroyed, Jews began to view charitable deeds as a replacement for the sacrifices they had once offered in the temple.[43] But as we learned from the books of Tobit and Ben Sira, that theological idea had already been in existence for several centuries.

10

salvation by works?

Your alms and prayers are like loans; in every location they enrich those who take them, while to you belongs the capital and interest. What you offer as a loan returns to you.

—St. Ephrem the Syrian

Many readers will find something unsettling about the matter-of-fact way I have interpreted Daniel's advice to King Nebuchadnezzar. Is the act of giving alms simply a financial exchange between the debtor and his God? If so, it would seem that human beings can "buy" their way out of their sinful state and that the critique of the Protestant reformers applies: humans save themselves by their good works.[1]

Roman Garrison has confronted this problem head-on in a book that examines the various ways the work of Christ can be described in the early church.[2] In it he illustrates those differences through the lens of two thinkers in the second century CE, the first being the anonymous author of the *Epistle to Diognetus,* and the second a church father, Clement of Alexandria.[3] Both writers employ the imagery of financial exchange to illustrate what the salvific process is about but understand that exchange in different ways.

In *Diognetus* (9:3–5) we read: "For what else could cover our sins but his righteousness? In whom was it possible for us, in our wickedness and impiety, to be made just, except in the Son of God alone? O the sweet exchange, O the inscrutable creation, O the unexpected benefits, that the wickedness of many should be concealed in the one righteous, and the righteousness of the one should make righteous many wicked!" Here the sweet exchange the writer has in view is the atoning death of Christ. No other covering for sin was possible "except in the Son of God alone." The gracious decision of Christ to die on behalf of humankind was so inexpressible that the proper response was simply awe.

When we turn to Clement of Alexandria, we find a similar elevated rhetoric about an exchange—though the subject matter is completely different. Rather than putting the emphasis on the divine work of salvation having been achieved by Christ, Clement seems to reserve his praise for the human act of giving alms. "O splendid trading! O divine business! You buy incorruption with money. You give the perishing things of the world and receive in exchange for them an eternal abode in heaven. Set sail, rich man, for this market, if you are wise. Compass the whole earth if need be. Spare not dangers or toils, that here you may buy a heavenly kingdom."[4]

For Garrison, these two texts provide a challenge for the theological reader. Clement's praise of a *human* work seems to share the same stage as the praise of Jesus Christ's divine work in the *Epistle to Diognetus.* If human agency (in the form of almsgiving) is sufficient to merit salvation, what need was there for a divine savior? This is the reason the exalted position of almsgiving in the early apostolic tradition of the church has been something of a stumbling block for Protestants. As Martin Hengel put it: "The idea of merit, taken over from Judaism . . . may be seen as a theological regression but it was this that provided a strong motive for concrete social and philanthropic action."[5] For T. F. Torrance, excessive claims such as Clement's suggested that the purity of the original Gospel message had fallen from view.[6] But this assessment puts Torrance in a peculiar predicament. The importance of almsgiving for the purposes of reconciliation is nearly universal in the early church. To say that it represents a departure from the Gospel implies that nearly every early Christian thinker got the matter wrong. That cannot be correct. Perhaps the problem is that we have not properly taken the measure of this important theological idea.

THE ENRICHER OF ALL BORROWS FROM ALL

St. Ephrem, a fourth-century Syriac poet and theologian, is a valuable witness on this subject, because as an Aramaic speaker he would have found it natural to refer to sins as debts. For Ephrem, one of the fundamental purposes of the incarnation is for Christ to void the bond of indebtedness that stands against us (see Col 2:14). But closely related to this is Christ's surprising intention to become a debtor to us. In his *Hymns on the Nativity,* Ephrem writes:

On this feast of the Nativity the openings in the curtains
are joyous, and the Holy One rejoices
in the holy Temple, and a voice thunders
in the mouth of babes, and the Messiah rejoices
in His feast as Commander of the host.

On the birth of the Son, the king was enrolling
the people in the census,
so that they would be indebted to him. To us the King came out
to cancel our debts, and He wrote in His name
another debt, so that He would be indebted to us. (5:11–12)[7]

Ephrem refers to the census reported in Luke's account of the nativity (see Luke 2:1–2). The emperor's motivation for the census was to facilitate taxation and conscription. By enrolling all their citizens, Roman officials could make sure all would be held accountable for their civic obligations. Ephrem, however, contrasts the interests of the state with the interests of heaven. Our king, the Messiah, Ephrem writes, came not only "to cancel the debts we owed him" but to write a new sort of bond, one that would make him a debtor to humanity.

God's intention, Ephrem concludes, was not simply to annul a bond that hung over the head of humanity, for what end would be accomplished by such a one-time declaration? As soon as the period of release was over—that is, after baptism—we would be back in the "market," ringing up debts on our spiritual charge cards. For this reason, Christ writes a new bond, the purpose of which is to complete the repair of our desperate state. Under the terms of this new bond, Christ will become obligated to us.

In this brief stanza Ephrem does not inform us as to what kind of bond has been bequeathed to the human race by Christ. But elsewhere in these hymns he provides the answer:

He Who is Lord of all, gives us all,
And He Who is Enricher of all, borrows from all.
He is Giver of all as one without needs.
Yet He borrows back again as one deprived.
He gave cattle and sheep as Creator,
But on the other hand, He sought sacrifices as one deprived. (Hymns on
   the Nativity, 4:203–5)[8]

Ephrem describes God as one who "borrows from all." By this he means that, in condescending to make a covenant with Israel, the Lord made promises that allowed and enabled Israel to serve him—even though he has no need of human service. In the Old Testament, this service took the form of offering sacrifices. At the altar the One who was "without needs" acted as "one deprived." But now, in the era of the new covenant, the "Enricher of All" has taken a new tack. Rather than request a donation of food, he seeks to borrow from our purse. The hand of the needy replaces the sacrificial hearth.[9]

For Ephrem, the religious life requires that God engage humanity at a personal level. Otherwise God would remain nothing more than the detached "unmoved mover" of Aristotle. This belief in God's gracious self-condescension is well in evidence in this hymn:

> Give thanks to him who brought the blessing
> and took from us the prayer.
> For he made the one worthy of worship descend
> And made our worship of him ascend.
> For he gave us divinity
> And we gave him humanity.
> He brought us a promise
> And we gave him the faith
> Of Abraham, his friend.
> For we have given him our alms on loan
> In turn, let us demand their repayment. (Hymns on Faith, 5:17)[10]

Here Ephrem praises the sort of commercial exchange that has been affected by the incarnation. In exchange for our prayer, God provides a blessing. In exchange for our humanity, he has given us divinity. He gave a promise, but we must have sufficient faith to rely on that promise. We give him a loan, and in return we can be assured that it will be repaid.

Ephrem believes that the one who makes a loan to God through alms-giving is not simply doing a human *work;* he is making a public testimony to his *faith.* In this view, alms are not so much a human work as they are an index of one's underlying faith. The relationship between belief and the granting of a loan is well reflected in a number of languages. In English, for example, the one who issues a loan is called a creditor (from *credere,* "to believe"), whereas in German the term is *Gläubiger* (from *glauben,* "to believe").[11] The widespread attestation of this semantic phenomenon makes semantic borrowing unlikely. The connection between issuing a loan and having faith must be so basic to human culture that it can arise in any language on its own. A midrash poignantly captures the linkage between faith and issuing a loan to the poor:

A certain philosopher asked a question of Rabbi Gamliel. He said to him, "It is written in your Torah: 'Give to (your needy kinsman) readily and have no regrets when you do so' (Deut 15:10). And do you have such a man that can give away his property to others and his heart would not be grieved? Such a person would eventually need to be supported himself!"

He replied to him, "If a man comes to borrow from you, would you give him a loan?" He replied, "No!" "If he brought you a deposit, would you give him a loan?" He replied, "Yes!"

"If he brought you someone that was not quite fitting to stand as surety would you give him a loan?" He replied, "No." "If he brought you as surety the head of the province would you give him a loan?" He replied, "Yes."

"Well then, is this not a matter of *a fortiori* logic? If when an ordinary mortal will go surety for him, you will issue the loan, how much the more so when He who spoke and made the world goes surety for him. For Scripture says, 'He who is generous to the poor makes a loan to God' (Prov 19:17)."[12]

No one gives away hard-earned money without some reasonable trust in the recipient. But if the recipient is God, R. Gamliel concludes, one should be supremely confident. Ephrem would concur completely. In the stanza I cited from his *Hymns on Faith*, four nicely balanced couplets set forth the expectations that govern the relationship between God and humanity:

> *God brings a blessing / we offer a prayer;*
> *God provides one worthy of worship / we offer worship;*
> *God provides something of his Godhead / we offer our humanity;*
> *God provides a promise / we supply the faith.*

There is asymmetry in these pairs. To offer a blessing is greater than the act of requesting one through prayer, and so the logic proceeds through the entire stanza. What God offers far exceeds what human beings provide in exchange. In the enacting of any of these modalities of relationship one is taught the radical dependence of the creature upon his creator. But Ephrem surprises us with his rhetorical flourish. His last two lines provide a commentary on how we might respond with faith to the promises God has made:

> *For we have given him our alms on loan,*
> *In turn, let us demand their repayment.*[13]

The boldness of these lines is surprising—can one really *demand* repayment from God? Yet for Ephrem, only one who truly believes in God as the ultimate guarantor of his loan to the poor would have the temerity to demand its repayment. Scripture, Ephrem reasons, has shown that God's promise of grace is to be found in the hands of the poor. Timidity about the reward for such a loan reveals nothing other than a lack of faith.[14] At this point, we are well beyond the standard contours of a debate about the merits of human works.

THE SAINTS AS HOLDERS OF A BOND

The reference to the saints' providing God with loans is so ubiquitous in Ephrem that one wonders whether the idea had shaken loose from its original biblical mooring and become a standard poetic trope. Indeed, all the acts of religious virtue practiced by the saints become a sort of currency that one could loan to God.[15] Ephrem says of Julian Saba, the fourth-century Syrian ascetic:

> *[God] will open his treasury and make you a*
> *possessor of notes of indebtedness regarding all that you lent him.*
>
> *Your prayers are recorded in his books;*
> *Your treasures are guarded in his treasury.*
>
> *Rise up O community of ours and give thanks*
> *before our Lord for Saba everyday.* (Hymns to Julian Saba, 6:14–16)[16]

Like Christ before him, Saba's religious fervor has made him into a creditor.[17] In his new financial standing he can "demand" that God repay what was lent to him. But the shocking boldness of making such a demand of God is nothing other than an index of the underlying faith (credo—"I believe") of the creditor who trusted God sufficiently to make the loan in the first place.

Ephrem returns to the theme of making a loan to God when he praises the merits of St. Abraham Kidunaya:

> *Two heroic commandments: to love one's neighbor and God. You bore them*
> *like a yoke. Between man and God you sowed a beautiful deposit.*
>
> *You listened in order to act. You acted in order to issue a loan. You issued*
> *the loan in order to believe. You believed so as to receive. You received so*
> *as to reign.*

Your alms and prayers are like loans; in every location they enrich those who take them, while to you belongs the capital and interest. What you offer as a loan returns to you.

The alms of the giver are like a loan that the just give. For it is in the full possession of both the borrower and the loaner. For it returns to him with interest. (Hymns to Abraham Kidunaya, 1:5–8)

What is striking in this poem is the phenomenological description of the life of faith. One might expect that faith would come first and that deeds would follow. For Ephrem, however, the order is reversed: first one hears the command to give a "loan" to the poor, then one puts it into action; after putting it into action, one comes to believe. Again, the nexus between belief *(credere)* and action (making a loan, becoming a creditor) does not allow us to parse the behavior of this saint along the standard axis of faith versus works. Through the "work" of giving alms one enacts his faith.

For most of us, language implying that God owes us something seems an unnecessary exaggeration that does not properly honor the Godhead. In Ephrem's view, however, the holy witnesses Julian Saba and Abraham Kidunaya are simply taking proper advantage of what God has promised in Scripture. They become creditors of God only because God has allowed himself to be approached this way in the economy of salvation. In being generous to the poor, Saba and Kidunaya are not saving themselves. Rather, they are trusting in the promises that God has freely and publicly made and are obeying divine commandments. In the Old Testament, God acted as though he was in need of food; in the new age he is short of currency. In the former, one could feed him at the altar; in the latter he is served through the hands of those in need.

But another part of Ephrem's text is worth noting—that is, his conception of the type of economy on display here. The person who loans to the poor turns out to be an extremely wise businessperson because of the way God has set up this system of exchange. No one gets cheated in this arrangement; from every angle the beneficence of God is on view. "In every location [your alms] enrich those who take them," Ephrem declares, "while to you belongs the capital and interest. What you offer as a loan returns to you." Clearly, the theology of Proverbs 19:17 undergirds this text. Because it is God himself who is the ultimate recipient of this loan to the poor, a different economic exchange comes into view. And it is perhaps no accident that rabbinic writers have a similar attitude toward the way alms work in the heavenly economy, for the Mishnah declares that the generous soul who gives alms will retain his principal and, in addition, gain interest.[18] The operative modality here seems to be the infinite goodness of God, who takes our small donations and multiplies them in heaven. This deeply Jewish notion of God's graciousness finds a classic expression in the Gospels, when Jesus tells his disciples that one who gives alms will receive back a hundredfold in this life and eternal life in the age to come.[19]

One should not be surprised that St. Augustine (d. 430)—the classic representative of the importance of grace over works—is in agreement with what the rabbinic and Syriac texts have articulated. In commenting on Psalm 37:26 ("the righteous man lends liberally at all times"), Augustine notes something odd about the verse: "If you have lent to someone—handed out money as a loan, I mean . . . you expect to get back from the other person more than you gave." But the only way to get back more is to charge interest, and that is an act which Scripture as a general rule says "deserves blame, not praise." So how is one to understand this verse, which praises the otherwise forbidden practice of usury? "Study the moneylender's methods. He wants to give modestly and get back with profit; you do the same. Give a little and receive on a grand scale. Look how your interest is mounting up! Give temporal wealth and claim eternal interest, give the earth and gain heaven. 'Whom shall I give it to?' did you ask? The Lord himself comes forward to ask you for a loan, he who forbade you to be a usurer [see Matt 25:34–36]. Listen to the Scripture telling you how to make the Lord your debtor, 'Anyone who gives alms to the poor is lending to the Lord.'"[20] Scripture, Augustine concludes, is not condoning collecting interest from another person. Rather, the only place where interest can be drawn is when one loans to God. This means that the treasure one establishes in heaven works by an entirely different set of rules than conventional savings programs. One would expect that the relation between a donation and its accumulation would be arithmetical. For every dollar donated, a dollar is accumulated—which is how a zero-sum economy works.

No earthly bank could provide its customers with a two-for-one sale, whereby one's money grows out of proportion with the dictates of financial markets. But heavenly treasuries know no such restrictions. It would be better to imagine the growth of one's heavenly investment as a geometric expansion, not unlike a graph showing the growth of an investment when its rate of return is compounded year after year. Or perhaps even more to the point, funding such a treasury is like getting in on a lucrative stock offering at the ground floor. Every dollar invested in yields growth by a hundredfold. The small amount deposited provides sufficient leverage to open the gates of immeasurable divine generosity (so Augustine: "Give a little and receive on a grand scale. . . . Give the earth and gain heaven"). If we understand Nebuchadnezzar's situation against this frame of reference, this human king is hardly repaying the full extent of what he owes for his sins. In sum, when we enter the realm of the heavenly treasuries we are a long way from *Selbsterlösung* ("self-redemption").

THE CRITIQUE OF THE REFORMATION ONCE MORE

If we return to the text in Daniel with the insights gained from Ephrem, we read it in a different light. And in light of this new reading, I think that much of the divisiveness about this text in the wake of the Reformation can be set to rest, as follows:

(1) The giving of alms need not be construed as a purely human work.[21] God has gamed the system, so to speak, in a way that allows our small donations to count against the immeasurable debt of our sins.[22] As St. Anselm of Canterbury said in the twelfth century, the doing of penance at one level makes no sense, for there is nothing that a human can give God that could repay the debt that is owed.[23] Anything one would give God is already his in the first place. Yet that does not mean that the practice of penitential deeds should be dispensed with. The sinner is like a child who wishes to purchase a present for his mother for Christmas. Given that his mother has provided the child with the funds, what does the child give her? At one level, the child gives nothing; he simply returns to his mother what was once hers. At another level, this gift allows the child to part with something in order to express his gratitude. The gift does not create the relationship—the child need not do anything in order to be loved by his mother—but it does in some sense enact the love that characterizes it.

So it is for King Nebuchadnezzar. By giving alms he is giving nothing of his own. He is returning to God what is God's. God is repaid with funds he provided in the first place. Yet at the same time, the king's gift is a free choice that enables him to display his gratitude toward his maker. By giving alms to the poor, Nebuchadnezzar is given the chance to enact a faith in the God he had once spurned (here it is worth recalling that one who gives a loan to the poor becomes a creditor in its etymological sense). In other words, the merit he will generate by giving alms is at the same time a declaration of faith and trust in the God he would wish to serve. As Ephrem wisely noted, it is not possible to divide the work from the faith it enables and generates.

(2) I have argued that if these alms are imagined as accruing in a heav-

enly treasury then a whole new set of rules takes effect as to how that treasury will accumulate. When doing business with God, either at the sacrificial hearth or through the medium of the poor, it is not a matter of a one-for-one exchange. The little that one gives to God is repaid a hundred-, nay, a thousandfold. Only a logic such as this can explain how the paltry alms of a sinner like Nebuchadnezzar could ever repay the unfathomable debt that he owed.

(3) There is yet another level to the problem the Reformation has bequeathed us. As we noted, the designation of alms as an act of ṣĕdāqâh ("righteousness") recalls the ritual of the Jubilee year, when the divine king established righteousness among his earthly citizens by mandating the release of all those who had fallen into debt-slavery. This act, whether done by the divine king in Israel or the human king in Mesopotamia, was an act of pure grace. Those who suffered from financial hardship had done nothing to merit this act of largesse. The only fit response of these debtors would be the expression of utter gratitude. By giving alms as his penance, King Nebuchadnezzar was enacting this model of divine love. Paradoxically, it was this imitation of divine grace that would secure his release from sin. Perhaps Nebuchadnezzar was to infer his standing in the eyes of God from the way in which the poor would view him. In both instances an individual was giving without any expectation of receiving something in return. Nebuchadnezzar was, of course, something of a debt-slave himself. By his enactment of grace toward the poor, he secured the showering of grace upon himself.

This understanding of Nebuchadnezzar's penance is nicely exemplified in St. Thomas Aquinas's *Summa Theologica*. As is his custom, he begins his discussion with a question: "Is almsgiving an act of charity?" He provides four reasons why one would think not. In one of them, he claims that almsgiving cannot be an act of charity because it was appointed to Nebuchadnezzar as a means of *satisfaction,* that is, a paying off of what was owed. Almsgiving pertains to the virtue of justice, not charity. Yet having subsequently established that Scripture itself understands almsgiving as an act of charity (in the *sed contra*), Thomas revisits the problem of Nebuchadnezzar's penance. Here he explains that almsgiving can both repay what is owed on a sin *and* be an act of charity. For insofar as the giver of alms directs his heart to God (and so gives alms with "pleasure and promptitude and everything else required for its proper exercise"), his act of serving the poor becomes an act of worshipping (*latria*) God. As such, the giving of alms is not simply concerned with satisfying a penalty but with loving God as he is found among the poor.[24]

(4) The sensitive reader will recognize that the discussion of this chapter is not too distant from another issue that created misunderstandings in the wake of the Reformation, that of indulgences. The granting of an indulgence was nothing other than the pope's authorization to use some portion of the "treasury of merits" that had been left to the church by the work of Christ and the saints. As one could infer, this idea is deeply rooted in Second Temple Judaism and has a clear parallel in the rabbinic notion of the zĕkût ābôt, or the "merits of the Patriarchs."[25] Although this idea could be subject to abuse (especially when the "treasury" was understood as the pope's personal bank account, which he could tap as needed), it is deeply rooted in the notion that outstanding acts of charity create a font of grace from which others can draw. Indeed, Anselm's notion of the atonement in *Cur deus homo (Why God Became Man)* rests on the notion that Christ's sacrifice created an infinite store of merit for which he had no need. In his love for humanity Christ ceded these immeasurable riches to the church. With the merits of Christ, any sinner could find the resources to cover his debts.

I think it fair to say that the issuance of an indulgence is not as unbiblical as one might have imagined. As early as the book of Tobit, the act of giving alms was seen as a deposit to a treasury that could save one from death. The "merits of the fathers" in Judaism and the "treasury of merits" in the church go beyond what is described in Tobit by presuming that other members of the faith community can derive benefit from the deposits of others. But this fact, in and of itself, need not cause alarm for the Christian reader, for Paul argued that the church is nothing other than the body of Christ and that what the head (Christ) has achieved redounds to the benefit of all members. The treasury of merits is nothing other than the boundless credit that Christ (and the saints by way of their imitation of and hence incorporation into the person of Christ) gained through his Passion. To pray that one might benefit from the power of those merits need not offend the theological sensibilities of a Protestant. On this score, the words of the early Luther are revealing. In theses 42 through 45 of the 95 theses that he posted on the Wittenberg door in 1517, he made a point of distinguishing his distaste for the way money was being raised for the rebuilding of St. Peter's in Rome from the act of donating goods to the poor.

42   Christians are to be taught that the pope does not intend that the buying of indulgences should in any way be compared with works of mercy [i.e., charity toward the poor].

43 Christians are to be taught that he who gives to the poor or lends to the needy does a better deed than he who buys indulgences [whose main purpose was to aide the rebuilding of St. Peter's].

44 Because love grows by works of love, man thereby becomes better. Man does not, however, become better by means of indulgences but is merely freed from penalties.

45 Christians are to be taught that he who sees a needy man and passes him by, yet gives his money for indulgences, does not buy papal indulgences but God's wrath.[26]

Luther's critique in these theses is hardly church-dividing. He is not opposed to good works per se—works of mercy toward the poor still appear to be meritorious. What offends him is the act of granting indulgences for the restoration of St. Peter's in Rome. At this point in his career, he is still a reformer within the Catholic fold.

The acquisition of merits through service to the poor, we might conclude, need not be the ecumenical stumbling block it is often claimed to be. That the Bishop of Rome might have some say in how those merits are distributed is, of course, a different matter. But that is a problem of how one understands the church (ecclesiology) rather than the saving work of Christ (soteriology) and stands outside the framework of the present concern.

11

a treasury in heaven

Heaven declared: "from me come the rains that descend upon the earth";
Earth replied: "from me come acts of charity that are stored in heaven."

—"A Syriac Dispute Between Heaven and Earth"

In the previous chapter, I noted that one of the principal characteristics of the treasury in heaven is its outstanding rate of return. As St. Augustine exclaimed: "Give a little and receive on a grand scale. Look how your interest is mounting up! Give temporal wealth and claim eternal interest, give earth and gain heaven." In this chapter I pursue this theme more deeply. One of the most distinguishing features of almsgiving is the way it dramatically alters the balance between one's debits and credits. For every unit of debt we take on, owing to various forms of wrongdoing, we must raise a similar amount of credit to keep our heads above water. But the logic of almsgiving will force us to reconsider this presupposition.

PRUDENTIAL ALMSGIVING

If giving alms is like making a bank deposit to an account in heaven, one might wonder how to maximize one's capital. One option is to follow the example of Tobit and make regular contributions so as to accumulate a generous nest egg. There is another advantage to regular donations to this account: the more regularly one contributes, the easier and more natural each donation becomes, thereby fulfilling the commandment "Do not let your eye *begrudge* the gift when you make it" (Tobit 4:7; cf. Deut 15:7b-8, 10a).

St. Paul may have recalled this advice when he wrote, in his famous address on love, "If I give away all my possessions . . . but do not have love, I gain nothing" (I Cor 13:3).

But there are more variables on the table. As any wise investment officer will disclose, future holdings depend on prudent investments. And so for almsgiving. If our donations are to make a difference, they must be done responsibly. On one hand, this requires careful scrutiny of the recipients. "To all those who practice righteousness," Tobit declares, "give alms from your possessions" (4:6–7). On the other, it is also important to give in proportion to one's means: "If you have many possessions, make your gift from them in proportion; if few, do not be afraid to give according to the little you have" (4:8). Giving too much, however, might mean cutting into principal. If that should occur too often, one would eventually become destitute and in need of alms oneself. This prudential judgment led the rabbis to codify the principle that one should give no more than one-fifth of one's principal at first and afterward only one-fifth of the interest earned on that principal.[1] Such stewardship nearly guarantees that one can continue giving alms year in and year out without becoming impoverished.

ALMSGIVING AND SACRIFICE

Because almsgiving was a way of depositing money directly into a heavenly treasury, it also intersected with another means of shipping goods to God: sacrifice.[2] One of the major purposes of the altar in ancient Israel was to convey the sacrifices made by an individual to God in heaven. For this reason the altar was thought to be the "most holy" *(qodeš-qodāšîm;* cf. Exod. 40:10) of structures, sharing the same degree of holiness as the inner sanctum of the temple, where God was thought to dwell. Proverbs 19:17 is an important biblical verse on the intersection of almsgiving and sacrifice: "He who is *generous* to the downtrodden *[ḥônēn dāl] makes a loan to the* LORD; He will repay him his due."[3] This surprising text suggests that when one deposits coins in the hand of a poor person they are simultaneously transferred to God in heaven. The almsgiver becomes the holder of a bond that has been "signed" by God himself. If ordinary investors are partial to United States treasury notes because the government stands behind them, what about the security one ought to feel if the Holy One of Israel is the borrower?

The Christian theologian Irenaeus of Lyons (second century CE) saw in Proverbs 19:17 a dramatic act of loving condescension on the part of God. Although God does not need our sacrifices or our money, he uses the altar and the waiting hand of the poor person as a means of approaching him.[4]

Now we make offerings to Him [at the temple], not as though He stood in need of it. . . . And even [though] God does not need our possessions, . . . we need to offer something to God; as Solomon says: "He who is generous to the downtrodden, makes a loan to the Lord" [Prov 19:17]. For God, who stands in need of nothing, takes our good works to Himself for this purpose, that He may grant us a recompense of His own good things, as our Lord says: "Come, ye blessed of My Father, receive the kingdom prepared for you. For I was hungry, and ye gave Me to eat: I was thirsty, and ye gave Me drink: I was a stranger, and ye took Me in: naked, and ye clothed Me; sick, and ye visited Me; in prison, and ye came to Me" [Matt 25:34–36].

As, therefore, He does not stand in need of these [services], yet does desire that we should render them for our own benefit, lest we be unfruitful; so did the Word give to the people that very precept as to the making of oblations, although He stood in no need of them, that they might learn to serve God: thus it is also His will that we, too, should offer a gift at the altar, frequently, and without intermission.[5]

In this text, Irenaeus links (1) sacrificial oblation, (2) almsgiving as a loan to God (Prov 19:17), and (3) the depiction of the last judgment in Matthew 25:31–46.[6] According to Matthew, we will be judged on the basis of our generosity to Christ, who is present in the poor.[7] Proverbs 19 serves as an Old Testament proof-text for the picture Christ draws in Matthew 25. In giving alms to the poor we are making a loan to the Son of Man.[8] But it is important to note that Irenaeus thinks of this "loan" not as a financial matter but as a liturgical act. Putting money in the hands of a poor person is like placing an offering on the altar. Just as God did not need the sacrifice of animals in the temple but desired that we give them to Him for our own benefit, so God does not need the alms we give but demands them from us in order that we might have some concrete means of displaying reverence.

If the giving of alms was akin to making a sacrificial donation, one must wonder whether Tobit's advice about prudent stewardship is the only way to calculate one's contribution. For some sacrificial laws, particularly those that concern obligatory contributions to deal with sin, there is a clearly constructed gradient as to what one must give, and the crucial variable is the wealth of the donor.[9] Some must offer an expensive animal, others a pair of birds, and still others just grain. But in nonobligatory sacrificial contexts, such as sacrifices that are vowed or freely given, the door is open for giving much more.[10] In this vein, one is reminded of the prophet Micah's sliding scale of values regarding sacrifice. He begins his oracle on this issue with a rhetorical question:

> *With what shall I approach the* LORD
>> *Do homage to God on high?*

In his answer, he provides three options:

> *Shall I approach Him with burnt offerings*
>> *With calves a year old?*
> *Would the* LORD *be pleased with thousands of rams*
>> *With myriads of streams of oil?*
> *Shall I give my first-born for my transgression*
>> *The fruit of my body for my sins? (Micah 6:6–7)*

It is fine and good, Micah reasons, to offer a few animals as a burnt offering; even better would be thousands of rams, but the supreme offering would be a firstborn son. As Abraham knew well, there could be no greater sacrifice. No doubt for this reason, some rabbinic texts could see the sacrifice of Isaac as the founding event of the daily liturgy of the temple.[11]

A similar logic held true for the giving of alms. If almsgiving was analogous to an offering on the altar, even a modest donation could have its effect. Yet among the truly devout, some would surely wish to go beyond the bare minimum.

THE RICH YOUNG MAN AND JESUS

There is no better example of this principle than the story of the rich young man found in the Synoptic Gospels.[12] I wish to discuss the version found in the Gospel of Mark (10:17–31; cf. Matt 19:16–30, Luke 18:18–30). But first it is important to consider its literary placement. The discourse occurs at the very center of the Gospel (Mark 8:27–10:52), a section that deals with Jesus's journey toward Jerusalem, where he will spend his last week. As such, it marks the crucial transition from Jesus's early ministry in the Galilee (1:1–8:26) to his last week in Jerusalem (11:1–16:8). This critical portion of the book is marked by three predictions of the Passion, one near the beginning (8:31–33), one in the middle (9:30–32), and one at the end (10:32–34).

In all three the disciples react in utter shock at what Jesus declares about the way his life will end. After the first prediction, Peter takes Jesus aside and tries to correct him. For this he is severely rebuked ("Get behind me, Satan!"). After the next two predictions, the disciples are still puzzled but wisely keep silent ("But they did not understand what he was saying and were afraid to ask him" [9:32].) The disciples clearly assumed that the Messiah of Israel would never have to suffer such a death. The cost of being the beloved Son of God was to come as a complete surprise.[13] But there is an additional irony here. Jesus adds that what is true for him will also hold true for those who wish to be his disciples: "If any want to become my followers, let them deny themselves and take up their cross and follow me. For those who want to save their life will lose it, and those who lose their life for my sake, and for the sake of the gospel, will save it" (Mark 8:34–35). Following Jesus means following him on the way of the cross.

Sandwiched between the second and third predictions is Jesus's encounter with the young man, which occurs immediately before the third and final prediction. As the great patristic commentator Origen (third century CE) saw, this literary juxtaposition was hardly accidental.[14] The giving up of all one's wealth was construed to be one way of losing one's life on behalf of the gospel. Just as the inner core of disciples found the crucifixion to be shocking, so the young man finds the giving up of all his wealth to be a sacrifice beyond calculation.

The story opens when a young man runs up to Jesus, kneels before him, and asks him what he must do to inherit eternal life. Jesus redirects the man's attention to the Ten Commandments that Israel heard at Mt. Sinai: "You know the commandments: 'You shall not murder; You shall not commit adultery; You shall not steal; You shall not bear false witness; You shall not defraud; Honor your father and mother.' He said to him, 'Teacher, I have kept all these since my youth.' Jesus, looking at him, loved him and said, 'You lack one thing; go, sell what you own, and give the money to the poor, and you will have treasure in heaven; then come, follow me.' When he heard this, he was shocked and went away grieving, for he had many possessions" (Mark 10:19–22).

Although the interaction with this man comes to an end, the overall narrative does not. For the disciples are understandably shocked at the implications of what Jesus has said. If this is what is required, they reason, what hope does anyone have? Jesus seems to be demanding the ultimate sacrifice of everyone. In response to their anxious query Jesus says, " 'For mortals it is impossible [to do this], but not for God; for God all things are possible.' Peter began to say to him, 'Look, we have left everything and followed you.' Jesus said, 'Truly I tell you, there is no one who has left house or brothers or sisters or mother or father or children or fields, for my sake and for the sake of the good news, who will not receive a hundredfold now in this age— houses, brothers and sisters, mothers and children and fields, with persecutions—and in the age to come eternal life' " (Mark 10:27–30).

Three aspects of this story demand our attention. First is the *particular selection* that Jesus makes from what is often known as the "second table" of the Ten Commandments.[15] The list begins with the sixth commandment ("you shall not murder") and continues in serial order to the tenth ("you shall not defraud"), but then it doubles back at the end and appends the fifth commandment ("honor father and mother").[16] These particular commandments pertain to interpersonal matters rather than the relationship of humans to God. The emphasis is *horizontal* rather than vertical.

Second is the young man's declaration that he has kept those six commandments since his youth. Are we supposed to believe that he has really fulfilled these obligations? And if so, how should we interpret the reply of Jesus that he still lacks one thing? Why does Jesus add the *new condition* that he must give all that he has to the poor?[17]

The third and final point is the *motivation* that Jesus provides the young man. He is not asked simply to part with his goods; rather he is encouraged to acquire "a treasure in heaven." This treasury, however, is not presented as an alternative to enjoying the goods of this world. Jesus does not say to suffer without these goods for now and revel in the wealth that will be waiting in the world to come. Instead he claims that one can enjoy the fruits of one's labors both now and in the hereafter. The economy of the Kingdom of Heaven does not appear to be a zero-sum affair. Jesus closes this literary unit by providing the disciples with an "insider tip" on how the heavenly stock exchange works. The way to make a fortune in this market is to sacrifice *all* that one has. Although the initial risk is considerable, the reward is beyond imagining ("you will receive a hundredfold *now* in this age . . . and *in the age to come,* eternal life"). The Kingdom of Heaven runs by a unique set of rules. That which is given benefits both donor and recipient—again we see a confluence between almsgiving and sacrifice. As I have argued elsewhere, the logic that governs donations to the temple is "I have given so little (a mere animal) and you have requited me so bountifully (fullness of life)."[18]

We therefore have three themes to explore: the selection of commandments and their horizontal rather than vertical orientation, the reason for the additional command that Jesus gives, and the status of the treasury that Jesus promises. All three can be illuminated by rabbinic texts.

THERE IS NO LIMIT TO ALMSGIVING

Of the three rabbinic texts I shall examine, the first is the Mishnah, a compilation of Jewish law whose final redaction took place in the late second or early third century CE. According to tradition, it contains laws that were passed on orally going all the way back to Moses himself. Modern scholars are dubious about the historicity of that claim; a more reasonable supposition is that some of the laws (which ones in particular is a subject of scholarly debate) go back to the turn of the Common Era, and some perhaps to a century or two before that. Alongside the Mishnah is the Tosephta, a word meaning "supplement." The traditional view has been that the Tosephta provides laws that were contemporary with those of the Mishnah but for some reason did not find their way into the Mishnah itself. Recent research, however, has suggested that the Tosephta should be seen as an earlier form of the Mishnah. If this is the case, a comparison of the Tosephta to the Mishnah will reveal how the editors of the Mishnah handled their source material.[19] The third source is the Jerusalem Talmud. Like its Babylonian counterpart, it is a commentary on the Mishnah and to a degree on the Tosephta as well. It was redacted in the land of Israel and dates to the fifth century CE.

In tractate *Peah* of the Mishnah, we find a discussion of the various biblical laws having to do with donations to the poor.[20] It is titled *Peah* because one way of making a donation to the poor in biblical times was to leave a corner—that is, a *peah*—unharvested: "When you reap the harvest of your land, you shall not reap to the very edges *[peah]* of your field, or gather the gleanings of your harvest" (Lev 19:9). But the opening section of the tractate is unusual, for it does not open with a consideration of *peah* per se, as we might expect. Rather it mentions a formal feature that is shared by five commandments: "These are matters that have no specified amount: *peah*, first fruits, the festival offering, charitable deeds, and Torah-study."[21]

The order of the commandments that have no specified measure is not random. I would outline them as follows:

1 *Peah*—donation for the poor
   2 First fruits—temple
   3 Festival offering—temple
4 Charitable deeds—donation for the poor
5 Torah-study.

The first and fourth items, which are provisions for the poor, constitute something of an outer frame for the inner two commandments that concern the temple. The only item that does not fit is Torah-study, and that may be one reason why the Mishnah describes it as "equal in value to all the rest."[22] It stands as a counterbalance to the first four. The Tosephta, we might add, begins almost exactly like the Mishnah, but it does not state that Torah-study is equal in value to all the rest. This is because the Tosephta will declare later in the tractate that "the giving of alms and works of charity are equal in value to all of the commandments in the Torah" (4.19). The Mishnah and Tosephta, then, represent differing views as to what is the most important of all the commandments, Torah-study or acts of charity.

The fact that gifts to the poor (*peah* and charity) provide an outer frame for two types of donations to the temple (first fruits and the festival offering) recalls the valuation of alms in Second Temple Judaism. In Ben Sira 35:2 almsgiving is compared to a thank offering. In 7:29–36 the sage urges his reader to honor priests and God through donations to the temple and to honor the poor with alms so that "your blessing may be complete." These are, in his mind, homologous activities.

The book of Tobit is more subtle. The work opens with a reference to Tobit's many acts of charity over the course of his life (1:4). And as soon as Tobit arrives in exile to Mesopotamia, we see him acting on this principle (1:16). Sandwiched in between is an account of Tobit's religious fervor while he resides in the land of Israel. There he is distinguished by his alacrity and zeal in bringing sacrifices to the temple (1:5–9). The point seems clear: sacrifices in the land of Israel have now been replaced by almsgiving and other acts of charity.[23]

There is an additional feature of this Mishnah. The opening line of the tractate states that even the slightest observance of these five commandments (*peah,* first fruits, festival offering, acting charitably, Torah-study) will suffice to fulfill one's obligation. But why was this so noteworthy that the Mishnah would make it the subject of its opening sentence? Saul Lieberman glossed this line thus: "The more one does, the more commandments one fulfills."[24] In other words, these commandments offer the possibility of making an *exceptional* display of one's piety, what Catholics would call works of supererogation. The more one does of any of them, the more merits *(zĕkūyôt)* one accrues. Hanokh Albeck says nearly the same with his annotation: "The more one does, the more praiseworthy he becomes."[25] The feature that distinguishes these commandments is the fact that *they provide an individual the opportunity to put his deep devotion to God into action.* If we take the sacrificial paradigm seriously, then the truly devout Jew will not be interested in making a minimal donation to charity. He may wish to imitate the sacrificial donation of Abraham and give away all that he holds dear. If there is no limit to almsgiving, and every coin I give adds to my merit, why not go all the way and donate *everything* to the poor?

It should be noted, however, that all commentators on the Mishnah—whether traditional or modern—close the door immediately on such a notion. The simple sense of this law—that almsgiving has no limit—must be qualified. One can take the Mishnah at face value only for charity that is interpersonal, such as burying the dead, tending the sick, or visiting those in prison. But when it comes to parting with money, prudent limits are put in place so that one does not become destitute.

JERUSALEM TALMUD: A LIMIT TO THE GIVING OF ALMS?

Commentators on the Mishnah derive these prudential concerns from the Jerusalem Talmud. Yet, as we shall see, the Talmudic discussion also reveals that some Jews understood this mishnah at face value. Regarding the statement that deeds of charity are subject to no limit, the Talmud says:

A   This concerns actions done with one's body (such as visiting the sick or burying the dead). With respect to the use of money [i.e., giving alms] there are limits.

B   This view accords with what R. Shimon b. Laqish said in the name of R. Yehudah b. Hanina: "At Usha they ruled that one may separate one-fifth of his possessions for alms-giving [*miṣwôt*]."[26]

C   R. Gamliel b. Ininya inquired of R. Mana: If one separates a fifth for every year, then after five years he will lose everything! R. Mana answered: At first one uses the principal but afterwards just the interest that accrues.[27]

The initial comment in A sets up a distinction between general acts of charity (*gĕmîlût ḥăsādîm*) and the specific act of donating money (*ṣĕdāqâh*). For the former there are no limits; one can visit the sick from dawn to dusk for as long as one wants. But monetary donations to the poor are subject to strict limitations. In the mind of R. Shimon (B), the rabbinic law court at Usha (mid-second century) was worried that individuals might read this mishnah as an invitation to give away all their goods. Hence the strict limit of a one-time gift of 20 percent followed by much smaller gifts from interest. No doubt this ruling was intended as an effective deterrent to overambitious generosity. Like the manager of any charitable endowment, R. Shimon knows that it is dangerous to spend down principal recklessly, lest one end up in need of charity oneself.

The ruling of the rabbinic court at Usha would seem to have solved the puzzle once and for all. Any possibility of heroic almsgiving has been ruled out *tout court*. Yet the next two units of the Talmud immediately qualify what had seemed to be a hard and fast conclusion.

D   It happened one day that R. Yeshebab (80–120 CE) decided to distribute all of his possessions to the poor. R. Gamliel sent a message to him: "Hasn't it been said: 'One-fifth of one's possessions can be given for alms?'" But did not R. Gamliel precede the council at Usha? R. Jose b. R. Bun, in the name of R. Levi said: "Such was the law that was once in their possession. But they forgot it and when a second generation arose, they framed the matter in accord with the opinion of the earlier generation."[28]

R. Gamliel is shocked at what R. Yeshebab has done. But the Talmud expresses puzzlement: How could Gamliel have known of this ruling given the fact that he lived prior to the council at Usha? R. Jose explains that the law itself had predated Usha but had been forgotten. The ruling at Usha, he claims, was simply the restoration of a lost legal tradition. It is hard to know whether R. Jose's account is historically true or just a means of accounting for the objection of R. Gamliel. Whatever the explanation, we can see from R. Yeshebab's actions that some Jews living in Palestine in the late first and early second century took the sense of this mishnah as a mandate for giving away all their goods.[29] And the later ruling about giving no more than 20 percent reflects the rabbis' fears that more would do the same.

Having accounted for R. Yeshebab's aberrant behavior, the Talmud considers another lawbreaker, but this time without any qualification. Rather, his deeds win him the highest praise:

E   Munbaz the king (of Adiabene) one day decided to distribute all of his possessions to the poor. Some friends sent word to him and said: Your fathers added to their wealth and that of their fathers but you have distributed what was yours and your fathers. He said to them: So much the more [that it be this way]. My fathers stored up [wealth] on earth and I stored up [wealth] in heaven.[30]

Not only is Munbaz's behavior subject to no rebuke, but as soon as the story is over, the Talmud takes this occasion to summarize its position and to speak to the importance of almsgiving in general:[31]

F   [And so one may conclude:] Almsgiving and charitable deeds are equal to all of the commandments in the Torah. But almsgiving is customarily done to the living while acts of charitable deeds are customary for both the living and the dead. But almsgiving is customary for the poor while acts of charitable deeds are customary for both the poor and the rich. But almsgiving is customarily done with money while acts of charitable deeds are customarily done with both one's money and body.

Munbaz's generosity provides the occasion for announcing that almsgiving and charitable deeds are equal to all the commandments.[32] Indeed, if we read F as a commentary on E, there are no qualifications associated with Munbaz's radical act of generosity; there is no hint of concern about the limits to what one can give away (A). Instead, the Talmud offers unqualified praise of this virtuous king.

ALMSGIVING IS *THE* COMMANDMENT

The Talmudic declaration that almsgiving is equal to all the other commandments in the Torah is a widespread motif not only in rabbinic literature but also in contemporary Hebrew and Aramaic idioms. Saul Lieberman, the leading Talmudist of the twentieth century, pointed out that the Hebrew and Aramaic term for commandment, *miṣwâh,* can often mean simply "almsgiving."[33] What does it mean to keep *the* commandment—give alms![34] Indeed, in Aramaic the phrase *bar miṣwĕtâʾ* does not mean "a son of the commandment" or "a commandment keeper" but, rather, "a generous person," that is, one who is in the habit of giving alms. This is exemplified in a fifth-century rabbinic commentary on the book of Leviticus known as *Leviticus Rabbah* (3:1): "Better is he who goes and works and gives charity of that which is his own, than he who goes and robs and takes by violence and gives charity of that belonging to others. . . . It is his desire to be called a man of charity *[bar miṣwĕtâʾ].*" The use of "commandment" as a cipher for almsgiving is also attested outside the rabbinic corpus. There is a tradition in the *Testament of Asher* (2:8) that closely parallels our text from *Leviticus Rabbah,* showing us that the tradition could go back to the Second Temple period itself: "And by the power of his wealth he ruins many; and out of [the wealth he secured through] his excessive wickedness, he gives alms." In Greek the last phrase of this text reads literally, "he does the commandments," but this would make little sense.[35] Lieberman is surely right when he observes that "the commandments" in the *Testament of Asher* must be a cipher for the giving of alms.

Even the book of Tobit is worth rereading with this in mind. When Tobit gives his son his last instruction in Torah, he emphasizes the value of almsgiving (4:5–11). And later in the tale, when Raphael gives his own instruction to Tobit, he summarizes the Torah in the command to give alms (12:8–10). At the end of the book, Tobit closes his deathbed address with a single command in view, alms (14:8–11).

TO CHARITY BELONGS BOTH PRINCIPAL AND INTEREST

Mishnah *Peah* claims not only that alms can be given without measure but that both "principal and interest" belong to the category of charitable giving. The text in question reads: "Regarding the following matters, a man may enjoy their fruit in this world and his principal will remain for him in the next: honoring father and mother, charitable deeds, establishing peace between a man and his friend; Torah-study is equal to all of them." The parallel text in the Tosephta gives us a similar picture of how certain sins are evaluated: "For the following matters, payment is extracted from a person in this world, while the principal remains for him in the next: idolatry, incest, murder, and gossip which is worse than all of them put together." To appreciate the nature of this claim we need to know something about the principle of a zero-sum economy that stands behind certain rabbinic texts.

In his recent work on the subject, Eliezer Diamond has shown that a number of rabbinic figures have been reluctant to enjoy the fruits of their merits in this world for fear of forfeiting them in the age to come.[36] And so he understands the following story from the Babylonian Talmud: "R. Yannai would check [a ferry to ensure that it was seaworthy] before crossing [in it]. R. Yannai [acted] in accordance with his own reasoning, for he said: One should never put oneself in a dangerous situation, saying that a miracle will be performed for him, lest the miracle not be performed. And if the miracle is performed, they will deduct it from his merits [i.e., they will lessen his reward in this world or in the next]. R. Hanan said: What is the scriptural source for the above? [The patriarch Jacob's declaration:] "[My heavenly account] has been drawn down due to all the kindnesses (ḥăsādîm) that you have so steadfastly shown your servant" (Gen 32:11).[37] The testimony of Jacob that Yannai cites comes just as he is about to ford the Jabbok River and return home to the land of Canaan (Gen 32:23–33). (And so the aptness of Yannai's citation of this particular biblical text: Jacob is about to become a ferryman, too.) When Jacob was in Aramea, he was destitute and dependent solely on the good graces of his God. Jacob had spent the last twenty years of his life in the service of Laban, his father-in-law. Although Laban tried to swindle him on several occasions, God continually came to Jacob's assistance. Yet when Jacob arrives back in the land of Canaan, his fortune takes a decided turn for the worse. His daughter is taken forcibly by the Shechemites (Gen 34) and while Jacob dawdles, his sons intervene violently to rescue her. His beloved son Joseph is then sold into slavery in Egypt and, as Jacob believes, is lost forever (Gen 37). Only many years later do his fortunes reverse. The midrash has observed this pattern in Jacob's life and interprets Jacob's remarks about his fears of reentering the land of Canaan accordingly. Rather than taking the Bible in its simple sense: "I am unworthy of [literally, "too small for"] the many kindnesses you have shown me," it understands the verse more literally: "I am too small—i.e., my merits have been decreased too much—due to your many kindnesses."

As Diamond observes, it is the worries of R. Yannai that need to be set against *m. Peah*.[38] Regarding the acts of (1) honoring one's father, (2) acting charitably, (3) bringing peace to disputants, and (4) studying Torah, one need not worry about benefiting from them in the present age. By doing so, one is only taking payment on the interest; the principal, on the other hand, will retain its full value in the world to come. Had R. Yannai's merits come from any of these actions, there would have been no reason to worry about using up their principal in the present age.[39] The interest earned on almsgiving can be spent down without worry of cutting into the principal.

Although his imagery is slightly different, Ephrem also marveled at the way charity stood outside the framework of normal spiritual commerce. Although we discussed Ephrem's words of praise for the saint Abraham Kidunaya, they are worth repeating here in briefer form: "Your alms and prayers are like loans; in every location they enrich those who take them, while to you belongs the capital and interest. What you offer as a loan returns to you. The alms of the giver are like a loan that the just give. For it is in the full possession of both the borrower and the loaner. For it returns to him with interest."[40] Ephrem uses the same economic idiom we find in rabbinic literature, but for him the giving of alms breaks the conventional rules of a zero-sum economy in a different way. Normally what one exchanges in a sale is conceived as a loss for the seller and a gain for the buyer. But in the case of almsgiving, Ephrem argues, both sides stand to gain, because both the borrower and the loaner possess the goods exchanged. The donor, however, stands to gain more than the receiver, because the giver of alms retains both the principal and the interest. If one gives one hundred dollars to a needy person, for example, that person is now richer by one hundred dollars, and the donor by one hundred dollars plus the interest that will accrue. The more rational economic decision, therefore, is to be profligate in one's generosity. In any event, both Ephrem and the rabbis, who are beholden to think of sin as a debt and virtue as a credit, outline the unique characteristics of almsgiving in identical financial terms.

THE GOSPEL OF MARK IN LIGHT OF TRACTATE *PEAH*

As noted, tractate *Peah* makes several points about charitable giving. First, giving alms to the poor is comparable to making a sacrifice in the temple; both are conveyed directly to God. Second, almsgiving has a special position among the commandments in that there is no specified minimal amount.

Because of this uncertainty, the religiously devout will be able to use this commandment as a means of demonstrating extraordinary piety, for as Lieberman remarked, the more alms that one gives, the more merits will be accumulated. Finally, almsgiving has a unique "ontological" status in the economy of heaven. It is not subject to the limitations that are part of a zero-sum economy. One can enjoy the fruits of one's merits both in this world and the next. With this in mind, let us return to the three questions raised by the story of the rich young man.

First, the majority of New Testament scholars have wondered why Jesus's commandments remain *on a horizontal rather than a vertical plane.* They concern what takes place between human beings rather than between human beings and God. But such a characterization does not fit the way almsgiving was viewed in contemporary Jewish material. To give alms to a poor person was just like bringing a gift to the temple. Just as the altar was a direct conduit of sacrificial donations to heaven, so, too, was the role of the poor person who receives another's coins. I would suggest that Jesus's injunction to give alms was meant to turn the young man's earthly focus heavenward through the agency of the poor. This would be in keeping with the contextual placement of this story amid three predictions of the Passion. Just as the crucifixion would constitute the supreme sacrifice of Christ on behalf of his allegiance to his divine Father, so would the distribution of all of one's goods to the poor.[41]

The second question concerned why Jesus felt the need to add another commandment to the six he drew from the Ten Commandments in order to see whether the young man was worthy of the Kingdom of God. To answer this, recall the opening line of m. *Peah,* which I paraphrase: "These are the commandments that have no fixed level of observance." If one of the distinctive features of almsgiving is the opportunity to distinguish oneself through generosity, then it is not surprising that Jesus would advise a prospective disciple to do just that. As the text recounts, the young man was able to keep the "second table" of the Ten Commandments with seemingly little effort.[42] After all, it is not that difficult to abstain from murder, adultery, theft, and fraud. But Jesus was looking for an additional command that would allow the man's true love for God to surface. And almsgiving was just such a commandment.

The third query raised about Jesus's teaching on alms was his promise that what was given to the poor would be returned to the donor a hundredfold in this world and still more in the next. This fits hand in glove with the tradition in *Peah.* Indeed, the single feature of charitable activity that the

Tosephta highlights is its singular position over all the other command-ments in the Torah. Although every act of Torah obedience will yield a merit (*zekût*), the uniqueness of almsgiving is that one acquires both principal and interest, which means the ability to benefit from one's charitable deeds both in this world and the one to come.

HEROIC ALMSGIVING IN JUDAISM AND CHRISTIANITY

The opening sentence of m. *Peah* states that five commandments share a common feature: they have no specified measure. One can give as little or as much as one wants. By framing the matter this way, the Mishnah throws open the possibility that certain persons may wish to distinguish themselves by prodigious generosity. Indeed tractate *Peah* could and did lead straight to the conclusion that we find in the teaching of Jesus. And an appeal to the Gospel is of value to the scholar of rabbinic Judaism, for it illuminates how this Mishnah might have been understood in first-century Palestine. Be-cause the Mishnah left open the possibility of giving much if not all of one's wealth to the poor—and certain individuals such as R. Yeshebab and King Munbaz did precisely that—the Talmud hedged in its simple sense by de-claring it applied only to charity done interpersonally (visiting the sick, burying the dead, and so forth) but not to the giving of alms. It is this Tal-mudic interpretation that has shaped Jewish thought ever since.

Yet the history of the Jewish people in the Mishnaic and Talmudic pe-riods complicates the picture that we find so clearly drawn in the Talmud. As Ephraim Urbach has noted, the ruling at Usha—in spite of the impor-tance it had for the editors of the Talmud—"did not prevent individuals from parting with a large percentage of their property."[43] Why, then, was the council so dedicated to putting a stop to a practice that seemed rather pop-ular? One reason, suggests Urbach, may have been that by the second cen-tury the practice of heroic almsgiving had become so popular among Chris-tians that its Jewish origins were obscured. On this reading, the rabbis issued their ruling to clarify the boundary between church and synagogue. Such a supposition would be supported by a recent essay of Daniel Schwartz, who shows that the Christian adaptation of certain legal positions once held by a particular circle of Jews often led to their rejection by later rabbinic fig-ures.[44]

Be that as it may, another explanation seems equally valid. It is striking that the New Testament story about the rich young man deals with a group of men who appear unbothered by responsibilities toward their families. The narrative takes no interest in depicting either Jesus, the young man, or any of the disciples as compromised by competing obligations to serve wife and children. They seem to have left *everything* to follow Jesus.[45] In the early church, this narrative depiction became a crucial element in the practice of heroic almsgiving. This sort of activity was most common among those who were single. Because of this, giving away all one's property did not have negative consequences for the family. But rabbinic Judaism had no place for such a lifestyle. Indeed in some texts, the choice to live a celibate existence was conceived as analogous to murder, for one was willfully preventing new life from coming into the world.[46]

Eliezer Diamond has recently argued that rabbinic stories about heroic almsgiving frequently involve tensions within the family. One such example concerns a second-century *hasid,* or holy man, by the name of Eleazar of Birta:

> When the charity collectors saw Eleazar of Birta they would hide from him, because whatever he had he would give to them. One day he went to the market place to acquire a dowry for his daughter. The charity collectors saw him and hid from him. He ran after them and said to them, "I abjure you, [to tell me] with what are you concerned at present?"
>
> They answered, "We are collecting money for the marriage of two orphans to each other."
>
> He replied, "By the Temple service, they come before my daughter." He took all that he had and gave it to them. One zuz remained; with it he bought some wheat, returned home and threw it in the storage room.
>
> His wife came home and asked her daughter, "What did your father bring you?"
>
> The daughter replied, "Whatever he brought he threw in the storeroom." She went to open the door of the storeroom and found that it was full of wheat, that the wheat was pouring out of the door's hinge-socket and that the volume of the wheat made it impossible to open the door.
>
> His daughter went to the study-house and said to her father, "See what the One who loves you has done for you!"[47]

This story is illuminating on several grounds. It is obvious that Eleazar has a reputation for outlandish giving, and, as a result, the charity collectors are reluctant to take his money. They believe that his funds would be of more use to his family.[48] When Eleazar sets out to purchase a dowry for his daughter, he learns of even greater need. Accordingly, he gives nearly everything he has to this cause. When he returns home and tosses the small amount of wheat he had purchased into the storehouse, the hand of heaven intervenes and exchanges it for a room that literally bursts open with grain. What better illustration could one find that almsgiving has both principal and interest? By giving away his money to the poor, he taps into a heavenly power that knows no bounds. God, it seems, has chosen to ignore the ruling at Usha. And had the story ended with the observation of the daughter, "See what the One who loves you has done for you," the reader could only stand in awe of this prodigious deed. Eleazar, to quote Jesus, had been repaid a hundredfold in this world and had stored up principal in the world to come.

Yet the story does not end in quite the same way that I cited it above. There is one crucial sentence at the very end that I left out: "[Eleazar] replied [to his daughter], 'By the temple service, you may benefit from the wheat no more than one of the poor in the land of Israel for the wheat is consecrated in relation to you.'" This shocking conclusion takes the reader by surprise and casts a pall over what had been a moving story about God's immeasurable grace. Rather than sharing with his daughter the proceeds of God's largesse, he declares that all the grain is hereby consecrated, by which we can assume he has vowed it all to the poor. As Diamond notes, the only other example in the Talmud of a father withholding property from a child was because of the child being unworthy. This story, obviously, does not make that point, but the Talmudic parallel does underscore the dramatic nature of Eleazar's actions. By acting in this way, Diamond argues, R. Eleazar "refuses to allow her to be the beneficiary of her relationship with him. She is not the daughter of Eleazar of Birta who has been blessed by God with great wealth; she is simply one of the poor in Israel."[49]

This rabbinic tale should allow us to read the story of the rich young man in a new light. When Jesus was making his way through the Galilee, he had in his company a band of followers who had left their families to follow him. The radical demands of the kingdom for this inner circle precluded, at least for a time, any involvement with family. When the Christian movement expanded in the second and third centuries, this form of heroic almsgiving was assumed to be the domain of holy men and women who were also leaving family behind in pursuit of the Kingdom of God.[50] Christianity was able to preserve the type of heroic almsgiving we find in the Gospel of Mark because it had a social context that was appropriate to its demands. (The Reformation, however, would make the interpretation of this story a complicated task, comparable in many regards to the Talmud's reception of m. *Peah*. For a similar point was at issue: Should the church give special honor to those who gave away all they had? And should the church extol the life of celibacy where such behavior was most naturally located? Like the Talmud, the Reformers expended considerable efforts to hem in the natural implication of what Jesus taught.) Such was not the case with rabbinic Judaism, yet it is a testimony to the power of the simple sense of our Mishnah that the Talmud contains several tales of rabbinic figures who continued to follow its inner logic.

THE DISTINCTIVE CHARACTER OF ALMSGIVING

To return to the original question in this chapter, how are we to understand the relation of debit and credit in the divine economy? At one level, they are proportionally balanced. If one sins, God then holds a bond on which he can collect when he sees fit. If one acts virtuously, one makes a deposit that can be drawn upon in the future. Such a closed universe of justice and mercy would naturally give rise to considerable anxiety. In *m. Avot* 3:6, R. Akiba states that God views the world as a store and himself as its shop-keeper. "The account books are open and the judge is seated. The collectors collect payments upon what is owed day in and day out, whether he knows it or not." This fear that God can draw down one's balance on the basis of whatever is taken led R. Yannai, as we noted above, to check his ferry every time he set off across the river, because should his ferry fail and should he be in need of a miracle to survive, an act of divine intervention would re-sult in a deduction from the merits he had stored in the heavenly treasury. In the terms of R. Akiba, God would deduct payment from the merits he had previously stored up. As Diamond observed, the worries of Yannai need to be set against the treatment of charity in m. *Peah*. For charity, Diamond contended, is not subject to the same cost accounting. In the case of human generosity, one need have no worries about not benefiting from them both in this world and in the world to come.

Another area in which the giving of alms plays a unique role is the prob-lem of drought.[51] Rain, or the lack thereof, has always been something of an objective gauge of where Israel stands in God's eyes. This point is made clearly in Deuteronomy 11:13–17:

> If then you obey the commandments that I enjoin upon you this day,
> loving the LORD your God and serving him with all your heart and soul.
> I will grant the rain for your land in season, the early rain and the late.
> You shall gather in your new grain and wine and oil. I will also provide

grass in the fields for your cattle—and thus you shall eat your fill. Take care not to be lured away to serve other gods and bow to them. For the LORD's anger will flare up against you, and He will shut up the skies so that there will be no rain and the ground will not yield its produce; and you will soon perish from the good land that the LORD is assigning to you.

The concern for rain in this text should not be surprising. Ancient Israel did not benefit from the sophisticated system of irrigation canals that led to the flourishing of the great civilizations of classical Egypt and Mesopotamia. The great wealth and prosperity of these parts of the world was guaranteed by an abundant food supply. Israel had no such infrastructure. There was no source of water save that which fell from the heavens. According to the words of Moses in Deuteronomy, rain was to be considered a gracious gift from God and as such would be dependent on Israel's obedience to the Torah. Indeed the presence or absence of rain was a barometer or index of the spiritual state of the nation. According to the prophet Amos, the sinfulness of the Northern Kingdom was so extreme that God would send such a terrible drought that "two or three towns would wander to a single town to drink water, but their thirst could not be slaked." And yet the brazenness of Israel was such that even in the face of such a judgment, "even then you did not turn back to Me" (Amos 4:8).

The significance of rain as a indicator of the nation's well-being did not cease at the close of the biblical period. The twice-daily recitation of Deuteronomy 11:13–21 as part of regular Jewish prayer (the Shema) made sure that this anxiety about the onset of the rainy season was retained. The Mishnah devotes an entire tractate to how the community was to deal with those times when winter rains did not arrive as expected. The tractate is appropriately named *Ta'anit*, or "fasting," because fasting was a sign of contrition intended to move God from a position of judgment to mercy. According to the tractate, a series of fasts was to be called, depending on the severity of the drought. During these, the congregation was to act "as persons who have been reprimanded by God" (*Ta'anit* 1:7). The tractate was trying to avoid the problem that the prophet Amos had bewailed: a brazen indifference to the judgment of God.

The Talmudic commentaries on this tractate are filled with stories of how individual communities handled the crisis of a drought and made their appeals for mercy. One such narrative in the Jerusalem Talmud tells of how the problem of drought, sin, and debt all came together.

One time they had to call a fast, but no rain fell. R. Yehoshua called a fast in the South and rain fell. Those who dwelt in Sepphoris said: R. Yehoshua ben Levi brings down rain for those in the South, yet R. Hanina prevents the rain from falling in Sepphoris.

So there was a need to call a second fast. R. Hanina sent for R. Yehoshua b. Levi and had him brought to Sepphoris. He said to him, "Would my Lord take note to come forth with us to engage in the fast?"

The two of them went forth to fast but rain did not fall. He entered and said to them: R. Yehoshua b. Levi does not bring down rain for those in the South, nor does R. Hanina prevent the rain from falling in Sepphoris. Rather the hearts of those in the South are soft; when they hear a word of Torah, they submit themselves to it. But the hearts of those in Sepphoris are hard. When they hear a word of Torah, they do not submit themselves to it.

When he entered, he lifted up his eyes and saw that the air was clear. He said, "Is it now to be thus (even after all this effort)!?" Immediately thereafter, it began to rain. He made a vow not to do such a [bold] thing again. He explained, "Why should I tell the holder of the bond not to collect what is owed him?" (JT *Ta'anit* 3:4 [66c–d])

This story provides a wonderful window into various aspects of rabbinic culture: the relation of the rabbi to his community, the spiritual prowess of one rabbi over another, and the camaraderie of the two rabbis over the claims of their respective communities. The ending, however, is most significant. Having failed to secure rain for the Sepphoris community, evidently because of its obstreperous nature, one of the rabbis turns boldly to God and issues a thinly veiled rebuke: "Is it now to be thus (even after all this effort)!?"

When rain does come, there is no spontaneous outburst of jubilation and praise but, rather, an expression of considerable trepidation. To provoke God to bring rain, when the community did not deserve it, was thought to be both brazen and dangerous. As the holder of a bond over the citizens of Sepphoris, God had every right to collect when he saw fit.

Yet it is not the case that every drought demanded such retributive justice. In some cases, as in the well-known stories about Honi the Circle-Drawer, it was the power of prayer alone that secured the needed rains.[52] In other cases, such as almsgiving, the rules that govern the balancing of the heavenly books were ignored. There is a beautiful illustration of this in the rabbinic commentary on the book of Genesis known as *Genesis Rabbah*.

This text, like the Jerusalem Talmud, comes from the land of Israel. Both are dated to the late fourth or early fifth century CE (though some would date *Genesis Rabbah* a bit later). The text I wish to discuss begins with a citation from the book of Psalms, "The LORD is gracious to all and his mercies extend over all his works" (145:9), and then turns to a moment when God shuts the sluice gates in heaven such that no rain can fall upon the earth.

> In the days of R. Tanhuma, Israel had to undertake a fast. They came to him and said: "Rabbi, decree a fast." He decreed a fast for one day, a second day and a third day but rain did not fall. He entered the synagogue and delivered a homily. He said to them, "My sons, be filled with mercy toward one another and then the Holy One (Blessed be He!) will be filled with mercy upon you."
>
> While they were distributing alms to the poor, a man was seen giving money to his divorced wife (and so was under the suspicion of having paid her for illicit sexual favors). Those [who had seen this] came before R. Tanhuma and said, "How can we just sit here in the face of this grave transgression?" He asked them, "What did you see?" They said: "We saw a certain man giving money to his divorced wife." Rabbi Tanhuma sent for them and they were brought forward. He said to the man: "Why did you give money to your divorced wife?" He said to him, "I saw her in great distress and I was filled with compassion for her."
>
> R. Tanhuma lifted his face toward the heavens and said, "O Lord of the Universe, this man who was under no legal obligation to provide her with sustenance saw her in distress and was filled with compassion for her. And about you it is written, 'The LORD is compassionate and merciful' (Ps 103:8). So I and your children, we who are the sons of the beloved ones, the sons of Abraham, Isaac, and Jacob—how much more should you be filled with compassion for us!" Immediately rain fell and the world was relieved of its distress. (*Gen Rab* 33.3)

In this remarkable narrative there is no hint of concern on the part of R. Tanhuma that he was too bold in his address to the Lord of the Universe. Like R. Hanina in the previous story, he is faced with a calamitous situation, and the normal recourse to fasting has not proven sufficient. The debt that the people have run up must be vast, and the holder of the bond was now taking payment in the form of bodily suffering.

When the community turns to almsgiving, however, the picture changes completely. The extraordinary act of a man giving alms to his divorced wife, toward whom he not only bore no obligation but also probably harbored hard feelings, changes the calculation of debits in heaven altogether. It may be worth pointing out that the story involves a divorced woman, because Israel was regularly thought of, both in the Bible and the Talmud, as God's bride, suggesting the following analogy: the Israelite man is to his divorced wife as God is to his [temporarily] estranged nation. But whereas this ordinary man finds it within himself to show mercy to one to whom he has no obligation, God—seemingly in the present moment—is not acting in such a manner toward a spouse that he had promised never to send away permanently. Almsgiving, in this instance, instantiates within the moral agent a disposition toward the world that is proper to the Godhead. As one midrashic text boldly puts it, a human being who feeds the poor is fulfilling an obligation that rests with God (*Lev Rab* 34.2). As such, the giving of alms is not founded on the limited economic plane of human obligation. It is just as the Mishnah and St. Ephrem had declared: Almsgiving involves both principal and interest.

ONE LAST GLANCE AT ALMSGIVING

In the previous three chapters, I have explored the way almsgiving functioned in the divine economy. The explorations of this ancient, widespread practice have yielded five important themes:

1. The Hand of the Poor as Altar

This idea was expressed prosaically in Ben Sira. In his mind, fearing the Lord means both honoring the priest—that is providing him with requisite temple donations—and stretching out one's hand to the poor. A slightly different reflection of the same can be found in Tobit, in which the main character displays his piety within the land of Israel by going to Jerusalem to offer sacrifices and provide the priests and poor with his tithes. When he is exiled to Assyria and donations to the temple become impossible, he begins to make direct donations to the poor. Several centuries later, rabbinic texts tell us that beggars addressed their benefactors with the phrase *zĕkî bî* —"acquire a merit [in heaven] through me" (i.e., by putting coins in my hand). Just as the altar in biblical times served to convey food from earth to heaven (sacrifices were frequently called the "food of God"), so the hand of the poor person served to conduct financial capital to heaven. This idea became especially important for Judaism after the destruction of the temple in 70 CE.

2. Almsgiving as *the* Commandment

In rabbinic Hebrew, the term *ha-miṣwâh* can be translated as both "the commandment" and "the giving of charity." So important was charity in rabbinic Judaism that it could be known as *the* commandment. (In addition,
the term *bar-miṣwâh* did not mean simply "son of the commandment" but
"a generous person"—i.e., one prone to giving alms.) Tosephta *Peah* (as
well as the Jerusalem Talmud) goes even further and declares that giving
charity is equal to keeping all the commandments.

3. Almsgiving and Faith

As Proverbs 19:17 declares, the one who gives to the poor is at the same
time making a loan to God. It is important that the one who issues such a
loan have sufficient faith that the borrower can repay. It is no accident that
in both English and German the terms for one who gives a loan literally
means "a believer" (*creditor* in English, from the Latin *credere;* and *Gläubiger* in German, from *glauben,* "to believe"). The whole industry of money
lending assumes a high level of risk. Both Syriac and rabbinic texts make a
big point of this fact by asserting that being generous to the poor tests one's
faith. The giving of alms is therefore not simply a good work; by giving alms
one enacts the faith one claims to possess.

4. Almsgiving Without Limits

The comparison of almsgiving to sacrifice naturally raises the issue of how
much to give: Is it most sensible to give in proportion to what one has (Tobit
4:6–7), or should one follow the more radical advice Jesus gives the rich
young man and sell all one has (Mark 10:17–34 and parallels)? As we saw,
the desire to make heroic gifts to the poor was attested elsewhere in contemporary Judaism, as made clear by the actions of R. Yeshebab and King
Munbaz. Although the example of the former could be excused on the
grounds that the halakhah about the limits of monetary donations had been
forgotten, that did not hold true for the latter, who was even the subject of
lavish praise in the Jerusalem Talmud. In general, however, one can safely say
that rabbinic Judaism did not approve of giving away all or a large proportion of one's wealth because of the deleterious effect it could have on the
family. In the early Christian movement, however, where renunciation of
the family was prized, so was the donation of all one's goods to the poor
(though many Christian writers were also quick to exempt those with families).

5. A Treasury in Heaven

In a worldview that construed sin as a debt and virtue as a credit, there was always a temptation to view the moral life as part of a zero-sum economy. Indeed, much criticism of the general thesis of my book comes from this starting point. There are many Christian writers who denigrate Judaism as a purely legalistic or even economic religion in which one's debits are mathematically balanced against credits. Yet rabbinic and Christian thinkers thought of almsgiving as having a unique set of "economic" properties. Whereas the rewards of other types of virtuous activity could be drawn down by the debit occasioned by sin, both the "capital" and the "interest" (rabbinic and Syriac texts are identical on this point) that accrued to almsgiving always remained to the credit of the giver. As Ephrem writes, "Your alms and prayers are like loans; in every location they enrich those who take them, while to you belongs the capital and interest. What you offer as a loan returns to you." Generosity of this sort participates in an alternative economy wherein both the giver and the receiver are enriched.

A second feature of the treasury in heaven is the rate of return it provides. Ephrem notes that the treasuries of the saints were unlike any treasury on earth, for the more the faithful plundered them, the more they grew! Evidently, in heaven there is no reason to fear a run on the bank. Augustine summarizes this well when he writes: "Study the money-lender's methods. He wants to give modestly and get back with profit; you do the same. Give a little and receive on a grand scale. Look how your interest is mounting up! Give temporal wealth and claim eternal increase, give the earth and gain heaven. 'Whom shall I give to?' did you ask? The Lord himself comes forward to ask you for a loan, he who forbade you to be a usurer. Listen to Scripture telling you how to make the Lord your debtor, 'Anyone who gives alms to the poor is lending to the Lord' " (Prov. 19:17).

In light of the character of the heavenly treasury, it is hardly fair to say that a religious system of debits and credits stands outside the framework of a gracious and loving God. Indeed, in giving alms to the poor one is imitating those very same qualities that exist within God. As we noted in our discussion of Daniel's advice to King Nebuchadnezzar, there is a paradox as to how almsgiving would serve to redeem him. On the one hand, we could say that the alms would flow into his heavenly treasury, where they would gradually grow such that his debts could be covered and his redemption achieved. Yet as the Christian theological tradition would assert, there is a sense in which the debts are so enormous that no amount of almsgiving could ever make a dent in what was owed. (St. Anselm is the clearest on this point, as we shall see in the next chapter.) One way to get around that impasse is to imagine a tremendous rate of return in heaven. By giving his goods to the poor it is as though King Nebuchadnezzar was able to purchase shares of a runaway growth stock at the price of its initial public offering. God, in essence, exchanges every dollar donated for hundreds upon hundreds of dollars. Another way to get at the problem is to attend to the utter graciousness of the act of almsgiving itself. Giving money to the poor was and still is an utterly gracious deed; nothing is required of the recipient. So in giving alms, Nebuchadnezzar was enacting the very same type of treatment for which he himself hoped. But either way, one can see that ancient Judaism and Christianity did not conceive of almsgiving as an act of *Selbsterlösung* ("self-redemption"), as it has often been characterized since the Reformation.

12

why god became man

No book on the history of sin as debt would be complete without a discussion of St. Anselm of Canterbury, who served as archbishop there from 1093 to 1109 and is perhaps best known among philosophers for his ontological argument in favor of the existence of God. As such, his work has spawned an enormous literature. Among theologians, however, he is best known for his classic work *Cur deus homo* (*Why God Became Man*), in which he articulates why it was necessary for the incarnation to take place.[1] In developing his argument, he provides an account of the sin of Adam and the great debt this sin occasioned. The metaphor of sin as a debt, as a result, informs every page of this book. There is no thinker in the Christian tradition for whom debt and atonement come together in such an integrated fashion. And, I might add, there is no thinker who is more roundly condemned for this fact. For dozens of modern thinkers, the notion that God the Father demanded the death of his Son as a means of repaying a debt borders on the barbarous. It seems to suggest that violence is inscribed within the Godhead itself.

Most interpreters of Anselm have not seen anything particularly *biblical* about his understanding of human sin; its more logical origin is often traced back to medieval feudal culture.[2] The failure to see the biblical grounds of this work is predictable for two reasons. First, few readers of Anselm recognize the deeply biblical roots of the debt metaphor (hence, one of the reasons for this book). In addition, Anselm claims his argument will demonstrate *remoto Christo* (that is, by bracketing what revelation says about Christ's divine nature) whether we need to affirm those very things to make sense of our salvation.[3] One should bear in mind, however, that his temporary bracketing of the church's claims about Christ does not require him to leave aside scriptural influences.

In spite of Anselm's claims to the contrary, his argument seems deeply biblical to me. And even more, his argument in many respects simply traces a path that the fathers of the church had marked out long ago. But before I address Anselm's work, let me summarize his argument:[4]

1 Humankind has been made for the purpose of enjoying the beatitude of God. All that they owe in return is to be obedient subjects of his will. When humanity refuses to pay God this honor they fall into debt.[5]

2 Because humanity has nothing of its own to give to God—everything they possess has been given to them—they possess no "currency" to repay their debt.

3 The situation viewed from the side of humanity is hopeless; eternal condemnation appears unavoidable. But this very predicament stands in contradiction to God's goodness. Were God to accept the status quo, he would be forced to watch helplessly as his created world fell apart.[6]

4 And so God's dilemma: Only He has the means to pay what is owed, but the responsibility for the debt rests with humanity. The only possible solution, Anselm concluded—and hence the title of his work, *Why God Became Man*—is for God to become incarnate.

5 Yet Christ, as man, also owes God the perfect obedience that is the responsibility of every son of Adam. If he lives out a sinless life, he will fulfill his own obligation but will not be able to benefit anyone else. But should Christ freely decide to surrender his life by undergoing the common penalty of humankind, he would go well beyond his obligation. As a sinless man, he does not owe his death; and as God, his life is of infinite value. This work of supererogation calls forth from God the Father some sort of compensation for the infinite value that has been surrendered.

6 But because Christ is God, he has no need for any reward from God; he wants for nothing. To whom shall this recompense be given? To those who approach God in the name of his Son, Jesus Christ, with the sincere desire to follow in his path.

The first question regarding Anselm's argument concerns its grounding in the Bible. Most summaries of Anselm's position trace his thought back no further than Tertullian (late first and early second century) and Cyprian (third century).[7] These are the thinkers who set forth the concept of making "satisfaction" for one's sins. I have argued, however, that the metaphor of sin as a debt is far older than that. To appreciate the biblical grounding of Anselm's position, let me review some of the points I have made in this book, focusing on two questions. The first is whether Anselm's position is biblical; the second, which is just as important, is how it is biblical.

IS ANSELM'S ARGUMENT BIBLICAL?

Years ago, while reading the *Damascus Covenant*, a text that relates how the sect at Qumran came together, I came upon a line that summarized the sins of ancient Israel: "Because [all] the former members of the covenant fell into debt, they were given over to the sword. They had forsaken the covenant of God and chosen their own will. They turned after their stubborn heart so that each did his own will" (*CD* 3:10–12).[8] The subject of this text is straightforward enough: after recounting the history of Israel from the era of the flood to the exile, it turns to the tragic ending: the Israelites, by following their stubborn hearts, had forsaken their covenantal responsibilities. The grammar is also simple for someone who knows biblical Hebrew. I was familiar with nearly all the vocabulary because it came straight from the Hebrew Bible. As we have seen, the covenanters at Qumran, wishing to place themselves within the trajectory of biblical history, imitated the literary style of the biblical authors.

But one word of the *Covenant* passage stuck out. Instead of saying that the Israelites had rebelled (*mārĕdû*) or sinned (*ḥāṭĕʾû*) against their God, the text read: "The former members of the covenant fell into debt" (*ḥābû*).[9] The line stopped me, not because the word was rare or difficult but because the word was not biblical. The only dictionary where one could find this root (*ḥ-w-b*) used to expresses the sense of personal culpability was rabbinic. I was struck by the fact that in the context of describing human sin, the biblical idiom the writer had been working so hard to maintain failed and in its place a verbal expression of his own day surfaced.

As I read further, I came to a bigger stumbling block: a section dealing with David and his noncompliance with a matter of Deuteronomic law. The example concluded with the remark that "God forsook/abandoned his sins."[10] Clearly the sense of the text was that God "forgave his sins," but why, I wondered, did the writer use such an odd term (*ʿāzab*) to mark the idea of forgiveness? The term occurs many times in the Hebrew Bible, but never with this meaning. It occurred to me that if I translated the word back into Aramaic, the sentence would make perfect sense, because the term in Aramaic (*šbaq*), which means "to forsake, abandon," has the extended meaning of "to forsake one's right to collect on a debt." Given that debt also means sin in Aramaic, this would make the sentence intelligible. That God had forsaken his right to collect on David's debt would mean that God had forgiven him. But the only way to explain this linguistic oddity was to assume that the scribe was thinking of a common expression in Aramaic and trying to find its near equivalent in colloquial Hebrew. This sort of misuse of a language is called a calque by linguists and occurs commonly among bilingual individuals.[11] When one is speaking a second language, it is almost impossible to keep aspects of the other tongue out of range completely. Later Hebrew (that is, the language spoken by the rabbis) used a different term altogether to mark noncollection of a debt or sin, m-ḥ-l. As a result, use of the term ʿāzab to mark forgiveness of sins was short-lived. We find the verb used this way only at Qumran and in the slightly earlier work of Ben Sira.[12]

Baruch Schwartz, in an essay written in the early 1990s, clarified that puzzle for me by emphasizing the metaphoric nature of the Hebrew expression "to bear a sin."[13] I was to discover that the matter was even more important than Schwartz had observed. Although the Bible uses many metaphors for sin, the most prevalent is the idiom of sin as a weight borne on one's back. But when one turns to the Second Temple period, this idiom disappears almost completely. To be sure, it does not vanish entirely because its presence in a canonical text guarantees frequent citations. But when writers at Qumran, in the Gospels, or in rabbinic literature tell their stories about human sin, they almost never use the imagery of weight or burden. Instead, the favored image is debt, as evidenced in the Aramaic translations of the Hebrew Bible (known as Targums), which systematically translate "to bear a sin" into a clause about the assumption of or release from a debt.

It should not be surprising that early Christian theologians who wrote in Syriac, a dialect of Aramaic, used the debt metaphor extensively in their works. Because they took St. Paul at his word (Rom 5) and traced the origins of human sinfulness back to Adam, it was natural to claim that Adam and Eve had signed a debt note in the Garden of Eden that put all their progeny in arrears. Only the coming of Christ could solve this "financial" crisis. But it was not the case that this Semitic idiom was the private possession of Aramaic-speaking Christians. Perhaps because of the presence of texts such as the Our Father in the New Testament or the influence of early Hebrew and Aramaic-speaking Christians, the image of the bond of Adam and Eve quickly spread throughout the Mediterranean basin.[14] One finds hundreds of references to the bond that Christ tore in two in both Greek and Latin sources. And the legacy did not remain tethered to the patristic period. In one of the most popular books of the medieval period, the *Golden Leg-*

end, one finds the following: "[Jesus] willed to shed his own blood, not the blood of a debtor, for which reason he withdrew from debtors. This sort of debt the apostle [Paul] calls a *chirograph* [Col 2:14], a handwritten bill, which Christ took and nailed to the cross. Augustine says of this bill: 'Eve borrowed sin from the devil and wrote a bill and provided a surety, and the interest on the debt was heaped upon posterity. She borrowed sin from the devil when, going against God's command, she consented to his wicked order or suggestion. She wrote the bill when she reached her hand to the forbidden apple. She gave a surety when she made Adam consent to the sin. And so the interest on the debt became posterity's burden.'"[15]

When I first came across texts like this in patristic and medieval sources I imagined two crews of miners tunneling under a mountain from opposite directions. Would they end up meeting in the middle? On one side of the mountain (let's call it the Old Testament side), we can see the development of the debt metaphor as it appeared in Leviticus 26 and Isaiah 40, the former specifying how Israel is to make satisfaction ("they shall repay the debts of their sins"), the latter announcing that satisfaction was an accomplished fact ("the debt of her iniquity has been satisfied"). On the other side (the world of early Christianity), we have an enormous amount of material that portrays the saving act of Christ as voiding a bond of indebtedness. How, one might wonder, are the two sides connected? The evidence of the Dead Sea Scrolls ("Israel fell into debt") and the New Testament ("Forgive us our debts" and "Christ has erased the bond of indebtedness") mark the path of the tunnel. I have hoped to show in this book that a text such as the one quoted from the *Golden Legend* is deeply biblical. There is a tunnel that leads straight back to the Bible. To slightly alter the metaphor of the miners: when we see the connection between the debt language of the church fathers and rabbis and its point of origin in the Second Temple period, we have hit the mother lode. With Isaiah 40:2, Leviticus 26, Daniel 4, and the book of Tobit, the developments that would follow become apparent.

HOW IS ANSELM'S APPROACH BIBLICAL?

Conceiving of the atoning work of Christ as an act of remitting debt does not completely solve the problem. It is not sufficient to say that the metaphor of debt is biblical. We need to ask how the metaphor is used. As Robert Jenson noted, neither the New Testament nor the Christian tradition has seen fit to articulate in a univocal manner *how* Christ redeems us for our sins. The creeds make clear that Christ died for humanity but say nothing about how his death atones. It has been the burden of the theological tradition to take up this task and assemble the biblical data into a meaningful whole.

Many of the earliest Christian thinkers commonly assumed that God had conceded to Satan the right to hold the bond of indebtedness that had been signed in the Garden of Eden. Because God had threatened Adam and Eve with death should they fail to keep his command, all their posterity was thought to fall under a bond held by Satan. The debt was collected in the form of death.

Modern theologians assert that the story of Christ's defeat of the devil and the voiding of this bond is a piece of mythology having nothing to do with biblical narrative.[16] One might be inclined to agree, based on the lengthy narrative that Narsai (fifth-century Syriac church father) composed about the conversations between Satan and Christ after his crucifixion but prior to his resurrection. The Gospel narratives, as Hans Urs von Balthasar has reminded us, say nothing about what happens between the final words of Jesus and his appearance in glory.[17]

However, given that early Christian writers were heir to a tradition that thought of sin as a debt and described the atonement as a release from a bond of indebtedness, it is not surprising that theologians and homilists would want to fill in the picture. As Ricoeur insightfully observed, "The symbol gives rise to thought." And for early Christians the primary symbol for sin was debt and the way to think through what that meant with respect to salvation in Christ was through narrative expansion. So, in my mind, the model of atonement that was central to patristic thinking, a model that Gustav Aulén called Christus Victor, was not quite as unbiblical as it is claimed to be. Narsai, in my opinion, was simply filling in the dotted lines left to him by an overly laconic biblical text.

But saying that it bears the imprint of biblical idiom is not the same as saying it represents *the* biblical portrait. Defining how an idiom is biblical is just as important as asking whether it depends on biblical ideas. As Ricoeur also noted, a particular metaphor does not necessitate a single narrative exemplification. We can therefore say with some confidence that the narrative of a goat that bears away Israel's sins in Leviticus 16 follows logically from the idea that sins are a burden on the shoulders of the offender. But we could not predict that a narrative such as this would be written by a culture that assumed sins were burdens. Many other narrative and ritual exemplifications could be imagined. The same thing holds true for cultures that construe sin as a debt. Although the combination of Colossians 2:14 and Romans 5:12–21 provides much of the Christus Victor model—Adam and Eve sign a bond involving all of humanity that is ultimately voided by Christ—many important details remain ambiguous. For example, do all human beings repeat the sin of Adam and Eve and so incur their own debt, or is the debt inherited? This is the classic question that divided Augustine from Pelagius. The latter believed each of us had the freedom to repeat or to refrain from the sin of Adam, whereas the former argued that the brokenness of Adam was passed on at birth as an inherited feature of our human condition.

Another, and more pressing, question concerns the bond signed by Adam and Eve: Who holds it, Satan or God?[18] In rabbinic thought, it is consistently said that God holds the bond (though the rabbis do not trace the signing of such a bond back to Adam and Eve). In the Christus Victor model that Narsai represents, Satan holds the bond. The idea behind Christ as victor is that he vanquished a worthy opponent. The dramatic character of this account requires a powerful agent of evil whom Christ can overthrow. Although the resulting "battle" between Jesus and Satan makes for a compelling story, it also creates a theological problem of considerable magnitude. As Gregory of Nazianzus stated in the fourth century CE, it was embarrassing to declare that a robber such as Satan should receive a ransom from God and that such an "extravagant price should be paid to his tyranny before [God] could justly spare us."[19] Is God answerable to the architect of evil?

It was these worries of Gregory that Anselm took up. He rejected the Christus Victor model entirely and stated that humanity's debt belongs not to the devil but to God (*Cur deus homo* 2.19). Like the fathers of the church, he grounds his approach in an exegesis of Colossians 2:14. But the bond that Christ is said to void is not, Anselm asserts, "a bond of the devil; it is a bond 'of the decree.' Now that decree was not a decree of the devil but of God. For it was decreed by the just judgment of God and, as it were, confirmed by a bond, in order that man, having sinned of his own free will, would not be able, through his own efforts, to avoid either sin or the punishment for sin" (*Cur deus homo* 1.8). What Anselm means is that Adam in the Garden had been given a command to which the penalty of death was attached. When he violated the command, he fell under the terms of the penalty that God had established from the first. In that sense, the bond that confirmed such a thing was held by God.

By declaring that God was the one who held the bond, Anselm solved one thorny problem while opening up another. The advantage of the classic Christus Victor approach was that it put God in the position of being the unqualified benefactor of humankind. In his passion, God acted on behalf of humanity to abrogate the rights that Satan had previously held. The story of the cross is a story of God's masterful victory over the evil one.

But if God is the holder of the bond, a point of tension can arise. It is possible to imagine God not as the champion of the human race but as an indignant being whose wrath against humanity must be appeased. Recall that in Isaiah 40:2 God could not forgive Israel until she had made full restitution for the debts she had accumulated ("[the debt due for] her iniquity has been satisfied"). The same picture was present in Leviticus 26 ("Israel shall repay the debt of her sins"), as well as in Daniel 9 ("to bring to completion the debt of their sin"). Israel's rebellion against her God led to the erosion of God's patience. When pushed to the extreme, God in his wrath decreed that Israel would be sent into exile. It was through the bearing of this punishment that Israel made amends and eventually was restored. If we extend that portrait into the New Testament, it would seem that the cross was nothing other than that moment in time when God extracted payment from humanity at large for the many debts it owed. The means of securing that price was to put to death an innocent victim who would stand in the stead of all humankind (the so-called "penal substitution" model). Christ's sufferings must be imagined as immeasurably great in order to counterbalance what is owed by the entire human race.

An idea like this poses a considerable theological challenge for understanding the passion narratives. Whereas in Isaiah 40 and Leviticus 26 we read about individuals who suffer the consequences of their misdeeds (hardly an injustice), the Gospels seem to portray God as demanding the death of an innocent. Is God such a vindictive figure that he demands the blood of his Son in order to discharge the debts that are indelibly inscribed in his account books? If this is all that is happening on Calvary, one might readily agree with the noted New Testament scholar Ernst Käsemann, who wrote that the Christian theologian must "abandon the ecclesiastical and biblical tradition which interprets Jesus' death as sacrificial."[20]

For many contemporary theologians, this is the danger that sits athwart the path Anselm has blazed. Yet we should be cautious about adopting this assessment too quickly. Those who have read Anselm closely—and many of his detractors clearly have not—have noted that he explicitly rejects the idea that God is exacting retribution from humanity at large by putting Christ to death on the cross. At a crucial point in the exposition of the problem, Anselm's interlocutor asks:

But how will it possibly be proved a just and rational thing that God treated, and allowed to be treated, in this way, the man whom he, as Father, called his beloved Son in whom he was well pleased, and whose nature he, as Son, took upon himself? For what justice is it for the man who was of all the most just to be put to death for a sinner? What man would not be judged worthy of condemnation, if he were to condemn someone innocent and release the guilty party? . . . If God could not save sinners except by condemning a just man, where is his omnipotence? If, on the other hand, he was capable of doing so, but did not will it, how shall we defend his wisdom and justice?

To this query Anselm then responds:

God the Father did not treat that man as you apparently understand him to have done; nor did he hand over an innocent man to be killed in place of the guilty party. For the Father did not coerce Christ to face death against his will, or give permission for him to be killed, but Christ himself of his own volition underwent death in order to save mankind. (*Cur deus homo* 1.8)

Anselm could hardly be more explicit—Christ does not atone for the sins of humankind by becoming a penal substitute.[21] He suffered death solely of his own choosing in order to redeem the human race. His divine Father took no pleasure or delight in the fact of his suffering or death. One can confirm this based on the religious life that Anselm lived. As Rachel Fulton has shown, Anselm avoided extreme acts of self-mortification as a means of doing penance, even though this was standard practice in the life of his contemporary Peter Damian. To be sure, when Anselm meditated on the cross, he saw the sufferings of Christ, but that suffering was a gift of God's love for the church that simply overwhelmed the debts of humankind. The divine Father was not so much collecting the punishment due on his bond as he was rewarding the self-donation Christ had made out of his love for humanity. It was that inestimable and unmerited gift, Fulton argues, that Anselm made the center of his devotional life.[22]

SATISFACTION OR PUNISHMENT

Fundamental to understanding Anselm is the crucial distinction he made between satisfaction and punishment that is lost on most modern readers.[23] Punishment, Anselm assumed, is suffering the just consequences for one's sins, something that happens to the sinner whether or not he or she wills it. Satisfaction, on the other hand, is a *voluntary* recompense for wrongdoing. Christ offers satisfaction in Anselm's view; he does not suffer punishment.

In the framework of this book, one must temper the penal dimension of a text like Isaiah 40:2 with the act of almsgiving that the prophet Daniel had commended (4:24—"Redeem your sins by almsgiving"). In Isaiah, Israel pays off her sins by way of suffering the consequences of her exile to Babylon. With the advent of the Persian empire, this prophet triumphantly announced that the debt owed on Israel's sins had been repaid. Daniel, on the other hand, took a different approach. Rather than imposing a severe punishment on King Nebuchadnezzar for his sins, the prophet urged him to earn his redemption monies through almsgiving. By acquiring this sort of treasury in heaven, his debt could be paid off or at least whittled down to a manageable size.

Because Anselm is interested in how Christ's sacrifice yields a surplus of merit, it is more appropriate to consider Christ's work as charity rather than as a punishment, which in Anselm's view, can only pay off what one owes; it can offer no additional credit that will benefit others. What has thrown off many readers of Anselm, of course, is the manner in which Christ shows this charity—that of suffering the consequences of the crime. But suffering the results of a crime can be construed as an act of love. The fathers of the church, for example, frequently compared Adam to Christ. According to one tradition, grounded in I Timothy 2:14 ("Adam was not deceived, but the woman was deceived and became a transgressor"), the real cause of the fall was not Adam but Eve. For Origen, this meant that Adam consented to eat the forbidden fruit not out of a desire to disobey a divine command but to avoid being separated from his spouse, Eve.[24] This interpretation depends on an allegorical underpinning: Eve represents the church and Adam Christ. On this reading, Adam loves Eve so deeply that he will share the consequences of her sin in order to redeem her from the exile she has been rightfully condemned to endure. The significance of this image cannot be understated: the *suffering* of Adam—and by extension, Christ—is not meant to be the primary subject of our attention. What the suffering of Adam (and therefore Christ) gives witness to is an immeasurable love for the sinner.

It is this model, many Christian theologians have argued, that best describes the work of Christ. Christ suffers to be sure, but not because paying a penalty is the central theme; he endures the penalty that is rightfully ours to reveal how deeply he loves us. If we were to return to the theme of Isaiah 40—that is, paying a penalty for one's sins—Christ could be likened to an innocent Jew who so loved his people that he chose to accompany them into exile to redeem them. By so doing, he would be enduring the wrath of God along with his countrymen, but by the same token he would be demonstrating such a deep form of charity that he would be at the same time amassing a great treasure in heaven. Joseph Cardinal Ratzinger gets the matter right when he criticizes the "much-coarsened version of St. Anselm's theology of atonement" that circulates in many theological handbooks.[25] "To many, many Christians," Ratzinger observes, "it looks as if the Cross is to be understood as part of a mechanism of injured and restored right. It is the form, so it seems, in which the infinitely offended righteousness of God was propitiated again by means of an infinite expiation. . . . This picture is as false as it is widespread. In the Bible the Cross does not appear as part of a mechanism of injured right; on the contrary, in the Bible, the Cross is quite the reverse; *it is the expression of the radical nature of the love that gives itself completely,* of the process in which one is what one does and does what one is; it is the expression of a life that is completely being for others."

Yet perhaps one question remains: How, we might ask, might such love be merit worthy such that it could cover the debts of others?

ISAAC AS A TYPE OF CHRIST

To answer that question let me turn to a different sort of tradition. In Second Temple and rabbinic Judaism there is, I believe, an analogy to a form of suffering that produced tremendous merits. I am thinking of the way postbiblical Jewish sources interpreted the story of the sacrifice of Isaac in Genesis 22. In the biblical story the reader's attention is drawn to the figures of God and Abraham. At the beginning we learn that God is going to put Abraham to a test, and at the climax that Abraham has passed that test. Isaac seems something of an accessory to the tale. He plays a crucial role, to be sure, but more as the object of his father's love than anything else.

These postbiblical sources took a great deal of interest in the person of Isaac. For many of them it was important to affirm Isaac's willingness to put his life on the line. Crucial to this transformation was the way this story was recontextualized during the execution of various Jewish families in the wake of the Maccabean uprising. In one text, when the Jews were given the choice to apostatize or suffer death, a set of brothers urged one another to show fidelity to the God of Israel by recalling the fate of Isaac: "Courage brother!" said one, and another, "Hold on nobly." And another, recalling the past, said, "Remember whence you came and at the hand of what father Isaac gave himself to be sacrificed for piety's sake" (IV Macc 13:10–12). By comparing their predicament to that of Isaac, they assumed that Isaac *chose* death as a way of sanctifying the name of God, that he put the love of God above all earthly competitors.

This free choice of a heroic death to the greater glory of God was construed as an act of unparalleled supererogation. As a result, great merits *(zekûyôt)* were recorded in his name. In one text I have already discussed, those merits were drawn upon when God threatened to do away with the entire nation of Israel after the sin of the golden calf. In his fervent prayer, Moses had implored God to "remember your servants Abraham, Isaac, and Jacob" (Exod 32:13). Whereas most modern commentators have understood the plea that God "remember" as a reference to the covenant God had made with his chosen nation in the book of Genesis, the rabbis understood this term to refer to the great acts of piety accomplished by the Patriarchs —in particular, Isaac's willingness to offer his own life as a sacrifice to God. The reasoning was that the merits Isaac had won at Mt. Moriah would far exceed the debts Israel had incurred at the foot of Mt. Sinai. So close is this analogy to Anselm's notion of the atonement that we can take his conclusion and, with a slight modification, make it appear Jewish. Anselm wrote: "What, indeed, can be conceived of more merciful than that God the Father should say to a sinner condemned to eternal torments and lacking any means of redeeming himself, 'Take my only-begotten son and give him on your behalf'" (*Cur Deus Homo* 2.20). This could be slightly altered to read: "What, indeed, can be conceived of more merciful than that the God of Israel should say to his people, 'Take Abraham's only-begotten son and give him on your behalf.'"

Moreover, in the rabbinic mind Isaac's willingness to die had won an ongoing role in Israel's sacrificial service just as the sacrifice of Christ did in the liturgy of the Mass. This is brought out in an imaginative midrash on Leviticus 1:11. In this chapter we learn the rules for sacrificing a bull (vv. 3–9), a sheep or a goat (vv. 10–13), and a bird (vv. 14–17). The Bible demands that the sheep or goat, unlike the bull or the bird, is to be slaughtered "on the *north* side of the altar." This geographical reference is odd—were the other animals sacrificed on a different side? Though modern readers pay little attention to it, rabbinic readers believed this unique rule could not be accidental; it must reveal some deeper truth. Why is the lamb distinguished from the other animals?

To understand how the rabbis solved this puzzle requires knowledge of two facts. First, every morning and evening in Jerusalem, a lamb was offered as a burnt offering in the temple (Exod 29:38–42 and Num 29:3–8).

Indeed, according to the book of Exodus, the sole reason for establishing a temple was to offer this particular sacrifice, which signified the gracious presence of the God of Israel dwelling amid his people. Second, it was at the future site of the temple that God had commanded the offering of Isaac. According to rabbinic readers, the sacrifice of Isaac was a foundational offering that paved the way for the ongoing liturgy in the temple.

The midrashic interpretation opens by citing the biblical verse "It shall be slaughtered on the north-side *(ṣāpônâh)* of the altar, before the Lord" (Lev 1:11). The exposition of the verse reads: "When our father Abraham bound Isaac his son, the Holy One (blessed be He!) established the institution of the two lambs, one in the morning and one in the evening [Exod 29:38–42]. Why so much? Because when Israel would sacrifice the daily offering on the altar and recite this verse ['on the *ṣ-p-n-h* side of the altar'], the Holy One (blessed be He!) would remember the binding of Isaac." I left *ṣ-p-n-h* untranslated because this is the key to understanding this text. The Hebrew Bible was originally written without vowels, and so the rabbinic reader always felt free to explore other ways of vocalizing a word. The consonants *ṣ-p-n-h* are commonly rendered *ṣāpônâh* and translated "north-side," as any modern translation of the Bible will confirm. But the rabbis eschewed the obvious sense of this word in order to link this text to the story of Isaac. They accomplished this by playfully misreading the word as *ṣĕpûnâh,* a feminine passive participle meaning "hidden." The word "hidden" would then refer to the story of the binding of Isaac (known in Hebrew as the *akedah* ["binding"], a feminine noun that would match our feminine passive participle). On this reading we could paraphrase the end of the midrash as follows: "Why sacrifice a lamb every morning and evening? Because when Israel would sacrifice those lambs on the altar and at the same time recite this verse—'hidden *(ṣĕpûnâh)* before the Lord'—the Holy One (blessed be He!) would remember the *akedah* of Isaac." In other words, in the rabbinic mind, Israel's daily sacrificial service was a way of memorializing the heroic self-offering of the patriarch Isaac. Every time Israel made her sacrifice on earth, God contemplated Isaac's merits that were stored in heaven. And perhaps even more surprising, especially to the Christian reader who is forever tempted to think of Judaism in narrow, parochial terms, is that this verse from Leviticus is imagined to have universal consequences. The text ends with a dramatic intervention on the part of God: "I call heaven and earth to witness against me: Whenever anyone—Gentile or Jew, man or woman, male or female slave, reads this verse ('on the north-side before the Lord'), the Holy One (blessed be He) remembers the bind-

ing of Isaac, as it is written: 'on the north side in the presence of the Lord'"
(*Lev Rab* 2.11).

The parallels between the *akedah* and Anselm are thought provoking. I
wish to make it clear that my argument has been analogical, not historical.
Anselm did not derive his theological insights from the writings of the rabbis. But given that both the rabbis and Anselm are beholden to the metaphor of sin as a debt and the idea that God is holder of the bond, it is not
surprising that their theological systems bear a strong resemblance. In both,
construal of sin as a debt to be repaid requires a holder of sufficient credit
to cover the sins of others.

Moreover, behind both systems is the matter of sacrifice. On the Jewish
side, the *akedah* became such a powerful narrative because it was understood
to be the foundational narrative for sacrifice in the temple. On the Christian
side, the sacrifice of Christ became the founding narrative for the Eucharis-
tic sacrifice. As Jaroslav Pelikan has stated: "As the central act of Christian
worship, the sacrifice of the Mass gave meaning to, and derived meaning from,
the image of the suffering and death of Christ on the cross as atoning sacrifice."[26] Indeed, the sacrificial understanding of both the Eucharist and the
atonement were "mutually reinforcing; in the words of Anselm, 'just as there
is one Christ who sacrificed himself for us, so there is one offering and one
sacrifice that we offer in the bread and wine.' More precisely, it was Christ the
Redeemer himself who 'every day without interruption . . . sacrifices the burnt
offering of his body and blood for us.'"[27] Of course, the intertwining of these
two sacrifices is not an innovation of the medieval era; it was already a well-
established fact in the patristic period. As noted earlier, Augustine argued that
his mother, Monica, should be worthy of entering the heavenly kingdom upon
her death because of her daily attendance at the Mass. There, Augustine reasoned, she was able to contemplate the price Christ had paid for her salvation
and allow herself to be remade into his image.

Let me express one final caveat. It has not been my point to close this
book with an unqualified recommendation of Anselm's construal of Christ's
sacrifice for the present day. That would be an act of hubris. Theologians far
more knowledgeable than I have wrestled with this problem, and from their
writings I have learned a great deal. I have, however, shown that Anselm's
much celebrated treatise owes its inspiration to the biblical metaphor of sin
as a debt. To the degree that one accepts this metaphor as a basic building
block for a doctrine of the atonement, Anselm's great work should remain
a point of departure for theological exploration.

NOTES

CHAPTER 1 **What Is a Sin?**

1 George Lakoff and Mark Johnson, *Metaphors We Live By* (Chicago: University of Chicago Press, 1980). Also worth consulting are the classic articles of Donald Davidson, "What Metaphors Mean," *Critical Inquiry* 5 (1978): 31–47, and Gottlob Frege, "On Sense and Reference," in P. Geach and M. Black, eds., *Translation from the Philosophical Writings of Gottlob Frege* (Oxford: Blackwell, 1966). Two recent theological treatments should be noted: Janet Martin Soskice, *Metaphor and Religious Language* (Oxford: Clarendon, 1985), and Colin Gunton, *The Actuality of Atonement: A Study of Metaphor, Rationality and the Christian Tradition* (Edinburgh: T and T Clark, 1988).

2 Lakoff and Johnson, *Metaphors We Live By*, 4–5.

3 Paul Ricoeur, *The Symbolism of Evil* (Boston: Beacon Press, 1967).

4 I follow Milgrom in his assumption that during the hand-leaning rite (Lev 16:21), Aaron transfers the sins of Israel onto the animal and that the animal then transports these sins into the wilderness. This ritual action is distinct from the act of wiping away the impurities *(kippēr)* that have adhered to the inner sanctum of the sanctuary. See Jacob Milgrom, *Leviticus 1-16* (AB 3; New York: Doubleday, 1991), 1041–45.

5 Baruch Schwartz, "Term or Metaphor: Biblical *nōśēʾ ʿāwōn/pešaʿ/ḥeṭʾ* " [in Hebrew] *Tarbiz* 63 (1994): 149–71. See also my article "From Israel's Burden to Israel's Debt: Towards a Theology of Sin in Biblical and Early Second Temple Sources," in E. Chazon et al., eds., *Reworking the Bible: Apocryphal and Related Texts at Qumran* (Leiden: Brill, 2005), 1–30.

6 See *Exod Rab* 44:5, from *Midrash Rabbah* (London: Soncino Press: 1939), 3:509–10: "Another explanation of '*remember Abraham, Isaac and Israel*'" (Exod 32:13). Why are the three patriarchs here mentioned? Because, said the Sages, Moses argued: [A] 'If it is burning that they deserve, then remember, O Lord, Abraham who jeopardized his life in the fiery furnace in order to be burnt for thy name and let his burning cancel the burning of his children. [B] If it is decapitation that they deserve, then remember their father Isaac who stretched forth his neck on the altar ready to be slaughtered for thy name and let now his immolation cancel the immolation of his children. [C] And if it is banishment that they deserve, then remember their father Jacob who was banished from his father's house to Haran. In summary, let all those acts [of the patriarchs] now atone for their act [in making the calf]'; this is why he said: '*remember Abraham, Isaac, and Israel*.'" For a full exposition of the merit of the patriarchs in rabbinic literature, see S. Schechter, *Aspects of Rabbinic Theology* (New York: Macmillan, 1909), 171–89, and Arthur Marmorstein, *The Doctrine of Merits in Old Rabbinic Literature* (1920; rpt., New York, KTAV, 1968).

7 The quotations are taken from *The Works of Emperor Julian*, ed. and trans. W. Wright (New York: G. P. Putnam's, 1933), 3:67–71.

8 Rodney Stark, *The Rise of Christianity: How the Obscure, Marginal Jesus Movement Became the Dominant Religious Force in the Western World in a Few Centuries* (San Francisco: HarperCollins, 1997), 88. Italics in the original.

9 Given our current times, it is worth mentioning that Islam was (and is!) also an heir to this tradition. The giving of alms became one of its five pillars, and its term for alms, *zakât*, was borrowed directly from the Hebrew-Aramaic term *zekût*.

10 See the wonderful treatment of Maureen Flynn, *Sacred Charity: Confraternities and Social Welfare in Spain, 1400–1700* (Ithaca: Cornell University Press, 1989). Many thanks to my colleague Carlos Eire for referring me to this work.

11 See Carter Lindberg, *Beyond Charity: Reformation Initiatives for the Poor* (Minneapolis: Fortress Press, 1993).

12 *T. Peah*, 4.19. See my discussion of this theme in Chap. 11.

CHAPTER 2 A Burden to Be Borne

1 Although I have relied on the NJPS version for a good portion of the translation of these and other verses in this chapter, I have modified them slightly to bring to the foreground the metaphoric imagery. The translations of all other postbiblical Hebrew texts are mine.

2 Baruch Schwartz, "Term or Metaphor: Biblical *nōśē ʿāwōn/peśaʿ/ḥeṭ*" [in Hebrew], *Tarbiz* 63 (1994): 149–71. Also see his "The Bearing of Sin in Priestly Literature," in D. Wright, D. N. Freedman, and A. Hurwitz, eds., *Pomegranates and Golden Bells* (FS Jacob Milgrom; Winona Lake, Ind.: Eisenbrauns, 1995), 3–21.

3 Schwartz, "Term or Metaphor," 158.

4 It is interesting to note that one can also indicate obligation in Hebrew with the preposition *ʿal*, meaning "upon." E.g., the phrase *ʿalay nedāreka*, which means "I am obligated to fulfil my vows to you," could also be translated "[a burden] is upon me to fulfil my vows to you."

5 Note that in a closely worded parallel, the biblical writer replaces *nāśā*, "to bear [away]," with *lāqaḥ*, "to take [away]": "Whose ass have I taken?" (I Sam 12:3). It is also worth noting that in modern Hebrew the verb *nāṭal* ("to bear," the nominal form meaning "a heavy burden") is used in the construction *neṭûl*-caffeine, meaning "without caffeine."

6 Reading *haśśôr* in place of *haśśaw*, a commonly suggested emendation of the Hebrew text.

7 *Leviticus 1–16* (AB 3; New York: Doubleday, 1991), 1072.

8 The translation is mine. The translation of the Hebrew root *k-b-ś* as, "to crush under foot," comes from the cognate term in Akkadian, *kabāsu*.

9 See the article by Hayim Tawil, "Azazel the Prince of the Steppe: A Comparative Study," *ZAW* 92 (1980): 43–59, and the discussion of Milgrom, *Leviticus 1–16*, 1072.

10 These two options are presented in the commentaries of Samuel R. Driver, *The Book of Genesis* (London: Methuen, 1913), 66, and Nahum Sarna, *The Jewish Publication Society Torah Commentary: Genesis* (Philadelphia: JPS, 1989), 34.

11 *Pesiqta deR. Kahana*, cited in James Kugel, *The Bible as It Was* (Cambridge: Harvard University Press, 1997), 96.

CHAPTER 3 **A Debt to Be Repaid**

1 The *TDOT* (vv. 561–62), though marred by overt anti-Jewish sensibilities, captures the shift well: "Later Judaism, which views the relation to God as a legal and business relation, often applies the metaphor of indebtedness to the ethical and religious relation between man and God. . . . Each transgression means indebtedness to the God who has given the Law. In heaven men's acts are entered into an account book *(šṭar ḥôb)* and the final reckoning decides whether the fulfillments of the Law or the transgressions are in the ascendancy. Because the individual is judged by the majority (i.e. of his works) . . . , man always appears to be in part righteous *(zaki)* and in part guilty *(ḥayyāb)*. If he keeps a commandment, well with him, for he has . . . inclined the scale on the side of merit" *(t. Qid* 1.14). It should be noted that what is said here is true not only for rabbinic Judaism but also for Syriac-speaking Christianity. The crucial variable in this new understanding of sin is not Judaism but, rather, Aramaic idiom.

2 One conspicuous exception would be Gen 15:16. See my discussion of this verse in Chap. 7. There are other examples as well, such as the frequent idiom of God "selling" Israel into the hands of foreign nations as a result of her sins (Judges 2:14, 3:8, 4:2, 10:7). The distance between this image and that of Israel making satisfaction for the debt of her sins after being "sold" into Babylon found in Isa 40:2 and 50:1 (see my discussion in Chap. 4) is not great. I do not intend to provide a complete list of idioms such as this. Suffice it to say that the image of sin as a debt that became so prominent in the Second Temple period did have a few examples from the First Temple period that it could build on.

3 This root also appears in Hebrew, but it probably derives from Aramaic. Indeed, the whole move toward such a commercial idiom is probably, at origin, the result of a borrowing from Assyrian-Aramean usage. On the influence of these words on Mishnaic Hebrew, see Eduard Y. Kutscher, *Words and Their History* [in Hebrew] (Jerusalem: Kiryat Sefer, 1961). On the importance of Aramaic as a conduit of legal metaphors and their influence on rabbinic religion, see Yochanan Muffs, *Love and Joy: Law, Language and Religion in Ancient Israel* (New York: Jewish Theological Seminary, 1992), 121–93.

4 The Aramaic Targums are relatively late compositions that are probably roughly contemporaneous with the other rabbinic writings. But given that their translations of terms for debt and forgiveness match up well with what we will see in both the Gospels and Qumranic literature (see my discussion later in this chapter), I think it fair to say that the Targums reflect an ancient translation practice.

5 A more literal translation would be "he assumes his debt," but "to assume a debt" seems more idiomatic to me.

6 This parallels nicely the usage of "to bear a sin" in the Bible. As Baruch Schwartz has also shown ("Term or Metaphor: Biblical *nōśē ʿāwōn/peśaʿ/ḥeṭ*" [in Hebrew], *Tarbiz* 63 (1994): 149–71), this idiom does not denote a punishment, as many have thought. Rather, it designates the state of culpability and says nothing about how the sin might be rectified. In the laws of Leviticus the culpability can be removed by making a *ḥaṭṭāʾt* sacrifice (5:1) or through a variety of punishments including dying childless (20:17), death by stoning (21:15), or death by divine agency (22:9).

7 Translation is mine.

8 BT *B.Bathra* 5a.

9 *Mekhilta deR. Ishmael,* at Exod 14:21.

10 BT *San* 100b.

11 BT *Ket* 90a.

12 *Gen Rab* 23:4.

13 Ibid., 85:2.

14 BT *Gittin* 26b.

15 BT *Taʿanit* 7b. I have adjusted the JPS translation to match how R. Tanhum has read the text.

16 Brown, "The Pater Noster as an Eschatological Prayer," *TS* 22 (1961): 175–208; reprinted in *New Testament Essays* (Milwaukee, Wis.: Bruce, 1965), 217–53. The citation is taken from the reprint, 244.

17 Brown, "Pater Noster," 245.

18 For a good discussion of current scholarship on this issue, see John P. Meier, *A Marginal Jew, Mentor, Message and Miracles,* vol. 2 (New York: Doubleday), 19–177.

19 *Early Biblical Interpretation* (Philadelphia: Westminster Press, 1986), 46.

20 *CD* 3:9–10.

21 The text actually reads, nonsensically, *hābû,* but it is regularly emended to *ḥābû.*

22 The major treatments of this text include Josef Milik, "Milki-sedeq et Milki-reshaʿ dans les anciens écrits juifs et chrétiens," *JJS* 23 (1972): 95–144; Paul Kobelski, *Melchizedek and Melchireshaʿ,* CBQMS 10 (Washington, D.C.: Catholic Biblical Association, 1981); Émile Puech, "Notes sur le manuscrit de 11QMelkisedeq," *RQ* 12 (1987): 483–514; and Florentino G. Martínez, *DJD* 23:222–41. The reading adapted here follows from Martínez's edition in *DJD.*

23 This text is a translation from a fragment found at Qumran. As a result there are numerous lacunae in the text that have been indicated by square brackets. The text found within the brackets has been filled in by Martínez (see n. 22). Points in the text where it is impossible to give a reasonable guess at reconstruction are indicated by a bracketed ellipsis: [. . .]. I added the references to the biblical citations for the benefit of the reader.

24 Not surprisingly, another text at Qumran, the Apocryphon of Joshua, dates the initial entry of Israel into the promised land in a Jubilee year. The text reads (ll. 5–6): "The sons of Israel crossed over onto dry land in the first month of the forty-first year since the exodus from Egypt. It was in the Jubilee-year that their entry into the land of Canaan had its beginning." In a symmetry that would not have surprised Hermann Gunkel, the end-time shall recapitulate the beginning of time.

25 Milik, "Milki-sedeq," 103, has restored the term *maśśā* (= "debt") as the object of the verb *ʿāzab,* "to release or forsake." His suggestion is grounded in the clause found in Neh 5:10: "I, my brothers, and my servants also have claims of money and grain against them; let us now abandon *(naʿăzôb)* those claims *(hammaśśā hazzeh)."* What appears to have happened in 11QMelchizedek (according to the way Milik has reconstructed the text) is that the financial image of Nehemiah 5:10 has become theological: "to abandon the (claims) that result from the debt of their sins." Elisha Qimron has proposed a simpler restoration. Rather than restoring the noun *maśśā,* he posits the direct object marker *et.* I would like to thank Professor Qimron for showing me his preliminary readings (forthcoming) for this text and several others.

26 This sort of calque on the root *ʿāzab* occurs a second time in the Qumran writings in the *Damascus Covenant* (5:5–6) regarding the forgiveness shown toward David when he

slept with Bathsheba. On this text, see Gary Anderson, "The Status of the Torah in the Pre-Sinaitic Period: The Retelling of the Bible in Jubilees and the Damascus Covenant," *DSD* 1 (1994): 1–29, esp. n. 35. Tadeusz Penar, *Northwest Semitic Philology and the Hebrew Fragments of Ben Sira* (Rome: Biblical Institute Press, 1975), was the first to make this suggestion on the basis of Ben Sira 3:13, but he did not observe that this meaning came from a calque on the Aramaic equivalent.

27 One problem created by this metaphor, however, is the question of who holds the bond of debt under which the Israelites are bound. Clearly no terrestrial adversary could wield such spiritual authority. The dualism of Qumranic theology provided a ready answer. Belial is declared to be in possession of this bond, and as such his power over Israel is not without some claim to legitimacy. This is a remarkable point that has not been noticed by those who have commented upon this text. It shows a striking correlation to a theme that would emerge in early Christianity, namely, that Satan justly holds a bond of indebtedness against humanity. On this, see briefly Gary A. Anderson, *The Genesis of Perfection* (Louisville, Ky.: Westminster John Knox, 2001), 158–61, and, in far greater detail, Michael E. Stone, *Adam's Contract with Satan: The Legend of the Cheirograph of Adam* (Bloomington, Ind.: Indiana University Press, 2002).

28 There are other instances of *ḥāb* and *ʿāzab* in the Qumran materials, and it is not my intention to run down the entire list (for *ḥāb*, see 4Q542 Testament of Qahat, frag. 1, 2.6, and 4Q179 ApocLamentations A 1.14; for *ʿāzab*, see 4Q271 [4QCD^t], frag. 3 3). More important, the idiom of sin as a failed financial venture can be found in other sorts of speech as well. E.g., in 4Q504, Words of the Luminaries, we find: "Through our sins we were sold [into exile]." This text is clearly built on the model of Isa 50:1. In 11Q5 19:10 we read: "I was near to death because of my sins, and my iniquities have sold me to Sheol."

CHAPTER 4 **Redemption and the Satisfaction of Debts**

1 One important exception to this rule would be those Second Temple texts that quote biblical texts that use the image of "bearing one's sin." A good example of this is John 1:29, in which Jesus is identified as the Lamb of God who takes away the sins of the world. The text appears to be a conflation of Lev 16 and Isa 53.

2 Gustav Aulén, *Christus Victor: An Historical Study of the Three Main Types of the Idea of the Atonement* (New York: MacMillan, 1969), 81.

3 For a convenient introduction to the problem, see Brevard Childs, *Introduction to the Old Testament as Scripture* (Philadelphia: Fortress, 1979), 311–38, and Marvin Sweeney, *The Prophetic Literature* (Nashville, Tenn.: Abingdon, 2005), 45–84.

4 It should be noted here that parts of Isa 1–39 are also thought to derive from a later hand.

5 Num 4:3, 23, 30, 35, 39, 43; 8:24, 25.

6 Gerhard von Rad, "*Kiplayim* in Jes 40,2 = Äquivalent?" *ZAW* 79 (1967): 80–82. For this usage of *mishneh*, see Deut 15:18.

7 Jan Koole, *Isaiah, part 3, volume 1, Isaiah 40–48* (HCOT: Kampen: Kok Pharos, 1997), 55.

8 Joseph Blenkinsopp, *Isaiah 40–55* (AB 19A; New York: Doubleday, 2000), 180.

9 *Sifre*, 32. L. Finkelstein, ed., *Siphre ad Deuteronomium* (New York: Jewish Theological Seminary, 1969), 57. The full text of R. Nehemiah's argument can be found at the end of this chapter.

10 See Sommer's annotations to Isa in *The Jewish Study Bible, JPS Tanakh*, ed. A. Berlin, M. Brettler, and M. Fishbane (New York: Oxford University Press, 1999), 885.

11 Elisha is able to provide the funds for the widow by recourse to a miracle: "2. Elisha said to her, 'What can I do for you? Tell me, what have you in the house?' She replied, 'Your maidservant has nothing at all in the house, except a jug of oil.' 3. 'Go,' he said, 'and borrow vessels outside, from all your neighbors, empty vessels, as many as you can. 4. Then go in and shut the door behind you and your children, and pour [oil] into all those vessels, removing each one as it is filled.' 5. She went away and shut the door behind her and her children. They kept bringing [vessels] to her and she kept pouring. 6. When the vessels were full, she said to her son, 'Bring me another vessel.' He answered her, 'There are no more vessels'; and the oil stopped. 7. She came and told the man of God, and he said, 'Go sell the oil and pay your debt, and you and your children can live on the rest'" (II Kings 4:1–7).

12 The careful reader will be aware of a subtle tension here. Although Isa 50:1 makes it clear that God is not Israel's creditor, a different picture seems to emerge from Isa 40:2 ("[the debt owed for] her iniquity has been satisfied; For she has received at the hand of the LORD double for all her sins."). There, Israel is said to have paid double for the debt of her sins. But to whom did she make this payment? The text seems to assume that the recipient of this payment was none other than the God of Israel! The tension between these two texts is unresolved in this book. In Chaps. 8 and 12 we shall see how Christian thinkers wrestled with the problem.

13 The verbal form in Isaiah is actually *nirṣâh* in the *niphal* conjugation, but I have put everything in the basic root form to make the argument clearer to the non-Hebrew reader.

14 *BDB*, for example, lists one of the standard meanings of the G stem as "to accept" (hence God "accepts" a sacrifice). This, in turn, leads to the meaning "to make acceptable," in the sense of "to pay off a debt" (so Lev 26:34 and 43). As will be seen below, this line of development is nearly correct, but it does not provide a means of understanding Isa 40:2. How is the "acceptance" of a sin related to "forgiveness"? *HALOT*, on the other hand, goes in a completely different direction and posits a second root meaning: "to pay off [a debt]."

15 The premodern commentators can be found in any *Miqrāôt Gedôlôt*. For the others, see Samuel R. Driver, *The Book of Leviticus in Hebrew* (Leipzig: Hinrichs, 1894), 102; Karl Elliger, *Leviticus* (HAT 4; Tübingen: Mohr, 1966), 378; S. Luzzato, *Commentary to the Pentateuch* (Tel Aviv: Dvir, 1965), at Lev 26:34, J. Milgrom, *Leviticus 23–27* (AB 3B; New York: Doubleday, 2000), 2323–24.

16 Here we can include *HALOT* and Tur-Sinai's corrections that have been incorporated into modern reprints of E. Ben-Yehuda's monumental dictionary, *Millon Ha-Lashon Ha-Ivrit*, 8 vols. (New York: Thomas Yoseloff, 1960), 6702–3.

17 So important is the notion of making such a sacrifice acceptable to God that a long set of criteria are enumerated later in the book: "And when a man offers, from the herd or the flock, a sacrifice of well-being to the LORD for an explicit vow or as a freewill offering, it must, to *be acceptable*, be without blemish, there must be no defect in it. 22. Anything blind, or injured, or maimed . . . you shall not offer to the LORD; you shall not put any of them on the altar as offerings by fire to the LORD. 23. You may, however, present as a freewill offering an ox or a sheep with a limb extended or contracted;

but it will not *be accepted* as a vow. 24. You shall not offer to the Lord anything with its testes bruised, or crushed . . . 25. nor shall you accept such [animals] from a foreigner for offering as food for your God . . . . They shall not *be accepted* in your favor. 26. The Lord spoke to Moses, saying: 27. When an ox or a sheep, or a goat is born, it shall stay seven days with its mother, and from the eighth day on it shall *be acceptable* as an offering by fire to the Lord. . . . 29. When you sacrifice a thanksgiving offering to the Lord, sacrifice it so that it may *be acceptable* in your favor. 30. It shall be eaten on the same day; you shall not leave any of it until morning; I am the Lord" (Lev 22:21–30).

18 This idiom occurs some thirteen times in the Bible, most of them in Ps (22:26, 50:14, 56:13, 61:9, 65:2, 66:13, 116:14,18).

19 One donated only the fat to the deity, whereas the priests received a portion of the thigh and breast (see Lev 7:28–34).

20 This sort of usage is common in Ps; see 50:14, 56:13, 61:9, 65:2, 66:13, 76:12, and 116:14, 18.

21 The word originated in Anglo-Norman and Old French, from whence it came into German. For the importance of quittance clauses, see Yochanan Muffs, *Studies in the Aramaic Legal Papyri from Elephantine* (Leiden: Brill, 1969). The term in question is an Aramaic phrase, "my heart is satisfied" *(tyb lbby)*, and its Akkadian cognate *(libbāšu ṭāb)*. Raymond Westbrook has taken issue with some of the argumentation of Muffs ("The Phrase 'His Heart Is Satisfied' in Ancient Near Eastern Legal Sources," *JAOS* 111 (1991): 219–24), but it does not alter materially what we wish to do here.

22 Muffs, *Studies,* 44.

23 Milgrom, *Leviticus 1–16* (AB 3; New York: Doubleday, 1991), 254–58.

24 For the source of this text see n. 9, above. It should be noted that because R. Nehemiah assumes that all sins are to be construed as debts, even biblical sacrifices for sin pay off debts. This was not, however, the way atonement sacrifices were conceived of in the Bible.

25 *BDB,* 953.

26 *HALOT,* 1280–82. See esp. the remarks on the top left column of p. 1282: "While it may be possible to draw [the conclusion that there are two roots] from biblical Hebrew alone, M[ishnaic] Hebrew, J[ewish] Aramaic, as well as Akk[adian] and O[ld] S[outh] Ar[abic] suggest that two homonymous roots should be recognized. In M[ishnaic] Hebrew [this meaning appears in the causative stem]: 1. to count out, carry forward a balance . . . and 2. to expiate, atone."

27 Blenkinsopp, *Isaiah 40–55,* 181.

CHAPTER 5 **Ancient Creditors, Bound Laborers, and the Sanctity of the Land**

1 On the basis of its distinctive vocabulary and theology, Lev 17-26 can be distinguished from the earlier portion of the book. Whereas chapters 1-16 (Priestly School) take care for the purity of temple and priest, 17-26 demonstrate a strong interest in the holiness of the people and the purity of the land. For an account of why the Holiness Code should be seen as later than the Priestly School, see the groundbreaking work of Israel Knohl, *Sanctuary of Silence* (Minneapolis: Fortress, 1995). For an outstanding account of the theology of the Holiness Code, see Jan Joosten, *People and Land in the Holiness*

Code: An Exegetical Study of the Ideational Framework of the Law in Leviticus 17–26 (New York: Brill, 1996).

2 The English verb *redeem* comes from the Latin *redimo,* "to buy back." God becomes the "redeemer" of Israel in biblical thought because as this people's near kinsman he is obligated to rescue her when she is in distress.

3 Another possibility, suggested to me by Baruch Schwartz (orally), is that the impoverished person does not sell his land but, rather, enters the household of a near relation as a dependent.

4 Jacob Milgrom, *Leviticus 23–27* (AB 3B; New York: Doubleday, 2000), 2208.

5 I have slightly altered the NJPS translation.

6 The idea that God is issuing warnings in this chapter rather than a set of punishments was first observed by Baruch Schwartz; see his annotations to Lev 26 in the *Jewish Study Bible* (New York: Oxford University Press, 2003), 273–277. I differ with him on one crucial point. Whereas he sees all the divine interventions as warnings, including the last one, I understand the logic to be four warnings and then a final punishment. This is partly due to the fact that Schwartz does not think that the chapter has undergone any significant redactional activity. As a result the return of Israel to her God is part of the original composition. On this view the destruction and exile are just like the other warnings—their function is to bring about the eventual turning of Israel.

7 The reconstruction of the various stages of redaction for this chapter is a complex business. The most intricate reconstruction is that of Karl Elliger (*Leviticus,* [Handbuch zum alten Testament; Tübingen: Mohr, 1966]). The simplest is that of H. L. Ginsberg, *The Israelian Heritage of Judaism* (New York: Jewish Theological Seminary, 1982), 80–81. I prefer the perspective of Ginsberg because it is far less speculative than Elliger's and is grounded in good textual parallels found elsewhere in the Bible. According to Ginsberg, the original layer of the final punishment consisted of vv. 27–33a and 37b–38. To this original layer was added the remainder of the chapter, which spoke to the presence of Israel in exile, the repayment of the debt that was owed, and God's covenantal obligation to restore his people (vv. 33b–37a, 39–45). It should be noted that Ginsberg further subdivides this secondary layer into two levels, though that part of his argument is not important for our purposes.

8 Ginsberg, *Israelian Heritage of Judaism,* 80.

9 There are other texts that follow this pattern as well. E.g., one thinks of the ten plagues that were sent upon Egypt (Exod 7–12). After each plague God provided respite so that the Egyptians could reconsider their ways and comply with the divine command to release Israel. At the conclusion of that sequence, when the series of escalating warnings fails to persuade Pharaoh, God takes drastic measures and enters the fray of human history. After the slaying of the firstborn sons of Egypt, Pharaoh is moved to contrition and tells Moses that he and his compatriots may set out on their journey. But no sooner has Israel embarked on her path than Pharaoh changes his mind and puts the chosen nation to flight (Exod 14:5–9). God, however, fights alongside the Israelites, and the end result is the destruction of Pharaoh and his mighty host in the waters of the Sea of Reeds (14:10–30). In this sequence we see a set of warnings give way to the final demise of a notable adversary. It should be noted, however, that this idea of warning Pharaoh with the hope that he and his subjects will relent is found only in the J version of the tradition; the P version entertains no such idea (my thanks to Baruch Schwartz for pointing this out to me).

10 The same sort of theological sensibility can be found in rabbinic thinking as well. The sages who resided in the land of Israel radically repunctuated the troublesome verse in Amos 5:2, which states: "She has fallen and will not rise again, the virgin of Israel," so that it would read: "She has fallen and will [fall] no more; rise, O Virgin Israel!" This particular midrash can be found in *BT Berachot* 4b. See the fine discussion of it in James Kugel's "Two Introductions to Midrash," *Prooftexts* 3 (1983): 131–55.

11 Let me summarize my opinion about the redactional development of this chapter. I presume that the original core of the composition consisted of vv. 27b–33a, 37b–38 and would have read as follows: "But if, despite this, you disobey Me and remain hostile to Me, I will act against you in wrathful hostility: I, for My part, will discipline you sevenfold for your sins. You shall eat the flesh of your sons and the flesh of your daughters. I will destroy your cult places and cut down your incense stands, and I will heap your carcasses upon your lifeless fetishes. I will spurn you. I will lay your cities in ruin and make your sanctuaries desolate, and I will not savor your pleasing odors. I will make the land desolate, so that your enemies who settle in it shall be appalled by it. And you I will scatter among the nations, and I will unsheath the sword against you. You shall not be able to stand your ground before your enemies, but shall perish among the nations; and the land of your enemies shall consume you." The secondary additions consisted of 33b–37a and 39–45.

12 I have adjusted the translation.

13 On the relationship between the Sabbath and divine ownership, see the brilliant article of M. Tsevat, "The Basic Meaning of the Biblical Sabbath," *ZAW* 84 (1972): 447–59.

14 This linguistic datum provides yet another argument for why this portion of Lev 26 is a secondary addition. As Ginsberg argued, the original form of the chapter probably took shape in the pre-exilic period, when the warnings were precisely that—warnings of the punishment that was to come should Israel prove recalcitrant in her disobedience. But after the destruction wrought by the invading Babylonian armies in 587 BCE, the original form of Lev 26 was expanded so that the final punishment of exile was transformed into a means for Israel and her land to repay the debts they owed. Milgrom, who wants to see the section on Israel's repayment of debt in Lev 26 as pre-exilic argues that II Isa (from the exilic period) has borrowed an image from this earlier source (i.e., Lev 26). See Milgrom, *Leviticus 23–27*, 2333. As I argued in Chaps. 2 and 3, however, this idiom was not borrowed by successive writers; rather, it reflects an innovation of the exilic and post-exilic period that follows from the introduction of a new metaphor into the Hebrew language. It must have been a commonly available idiom to all writers in this period.

15 Milgrom, *Leviticus 23–27*, 2323.

16 See Schwartz's annotations to Lev 19 in the *Jewish Study Bible*, 252.

17 As we noted at the beginning of this chapter, it could also be considered in its most pristine and archaic form as a summary of the laws of the Holiness Code alone (Lev 17–26).

18 The best place to see this illustrated is in the commentary of Rashi (eleventh-century France) on these verses. His commentary is not original; he is making use of earlier rabbinic sources.

19 The reference to "at Mount Sinai" could also prove to be logically confusing. If the reference is to what Moses heard on the mountain, the text is out of chronological

order. Moses heard the instructions about how to build the Tabernacle only on Mt. Sinai (Exod 25–31); the rest of the commandments he heard within the Tabernacle. On the other hand, some have noted that the preposition "at" is different from "upon" and that the reference to "at Mount Sinai" is simply another way of referring to the Tabernacle, which was initially set up beside that holy mountain. However one would wish to solve the problem, it is still unusual that in precisely this location the writer has used this odd locution twice to bracket the material within chaps. 25–26.

20 See Milgrom, *Leviticus 23–27,* for a number of explanations as to why this narrative was thought to have been revealed at Mt. Sinai. B. Schwartz (*The Jewish Study Bible,* 269) argues that the Hebrew phrase *be-har sinay* means "at (but not on) Mt. Sinai." In other words it is simply a reference to the regular spot of revelation, the Tabernacle, which stood beside Mt. Sinai. Although this is eminently possible and reasonable, it does not explain why such a locution is used in this specific portion of Lev to identify the location of the Tabernacle.

21 See the article by B. Schwartz on this subject: "Reexamining the Fate of the 'Canaanites' in the Torah Traditions," in Ch. Cohen et al., eds., *Sefer Moshe: The Moshe Weinfeld Jubilee Volume* (Winona Lake, Ind.: Eisenbrauns, 2004), 151–70.

22 Milgrom, *Leviticus 23-27,* 2278; see, as well, his discussion of the keeping of the Sabbath in his commentary on Lev 23:1–3 (1951–64)

23 See the comments of William Holladay, *Jeremiah 1* (Hermeneia; Philadelphia: Fortress, 1986), 509–11, esp. his remark on 511. In commenting on the need to keep the Sabbath as articulated in Jer 17:19–27, he writes: "The survival of the community depends upon the observance of the Sabbath. It is not, we conclude, a word from [Jeremiah], but it is a word that helped to shape the outlook of the post-exilic community."

24 With respect to Isa 56:2, Joseph Blenkinsopp writes (*Isaiah 56–66* [AB 19B; New York: Doubleday, 2003], 135): "It will seem somewhat surprising that the quite general injunction to avoid evildoing is linked with the very specific point of Sabbath observance. . . . [By doing this], the passage betrays affinity with the perspective of the priest scribes who authored the Priestly History in the Hexateuch."

25 See Tanhuma (Buber) to Lev 25.

26 Milgrom, *Leviticus 23-27,* 2149–51; he repeats his argument (as well as the midrash!) on 2274–75.

CHAPTER 6 Lengthening the Term of Debt

1 On this point, see the seminal article of Michael Knibb, "The Exile in the Literature of the Intertestamental Period," *Heythrop Journal* 17 (1976): 253–72.

2 This is most likely not from the prophet himself but, rather, from a later (probably Deuteronomic) editorial hand. But to avoid awkward circumlocutions, I shall refer to texts from the book of Jer as coming from Jeremiah.

3 See the most recent discussion of the problem by Israel Ephal, "The Conceptual Timing of Salvation in the Restoration Period [in Hebrew], *Tarbiz* 76 (2007): 5–16.

4 There need be no contradiction between the suggestion of Ephal and the innerbiblical explanation that seventy years is the life span of the individual. They could both be true. Indeed, perhaps the biblical author was drawn to the ancient Near Eastern motif because it fit so well with this innerbiblical idea.

5 Michael Fishbane, *Biblical Interpretation in Ancient Israel* (New York: Oxford University Press, 1985), 479–85, esp. 481.

6 I have altered the NJPS translation so that the similarities found in the original Hebrew will be more obvious to the reader.

7 This is a significant text for a number of reasons, perhaps the most important being that it shows the growing importance of sacred texts in the exilic and post-exilic periods. To explain what has happened in this text from Chron we must assume that the writer has in front of him the books of both Lev and Jer. He must hold both these works as sufficiently sacred to require some means of correlation between their respective prophecies. In other words, for the writer of Chron (often called "the Chronicler") both Lev and Jer must have divine authority; the question, then, is how are they related to one another? The Chronicler provides a window into how an ancient Jewish scribe would interpret scripture.

8 See R. Albertz, *Israel in Exile: The History and Literature of the Sixth Century B.C.E.* (Atlanta: Society of Biblical Literature, 2003), for a typology of how the exile was viewed by various writers.

9 See the article of Bradley Gregory, "The Postexilic Exile in Third Isaiah: Isaiah 61: 1–3 in Light of Second Temple Hermeneutics," *JBL* 126 (2007): 475–96.

10 See Knibb, "Exile in the Literature of the Intertestamental Period."

11 It should be noted that according to the book of Kings, the cause of the exile was put in the lap of Manasseh (II Kings 21), a king who ruled several generations prior to the tragic event itself. In Chron, however, this explanation was rejected (see its account of Manasseh's reign and apostasy in II Chron 33) in favor of the notion that blame should be put on the Zedekiah and his generation, the last king of Judea (II Chron 36:11–21).

12 As Daniel puts the matter, it is not seventy years that have been forecast but "seventy weeks [of years]" (9:24). That is, Jeremiah was not thinking of a simple calendrical unit of seventy consecutive years but of seventy individual sabbatical years that would need to be made up. Since the word "seventy" and the word "weeks" look identical in the consonantal text of the Hebrew, it took only a slight tug on the imagination to convert seventy years into seventy weeks of years.

13 John Collins, *Daniel* (Hermeneia; Minneapolis: Fortress, 1993), 354.

14 Adele Berlin, *Lamentations* (OTL; Louisville, Ky.: Westminster John Knox, 2002), 114.

15 There are some textual problems in these two verses. The solution to 8:23 is not complicated and is followed by nearly everyone. Whereas the Hebrew text has been vocalized to read "with the bringing to completion of the sinners," most would revocalize this to read "when their sins have been completed." The difference is whether we read *hap-pōšĕ'îm* ("the sinners") or *hap-pĕšā'îm* ("the sins"). In 9:24 the Hebrew consonantal text reads "to seal the sins," but it has been vocalized so as to read "to bring the sins to completion." Almost all commentators follow the vocalization.

16 For the text, see 4Q389, col. 2, frag. 9: 4–6. For the original publication, see *DJD* 30, 228. I have emended the second usage of the root *šālēm*. The text reads *bšlm 'wnm*, but I would suggest *bšlm 'wnm*. It is common in this period for an intervocalic *heh* to drop out.

17 In the *piel* conjugation rather than the *hiphil*, as we find in the Apocryphon of Jeremiah. I might add at this point that the various terms whose root meaning is "to bring [something] to completion" are used only to mark the "forgiveness of sins" in late biblical and Mishnaic Hebrew. Significantly, they are used regularly in these later dialects for precisely this purpose. This is as good an indicator as any that these words refer to

the completion of a payment due on a sin, for that is the predominant metaphor of this period. And besides, how else would one explain the usage of "completion" to mean "forgiveness"?

18 See Gary Anderson, "Two Notes on Measuring Character and Sin at Qumran," in E. Chazon, D. Satran, and R. Clements, eds., *Things Revealed: Studies in Early Jewish and Christian Literature in Honor of Michael Stone* (Leiden: Brill, 2004), 141–48. The question of scales as a source of rich metaphors is in need of a careful investigation.

19 New Testament commentators generally tied this verse to the notion of wages owed a soldier. So Joseph Fitzmyer (*Romans* [AB 33; New York: Doubleday, 1993], 452) writes: "Paul reverts to a military figure and uses *opsōnion* 'ration (money),' paid to a soldier. Underlying the figure is the idea of regularly recurring payment. The more one serves sin, the more pay in the form of death one earns. Such 'wages' are paid out as death to those who serve sin." But I would concur with Fredrick Danker in his revision of *A Greek-English Lexicon of the New Testament and Other Early Christian Literature* (Chicago: University of Chicago Press, 2000), 747, where he notes that the use of *opsōnion* in Romans 6 is distant from the military scene and better understood in the generic sense of "reward, compensation." If he is correct, then the overlap with the rabbinic term *śākār* is almost exact: what is owed for a life of sin is death.

20 See *m. Avot 3.17*: "R. Akiba used to say: 'All is given against a pledge, and the net is cast over all living; the shop stands open and the shopkeeper gives credit and the account-book lies open and the hand writes and every one that wishes to borrow let him come and borrow; but the collectors go their round continually every day and exact payment of men with their consent or without their consent.'" Jonathan Schofer, *The Making of a Sage: A Study in Rabbinic Ethics* (Madison, Wis.: University of Wisconsin Press, 2005) provides an admirable summary: "The passage employs two powerful metaphors to describe God: a storekeeper with a ledger and a judge in charge of collectors. God sells goods on credit, implying that physical and material benefits come with an account, and humans have to pay for them through right action. For those in debt God acts as a judge who decrees judgment and sends out collectors to mete out punishment." Of course the two metaphors are not independent. The action of the judge to initiate collection stems from a form of "fiscal" malfeasance.

21 The translation is taken from Jonathan Goldstein, *II Maccabees* (AB 41A; New York: Doubleday, 1983), 269.

22 See "Is *Divrei ha-Meorot* a Sectarian Prayer?," in Devorah Dimant, ed., *The Dead Sea Scrolls: Forty Years of Research* (Leiden: Brill, 1992), 3–17, and "Prayers from Qumran and Their Historical Implications," *DSD* 1 (1994): 265–84, esp. 271–73.

23 The text I have cited from *Divre Ha-Me'orot* is found in 4Q504, frag. 1-2, col. 6:4-8. For a much fuller discussion of this passage, see my article "From Israel's Burden to Israel's Debt: Towards a Theology of Sin in Biblical and Second Temple Sources," in E. Chazon et al., eds., *Reworking the Bible: Apocryphal and Related Texts at Qumran* (Leiden: Brill, 2005), 26–29.

24 The reference to the *Merchant of Venice* is deliberate in that the entire play depends on the image of a bond to make a theological point about the relationship of justice to mercy. Tragically, the play suffers greatly from setting this theme within an anti-Semitic context.

CHAPTER 7 Loans and the Rabbinic Sages

Epigraphs: Jerusalem Talmud *Peah* 5a; Thomas Aquinas, *Summa Theologica I*, q. 21, a. 3.

1 Scholars vary in their opinions as to how fluent Jesus was in the various languages with which he was familiar (Aramaic, Hebrew, and Greek). Most New Testament scholars assume that Aramaic was his mother tongue and that Hebrew was a secondary language. For a good survey of such issues, see Joseph Fitzmyer's classic essay "The Languages of Palestine in the First Century AD," which has been reprinted in Stanley E. Porter, ed., *The Language of the New Testament: Classic Essays* (JSNTSS 60; Sheffield, Eng.: Sheffield Academic Press, 1991), 126–62. Although he sides with the view that Aramaic was probably the mother tongue of Jesus, he does concede that there is good evidence for Hebrew as well. Part of the problem is that the best scholarship on the Hebrew of the late Second Temple period is being done at the Hebrew University and is written in modern Hebrew. Only a handful of New Testament scholars could follow this discussion, and I know of none who do. As a result, the case being made for Hebrew as a living language in the first and second centuries CE has gone unnoticed.

2 See my discussion in Chap. 3.

3 Eliezer Diamond, *Holy Men and Hunger Artists: Fasting and Asceticism in Rabbinic Culture* (New York: Oxford University Press, 2004), 67.

4 See the entry "*ṭuppum*" in the *CAD* for numerous examples of how the term functioned.

5 Perhaps not accidentally, the term for such a note, *šṭar,* was a loan word from Akkadian, the language of classical Mesopotamia. In Akkadian, however, the verb *saṭāru* meant simply "to write," whereas the noun *šṭar,* which came into both Hebrew and Aramaic, referred to a specific form of writing, namely, a legally binding document.

6 Interest was, of course, not allowed on loans that were made between Jews. If a loan was not subject to interest, it was common to demand that something be put up as a pledge that the loan would be paid in the future. On the matter of securing a loan in the Bible, see the excellent discussion of Isac Seeligmann, "Darlehen, Bürgschaft und Zins in Recht und Gedankenwelt der Hebräischen Bibel," in *Gesammelte Studien zur Hebräischen Bibel* (FAT 41; Tübingen: Mohr Siebeck, 2004), 319–48.

7 For the details, see Josephus, *Jewish War* 2.247. For a good discussion of the problem of personal indebtedness in this period, see Martin Goodman, *The Ruling Class of Judaea: The Origins of the Jewish Revolt Against Rome, A.D. 66–70* (Cambridge: Cambridge University Press, 1987), 57–58; and "The First Jewish Revolt: Social Conflict and the Problem of Debt," *JJS* 33 (1982): 417–27.

8 *Gen Rab* 23:4.

9 Ibid. 85:2. I have used the edition of J. Theodor, with corrections and additions by Ch. Albeck (Jerusalem: Wahrmann, 1965), 2:1033.

10 The translation is mine.

11 *Gen Rab* 85:2.

12 My reading of this portion of the Joseph story depends on the brilliant discussion of J. Levenson in *The Death and Resurrection of the Beloved Son* (New Haven: Yale University Press, 1993).

13 *Gen Rab* 82:13

14 Theodor and Albeck, *Bereshit Rabba*, 2:992. See the note to line 4.

15 Just after God tells Abraham, "I am the LORD who brought you out from Ur of the Chaldeans to assign this land to you as a possession," Abraham responds, "O LORD God, how shall I know that I am to possess it?" (Gen 15:7–8). The announcement God makes ("I am the LORD who brought you out from Ur of the Chaldeans") clearly foreshadows the words God will use when he brings Israel to Sinai and proceeds to give Israel the Torah ("I am the LORD who brought you out of the land of Egypt" [Exod 20:2]). But whereas Israel will respond unanimously and with alacrity: "We will do and we will hear" (Exod 24:7), Abraham expresses more than a modicum of doubt. Another possibility is that Abraham's offspring will be punished as a result of his urging his wife to lie about her marital status in Gen 12:11–13 (so was proposed by the medieval Jewish commentator Nachmanides).

16 Moshe Mirkin, ed., *Midrash Rabbah: Be-Midbar Rabbah* (Tel Aviv: Yavneh, 1987), 2:231–32.

17 Hermann Strack and Paul Billerbeck, *Kommentar zum neuen Testament aus Talmud und Midrasch,* 6 vols. (Munich: Beck, 1924–61).

18 E. P. Sanders, *Paul and Palestinian Judaism: A Comparison of Patterns of Religion* (Philadelphia: Fortress, 1977).

19 Ibid., 42–43.

20 Ibid., 43.

21 It is true that the image of a set of scales does conjure the notion of weight—for it is the weight placed on the pan that will determine what the price of a certain set of goods will be. But here the idea of weight has been fully subsumed into a commercial context. What is being weighed are not the sins of the individual but the bonds that those sins have created. It should be recalled that sin has a certain "thing-ness." In the First Temple period the "thing" that is created at point of sin is a weight that is loaded upon one's shoulders. That weight could be so heavy that one would have to load it upon carts into order to transport it. In the Second Temple period, the picture is wholly transformed: a bond is drawn up that must be repaid. In this particular midrash it is the bonds that are put in the pan of a set of scales; this is very different from the picture one finds in First Temple texts.

22 See the examples found in Peter Shäfer, *Rivalität zwischen Engeln und Menschen: Untersuchungen zur rabbinischen Engelvorstellung* (Berlin: de Gruyter, 1975).

CHAPTER 8 **Early Christian Thinking on the Atonement**

1 See my discussion of this in Chap. 3.

2 For an outstanding introduction to the thought of St. Ephrem, see Sebastian Brock, *The Luminous Eye: The Spiritual World Vision of Saint Ephrem the Syrian,* Cistercian Studies Series, 124 (Kalamazoo, Mich.: Cistercian, 1985).

3 The three mentions I have found (there may be more) are "Homily on Our Lord," in Joseph Amar and Ed Matthews, trans., *St. Ephrem the Syrian: Selected Prose Works* (FC 91; Washington, D.C.: Catholic University of America, 1994), sect.16, pp. 290–91; *Carmina Nisibena* 60:1–8 (for the original Syriac, see Edmund Beck ed., *Des Heiligen Ephraem des Syrers: Carmina Nisibena* (CSCO 240; Louvain, 1963); and his commentary on the Diatessaron, in Carmel McCarthy, *Saint Ephrem's Commentary on Tatian's Diatessaron* (JSSSuppl 2; Oxford: Oxford University Press, 1993), pars. 8–10, pp. 170–71.

4 One can compare the translation of Amar and Matthews, *St. Ephrem the Syrian*, 290–91. I have translated directly from the Syriac; see E. Beck, ed., *Des Heiligen Ephraem des Syrers: Sermo de Domino Nostro* (CSCO 270/71: Louvain, 1966).

5 The history of the exegesis of this verse remains to be written. For now see the work of Eugene Best, *An Historical Study of the Exegesis of Colossians 2:14* (Rome: Pontificia Universitas Gregorian, 1956).

6 The Jewish thinker Philo of Alexandria used this term in precisely this way to refer to the generous actions of creditors toward their debtors when they canceled a loan *(ta daneia)* in the seventh, or better, sabbatical year *(Spec. Leg.* 2.39). Philo has in mind the law found in Deut 15:2, which requires that every seven years one must waive or release *(aphiemi;* the same term as in the Our Father) one's rights to collect on debts that are owed. The Greek translation of the Hebrew original reads: "You shall *release (aphiemi)* every debt which your neighbor owes you *(ophelei,* the same root as "debts" in the Our Father) and not seek payment of it from your brother. For (this year) is called by the Lord, your God, the (year of) *release (aphesis).*" In Philo's summary of the law he has simply replaced the more conventional word for release—*aphiemi*—with a less common variant, *charizo.*

7 See the classic work of Gustav A. Deissmann, *Light from the Ancient East: The New Testament Illustrated by Recently Discovered Texts of the Graeco-Roman World* (New York: George H. Doran, 1927).

8 Wesley Carr, *Angels and Principalities* (Cambridge: Cambridge University Press, 1981), 52–66, is well aware of the problem and tries a creative—but in my view faulty—solution to the problem.

9 It should be said that as soon as a sin was understood to be a debt *(ḥôb)* this would naturally have been associated with the legal document *(šṭar)* upon which the debt was drawn up. The linkage between *ḥôb* and *šṭar* must have been quite early.

10 The manner in which the bond works in this book is not altogether clear. Joseph Fitzmyer, in *Tobit* (New York: de Gruyter, 2003), 186, attempts to solve the puzzle thus: "The idea seems to be that there were two bonds, one from Tobit and one from Gabael, which were both divided in two. Apparently, Tobit retained two parts, one that matched the half of the bond that Gabael retained, and the other that matched the half of one left with the money. These two halves are what Tobias would carry with him on his journey to Rages so that he could match them with the half that Gabael retained and the half that was with the money. The two halves constituted in effect one bond; hence Tobit refers to it as 'one.'"

11 The translation comes from the Douay-Reims version of the Vulgate.

12 For a discussion of the Aramaic form of the book that Jerome claims to have used, see Fitzmyer, *Tobit,* 19–21, and the dissertation of his student Vincent T. M. Skemp, *The Vulgate of Tobit Compared with Other Ancient Witnesses* (SBLDS 180; Atlanta, Ga.: Society of Biblical Literature, 2000).

13 We will discuss this theme at length in Chap. 10. For now, see the discussion of Seeligmann, "Darlehen, Bürgschaft und Zins in Recht und Gedankenwelt der Hebräischen Bibel," in *Gesammelte Studien zur Hebräischen Bibel* (FAT 41; Tübingen: Mohr Siebeck, 2004), 319–48.

14 Although this is most likely not the original sense of the book, it has the benefit of turning this financial exchange into a no-interest loan which was thought to be, in

some Jewish circles, the kindest way to convey money to the needy. For an interest-free loan protected the dignity of the recipient by presuming that he would have the means to repay in the future.

15 Although modern scholars suspect that Paul did not write Colossians, early Christian readers had no such problems. As Harry Gamble has argued in his *Books and Readers in the Early Church: A History of Early Christian Texts* (New Haven: Yale University Press, 1995), 98–100, the circulation of letters in antiquity was different from that of our own day. From a very early date Paul's letters began to circulate to a wider set of communities than their original addressees might imply (to the Romans or Corinthians, for example). As these letters took on this larger role, the communities themselves assumed an active part in the copying, editing, and distribution of them. Paul was no longer the sole proprietor of them. This made it very easy and natural for other individuals to edit the existing correspondence and even write new letters in the name of Paul. This was not an act of forgery, as we might conceive the matter, but simply an extension of the authoritative voice of Paul in a new but related direction. It is the supposition of some that this collection of Pauline letters was in circulation even in Paul's day and that he himself may have contributed to the literary process that would have made such an anthology possible. If he was involved in the editorial process, he would have been aware that the letters could be edited on site, and he may have already designated a person whom he trusted to oversee the process. However that might be, from an extremely ancient period, the letters of Paul were interpreted as a coherent theological expression of the Christian faith.

16 See Deissmann, *Light from the Ancient East.*

17 St. Irenaeus, *Against Heresies,* bk. 5:17.

18 Paul Bedjan, ed., *Homiliae selectae Mar-Jacobi Sarugensis* (Paris, 1905), 1:225. All Syriac translations in this chapter are my own.

19 Gustav Aulén, *Christus Victor: An Historical Study of the Three Main Types of the Idea of the Atonement* (New York: Macmillan, 1951).

20 For the text of Narsai's "Homily for the Great Sunday of the Resurrection," see Frederick McLeod, "Narsai's Metrical Homilies on the Nativity, Epiphany, Passion, Resurrection and Ascension," in *Patrologia Orientalis* 40 (1979): 136–61.

21 See the important article by Veselin Kesich, "The Antiochenes and the Temptation Story," *Studia Patristica* 7 (1966): 496–502, and the following two monographs: Klaus-Peter Köppen, *Die Auslegung der Versuchungsgeschichte unter besonderer Berücksichtigung der Alten Kirche: Ein Beitrag zur Geschichte der Schriftauslegung* (BGBE 4; Tübingen: Mohr-Siebeck, 1961), and Martin Steiner, *La tentation de Jésus dans l'interprétation patristique de Saint Justin à Origène* (EtB; Paris: Gabalda, 1962).

22 Most commentators believe that this moment takes place during the passion and cite Luke 22:3 in support of this: "Then Satan entered into Judas, called Iscariot, who was one of the twelve." H. Conzelmann goes the furthest here when he asserts that the interval between the temptations and the passion was a "Satan-free period." See his *Theology of St. Luke* (Philadelphia: Fortress, 1961), 16, 27–29, 80–81.

23 This position is also followed by some modern commentators. See, most recently, Joel Marcus, *Mark 1–8* (AB 27; New York: Doubleday, 2000) 169–171.

24 All citations from Narsai are from his "Homily for the Great Sunday of the Resurrection" and are cited according to the line numbers that F. McLeod provided in his edi-

tion (see n. 20, above). In this section there appears to be a typographical error in the Syriac text. In order to read "insatiable," I had to restore an initial *yod* to yield the form yā‛nâ.

25 In legal contracts from the ancient world it was important to establish that the contracting parties entered the agreement by their own free choice. If this was not the case, the contract could be contested in court at a later date. On this point see Yochanan Muffs, *Studies in the Aramaic Legal Papyri from Elephantine* (Leiden: Brill, reprint, 2003), 128–41. In our text, Satan makes it clear to Christ that Adam and Eve had freely chosen to sign this bond, making it all the harder to dissolve it.

26 This point is made later on, see ll. 291–92: "That wrongful bond he brought forth and demonstrated [legally] / that it was not sealed with a signature before proper witnesses."

27 See ll. 295–96: "And since I have conquered *(z-k-y)* and the hater of our race has been defeated *(ḥāb)* / I will allow my companions to share in the greatness of my victory." It is worth noting that in Syriac *ḥāb* does not always refer to "debt". Its most basic meaning is "to lose" from which comes the meaning "to owe" since those who lose in court or in battle have to pay some sort of penalty (a form of punishment, or the imposition of tribute).

28 In Syriac thought the mark of the fall was the change from an angelic constitution to a mortal human body. Here the lesions on the flesh indicate that onset of the mortal state. See the classic essay of Sebastian Brock, "Clothing Metaphors as a Means of Theological Expression in Syriac Tradition," in M. Schmidt and C. Geyer, eds., *Typus, Symbol, Allegorie bei den östlichen Vätern und ihren Parallelen im Mittelalter* (Regensburg: Friedrich Pustet, 1982), 11–37, as well as Gary A. Anderson, "Garments of Skin in Apocryphal Narrative and Biblical Commentary," in J. Kugel, ed., *Studies in Ancient Midrash* (Cambridge, Mass.: Harvard University Press, 2001), 101–43.

29 This selection is from the "Homily on Fasting." The Syriac text was edited by Frédéric Rilliet, "Jacques des Saroug: Six Homélies Festales en Prose," *Patrologia Orientalis* 43 (1986): 568, 570.

30 See also Epistle to the Heb 1:14, 6:12,17, and Rom 8:17. Matt 21:33–44 is probably also relevant.

31 From the "Homily on Good Friday." For the Syriac, see *Jacques des Saroug*, 612.

32 *Jacques des Saroug*, 626, 628.

33 Robert Jenson, *Systematic Theology*, vol. 1: *The Triune God* (New York: Oxford University Press, 1997): "It is one of the more remarkable and remarked-upon aspects of theological history that no theory of atonement has ever been universally accepted. By now, this phenomenon is itself among the things that a proposed theory of atonement must explain" (187).

34 "On the Incarnation," par. 6. For the text, see E. Hardy and C. Richardson, eds., *The Christology of the Later Fathers* (LCC; Philadelphia: Westminster, 1977), 60–61.

35 For one example of such criticism, among many, see Jenson, *Systematic Theology*, 1:188. Aulén's broadside against St. Anselm was grounded somewhat differently. Aulén held that the notion of making satisfaction for sin conceived of as a debt was a product of the Latin (i.e., Catholic) imagination. But, as we have seen, the idea is deeply biblical. For the continuity between Anselm and the Greek patristic tradition on the matter of the atonement (contra Aulén and many others), see David Hart, "A Gift

Exceeding Every Debt: An Eastern Orthodox Appreciation of Anselm's *Cur Deus Homo*," *Pro Ecclesia* 7 (1998): 333–49.

36 This matter deserves further study. For now, see the work of Best cited in n. 5.

37 The section I will be addressing is in bk. 9, chap. 13, pars. 35, 36.

38 My citation is from the translation of Rex Warner, *The Confessions of St. Augustine* (New York: New American Library, 1963), 208.

CHAPTER 9 Redeem Your Sins with Alms

1 The one who owed a sin offering was called *ḥayyāb ḥaṭṭāʾt*; one who owed a lashing, *ḥayyāb makkôt*; one guilty of a capital crime, *ḥayyāb mîtâh*.

2 It is worth noting that M. Sokoloff, in *A Dictionary of Jewish Palestinian Aramaic* (Ramat Gan, Israel: Bar Ilan University Press, 1990), 177, lists as the basic meaning of the root *z-k-y* "to be innocent" and adds an important derived sense, "to gain possession [of something]." One could explain the relationship between the two meanings in two ways. On one hand, someone who was declared innocent in a trial over contested property would be entitled to that piece of property. So innocence in court and the subsequent possession of property could be closely related. On the other, if we take the Akkadian evidence seriously (see the entry on *zakû* in *CAD* vol. 31, 23–32), the root would have originally meant "to be clean," and then "cleansed," or better "cleared of legal claims." In legal contracts to clear a piece of property from claims is tantamount to purchasing it, hence the development from cleansing to gaining possession.

3 This sort of semantic development is very well attested in Hebrew, Aramaic and Akkadian material. See the detailed discussion of Eduard Y. Kutscher, *Hebrew and Aramaic Studies* (Jerusalem: Magnes, 1977), Hebrew Section, 417–30.

4 See the tractate, *Peah* 5a, in *The Jerusalem Talmud. First Order: Zeraim. Tractates Peah and Demay,* ed. Heinrich W. Guggenheimer (Berlin: de Gruyter, 2000).

5 Isaac's own role in the sacrifice that Abraham is commanded to carry out is never highlighted in the Bible. However, rabbinic tradition transforms Isaac into a willing participant who consents to his father's bidding. The importance of Isaac's participation is a familiar subject in rabbinic literature. See my discussion of how Moses' prayer of intercession in Exod 32 in interpreted in *Exod Rab* in Chap. 1.

6 It should be noted that the "treasury of merits" was subject to considerable theological reflection and it was not the case that this treasury could be invoked by just anyone at anytime. Nor were the merits inexhaustible. Some rabbis, in fact, rejected the value of the treasury altogether and put the full onus of moral responsibility on the individual. Others argued that the treasury had been exhausted by Israel's past sins and now Israel was dependent solely on the covenantal fealty of God alone. For details on this see the discussion in Solomon Schechter, *Aspects of Rabbinic Theology,* 171–89.

7. Ephrem, *Hymns on Fasting,* 1:14. For the Syriac, see E. Beck, ed., *Hymnen de Ieiunio* (CSCO 246; Louvain: Secrétariat du CorpusSCO, 1964).

8 The translation is mine. Conventional translations vary considerably for reasons that will become clear below.

9 It is a curious accident that the English word "alms" is nothing other than a corruption of the Greek term *eleēmosynē*. It is significant as well, as Jan Joosten has shown, that the Septuagint was aware of the rabbinic meaning of both *ṣĕdāqâh* and *ḥesed* as acts of mercy toward the poor. See his "*Ḥesed* 'bienveillance' et *eleos* 'pitie': Reflexions

sur une equivalence lexicale dans la Septante," in *"Car c'est l'amour qui me plaît, non le sacrifice . . .": Recherches sur Osée 6:6 et son interprétation juive et chrétienne,* ed. Eberhard Bons (SJSJ 88; Leiden: Brill, 2004), 25–42.

10 See the collection of proverbs known as 4Q424 or 4QWisd, Fragment 3:7–10 of which reads: "A man of means is zealous for the law—he is a prosecutor of all those who shift boundaries. A merciful and gracious man gives alms *(ṣĕdāqâh)* to the poor—he is concerned about all who lack monetary capital." Though the original edition (prepared by Sarah Tanzer in *Qumran Cave 4; Cryptic Texts and Miscellanea Part 1, DJD* 36 [Oxford: Clarendon Press, 2000], 342) testifies to the reading, *ṣĕdāqâh,* I am dependent on Elisha Qimron's new readings (unpublished) for the rest of the line. Also note that the word occurs in the Qumran fragments of the book of Tobit (4Q200, 2:9 —*[ba-ʿăś]ōtekā ṣĕdāqâh śîmâh ṭôvâh,* "through your giving of alms, there will be a good treasure"). For the text, see Florentino García Martínez, *The Dead Sea Scrolls Translated: The Qumran Texts in English* (Leiden: Brill, 1994). For a discussion of these lines, see Joseph A. Fitzmyer, *Tobit* (Commentaries on Early Jewish Literature; Berlin: Walter de Gruyter, 2003), 171.

11 Rosenthal, "*Ṣĕdāqâh,* Charity," *Hebrew Union College Annual* 23 (1950–51): 411–430.

12 In this chapter, I have slightly altered the translation of texts from Ps and Pro from the JPS version both for accuracy and to make my point more clearly.

13 Isac Seeligmann has astutely observed that the verb *nôtēn* frequently has the technical sense of "to issue a loan" (see Deut 15:7–11, especially the use of the verb *nātan* in v. 10). In that case, the verse from Psalms would be telling us that the righteous are quick and generous in their loans to the poor—loans which they may not be able to collect upon. See Seeligmann, "Darlehen, Bürgschaft und Zins in Recht und Gedankenwelt der Hebräischen Bibel," in *Gesammelte Studien zur Hebräischen Bibel,* ed. I. Seeligmann, I. Leo, R. Smend, and E. Blum, FAT 41 (Tübingen: Mohr Siebeck, 2004), 319–48.

14 Here, I am dependent on Avi Hurwitz's excellent article, "Reshitam Ha-Miqra'it shel Munahim Talmudiyyim—Le-Toledot Tsemihato shel Musag Ha-Sedaqâh," in *Mehqarim be-Lashon* 2–3 (Jerusalem: Center for Jewish Studies, 1987), 155–60.

15 Seeligmann writes ("Darlehen, Bürgschaft und Zins," 319): "Special insight into social conditions in Israel can be found in the popular aphorisms handed on to us in Proverbs. This is true, too, with some psalms, especially the wisdom psalms."

16 In the Bible the act of honoring God is frequently conjoined with the delivery of some specific gift such as an oblation or sacrifice. "To honor" someone entailed some sort of external display. (For this, see Num 22:17 [cf. 22:37], where the king Balak promises to honor Balaam for his services, by which he means that he will pay him handsomely.) It is altogether appropriate, then, that the act of honoring God in this proverb is fulfilled by being generous to the poor. A charitable gift stands in the place of a sacrificial offering.

17 See the BT *B. Bathra,* 10a.

18 The Syriac reads: "He who accompanies [*metlawwe*—same root as the Hebrew term for loaning but a different meaning] the Lord shows mercy on the poor, he will be repaid according to his deeds." But the concept of making a loan to God was not unknown in the Syriac tradition. This wisdom teaching from Proverbs, though slightly reworked, found its way into the Peshitta version of Ben Sira. "Give to God as he gives to you with

a good eye and a large hand; for he who gives to the poor, lends to God; for who is a re-payer if not he? For he is God who repays and he will repay you ten thousand times ten thousand" (35:10–11). And strikingly, one Hebrew manuscript of Ben Sira includes similar wording in the same location in a marginal note. See Pancratius Beentjes, *The Book of Ben Sira in Hebrew: A Text Edition of All Extant Hebrew Manuscripts and a Synopsis of All Parallel Hebrew Ben Sira Texts* (Leiden: Brill, 1997), 61.

19 In the Jewish Bible it is the earliest text to do so; in the larger canon of the Christian Old Testament one can find the term functioning in this fashion in Tobit and Ben Sira.

20 The translation is mine.

21 There is a vast literature on this subject, but the best discussion of it and its implications for the Bible remains that of Moshe Weinfeld, *Social Justice in Ancient Israel and the Ancient Near East* (Minneapolis: Fortress, 1995).

22 See *"Anduraru,"* in *CAD*, vol. 1, pt. 2, pp. 115–17.

23 On the Jubilee year and the early history of its interpretation, see John S. Bergsma, *The Jubilee from Leviticus to Qumran: A History of Interpretation* (SVT 115; Leiden: Brill, 2007).

24 In the Bible *mîšôr/mêšar* often stands in parallel to *ṣedeq/ṣĕdāqâh.* As an example, note Ps 9:7–9, "It is [the Lord] who judges the world with righteousness *(ṣedeq),* / rules the peoples with equity *(mêšarîm).* The Lᴏʀᴅ is a haven for the oppressed, / A haven in times of trouble." In these verses, righteousness and equity are singled out as divine qualities that have a special concern for the rights of the poor.

25 For the text, see Jacob Lauterbach, *Mekilta de-Rabbi Ishmael,* 3 vols. (Philadelphia: Jewish Publication Society, 1935), 3:86–87.

26 Some would translate the term "to break off." Originally the term meant "to untie, dismantle" or even "to take apart." It was often used to describe the action of removing a yoke from an animal or a slave. From there it assumed the secondary sense of "to redeem," since redemption of a slave is the removal of a type of "yoke" that binds him to his master. Because of the financial imagery of giving alms, it seems wisest to assume that *praq* is to be translated "redeem."

27 I have altered the NJPS translation for clarity.

28 In the Septuagint translation one finds a variant of the Greek word *lytrōsis,* which means "redemption" or "ransom price."

29 Note that the person here is not technically a slave, according to the theology of Leviticus. For our purposes, however, this fine point is not significant. On this problem, see the discussion of Jacob Milgrom, *Leviticus 23–27 (AB* 3B; New York: Doubleday, 2000), 2212–41.

30 In Isa 40:2, we read that Jerusalem can now be consoled because "her term of service [as a debt-slave] is over, her iniquity has been paid off." On the translation of this verse, see Chap. 4, and Anderson, "From Israel's Burden to Israel's Debt," in E. Chazon et al., eds., *Reworking the Bible: Apocryphal and Related Texts at Qumran* (Leiden: Brill, 2005), 19–24. In Isa 50:1, Israel is described as not being sold into slavery by God but as having sold herself through her iniquities: "And which of my creditors was it to whom I sold you off? You were only sold off for your sins." The subject of Israel as a debt-slave in Isaiah has been discussed by Klaus Baltzer, "Liberation from Debt Slavery After the Exile in Second Isaiah and Nehemiah," in *Ancient Israelite Religion: Es-*

says in Honor of Frank Moore Cross, ed. Patrick D. Miller, Jr., Paul D. Hanson, and S. Dean McBride (Philadelphia: Fortress, 1987), 477–84.

31 For many early Christian writers, almsgiving was the single most important means for taking care of sins that occurred after one's baptism. A classic exposition of the matter can be found in Cyprian's "Works and Almsgiving," written in the third century. For the text, see *Saint Cyprian: Treatises,* ed. and trans. Roy J. Deferrari (FC 36; Washington, D.C.: Catholic University of America, 1958), 225–56. See also the discussion in Roman Garrison, *Redemptive Almsgiving in Early Christianity* (JSNTSS 77; Sheffield: JSOT Press, 1993).

32 I have altered the NJPS translation here for clarity.

33 Jesus depicted the dangers of this proverb: "Then [Jesus] told them a parable. 'The land of a rich man produced abundantly. And he thought to himself, "What should I do, for I have no place to store my crops?" Then he said, "I will do this: I will pull down my barns and build larger ones, and there I will store all my grain and my goods. And I will say to my soul, *Soul, you have ample goods laid up for many years; relax, eat, drink, be merry.*" But God said to him, "You fool! This very night your life is being demanded of you. And the things you have prepared, whose will they be?" So it is with those who store up treasures for themselves but are not rich toward God' " (Luke 12:16–21). Jesus is not critical of how this man acquired his wealth. He may have been the most moral farmer in town. The subject of his critique has to do with where the man has put his confidence. In Jesus's mind, this person had made the mistake of assuming that an *earthly* treasury would deliver him in a day of distress (see Luke 12:19, in particular).

34 This book is difficult to place in terms of date and provenance, but I incline toward the view of those who date it to the third century and place it in Mesopotamia. Because we have fragments of the book in both Hebrew and Aramaic from Qumran, we know it cannot be any younger than the mid-first century BCE.

35 *Lev Rab* 34:7, in H. Freedman and Maurice Simon, *Midrash Rabbah,* vol. 2 (London: Soncino, 1939).

36 So Shlomo Naeh, Talmud Department, Hebrew University, personal communication.

37 His acts of charity parallel his sacrificial activity in another fashion as well. Both are done against the backdrop of a less than obedient set of Jewish peers. Just as his devotion to the temple sets him apart from his neighbors ("I *alone* went often to Jerusalem for the festivals" [1:6]) so, too, did his deeds of charity. In the end, he is mocked for tending to Israel's dead (2:9). The point seems clear: his sacrificial service in the land of Israel came at considerable personal cost, as did his almsgiving and charity in the Diaspora.

38 This text has set in parallelism the keeping of the commandments and the giving of alms. I shall return to this theme in Chap. 11. For now, one may wish to note that the term *ham-miṣwâh* in rabbinic Hebrew or *miṣwětā'* in Aramaic normally means "the commandment." It can be a shorthand expression for "almsgiving." In other words, almsgiving is *the* commandment. And accordingly, *t. Peah* 4:19 (see the discussion of this text in Chap. 11) will declare that the giving of alms is equal to all the other commandments in the Torah.

39 The text of the Hebrew (translated here as "will be credited") is difficult; the translation I have used too confidently conveys a monetary idiom. M. Kister, in "Romans 5:12-21 Against the Background of Torah-Theology and Hebrew Usage," *HTR* 100

(2007): 394–95, has recently made a brilliant suggestion about the initial phrase of v. 14. He understands the phrase "kindness [*sĕdāqâh*] to a father" as "the merits belonging to the father." If he is correct, this would be one of the earliest examples of *ṣĕdāqâh* used as a merit in a financial sense that is balanced against sins. It would be a remarkably close parallel to the rabbinic term *zĕkût*, especially in the idiom "the merits of the fathers."

40 BT *B. Bathra* 10a.

41 *2 Clement* 16:4. For the text, see *The Apostolic Fathers*, ed. and trans. Bart D. Ehrman (LCL 24; Cambridge: Harvard University Press, 2003).

42 *Didache* 4:5–6. For the text, see *The Didache, The Epistle of Barnabas, the Epistles and Martyrdom of St. Polycarp, The Fragments of Papias, The Epistle to Diognetus*, trans. and annotated by James A. Kleist (ACW 5; New York: Newman, 1948).

43 Rabbinic literature makes a legal distinction between almsgiving proper (*ṣĕdākâh*) and charitable deeds (*gĕmîlût ḥăsādîm*) in general (see my discussion of this in Chap. 11). It is not clear to me that such a distinction exists in earlier literature, nor that the distinction is maintained in nonlegal portions of the rabbinic corpus. This matter should be the subject of further study. For now, given that deeds of charity are thought to pay down a debt, I assume that the most obvious manner of doing such would be through the giving of alms. It is from the prestige of almsgiving that the other charitable deeds acquire their value.

CHAPTER 10 Salvation by Works?

Epigraph: St. Ephrem the Syrian, *Hymns to Abraham Kidunaya* 1:7.

1 As James A. Montgomery notes, this formula has been a *locus classicus* between Catholic and Protestant interpreters over the centuries. He quotes the tart conclusion of Matthew Pole in 1694: "Pontificii ex hoc loco satisfactiones suas et merita colligunt." Loosely translated: "The papists gather from this verse their notions of satisfaction and merits." See Montgomery, *A Critical and Exegetical Commentary on the Book of Daniel* (ICC 24; Edinburgh: T and T Clark, 1927), 238. The wealth of textual material on this verse that the debates of the sixteenth century spawned is immeasurably vast and merits a study in its own right.

2 See Roman Garrison's discussion in *Redemptive Almsgiving in Early Christianity* (JS-NTSS 77; Sheffield: JSOT Press, 1993), 11. In relation to the texts of Clement and the Epistle to Diognetus, he writes, "The early Christian belief that the death of Jesus is the unique atonement for sin seems to be incompatible with the doctrine of redemptive almsgiving."

3 The translation of the *Epistle of Diognetus* is from J. B. Lightfoot, *The Apostolic Fathers* (London: Macmillan, 1926). For Clement, see n. 4, below.

4 Clement of Alexandria, "Who Is the Rich Man That Would Be Saved?," in *Clement of Alexandria: With an English Translation*, ed. and trans. G. W. Butterworth (LCL; London: W. Heinemann, 1919), 32.

5 Martin Hengel, *Property and Riches in the Early Church* (Philadelphia: Fortress, 1974), 82.

6 T. F. Torrance, *The Doctrine of Grace in the Apostolic Fathers* (London: Oliver and Boyd, 1948).

7 The translation is taken from Kathleen McVey, *Ephrem the Syrian: Hymns* (Classics of Western Spirituality; Mahwah, N.J.: Paulist, 1989), 107.

8 Ibid., 103.

9 One should note that in the Gospel of Mark, the story of the rich young man (10:17–31) occurs within Jesus's threefold prediction of his own death and resurrection (8:31–33, 9:31, 10:33–34). The Gospel imagines that the donation of all one's goods to the poor is something equivalent to the demand to take up one's cross. This reading is confirmed by the disciples' reaction. When Jesus says that he must die by crucifixion, this is simply unimaginable to his followers (8:32). They are similarly shocked by Jesus's demand of the rich young man to give all that he has to the poor (10:26). I would suggest that Ephrem also understood the distribution of all one's wealth to the poor and the crucifixion as homologous acts of self-donation. Almsgiving becomes part of the economy of salvation that Christ has graciously bequeathed to the church.

10 Text in Edmund Beck, ed., *Des Heiligen Ephraem des Syrers: Hymnen de Fide* (CSCO 154–55; Louvain: Imprimerie Orientaliste, 1955).

11 One should note that the same phenomenon can be found in Hungarian (the verb *hitelező* means "one who issues a loan" while the nominal form means "faith") and Akkadian (see the entry for the verb *qâpu/qiāpu* in *CAD* vol. 13 [Chicago: University of Chicago Oriental Institute, 1982], 93–97). One of the meanings of *qiāpu* is "to have faith, believe" ("as for the words that So and So said to you, you said thus: I do not believe it *[ul qīpāku]*"), while another meaning is "to issue a loan" ("a woman tavern keeper who made a *qīptu* loan of beer or barley cannot collect anything that she has loaned out [after the remission of debts announced by the king]").

12 Text in *Midrash Tannaim zum Deuteronomium*, ed. David Hoffmann (Berlin: Ittzkowksi, 1908), 84.

13 *Hymns on Faith* 5:17. The reference to giving alms on loan must derive originally from Prov 19:17 (though on the problem of this verse in the Syriac, see n. 18 in Chap. 9). The italics are mine.

14 See note 15.

15 Ephrem treats the treasuries of the reliquaries in Edessa in a similar fashion in *Carmina Nisibena* 42:4. These boxes, which contain the bones of the saints, are thought to house something of the inexhaustible power of resurrection itself; for the bones of the saints were thought to participate proleptically in those very benefits. Ephrem argued there that the spiritual treasures they contain will actually grow in size the more they are plundered by the faithful. These treasuries did not follow the rules of a zero-sum economy. It is as though the natural world has various apertures of grace that God has designated for the use of his faithful. One demonstrates faith in God by availing oneself of their riches.

16 The text is from E. Beck, ed., *Des Heiligen Ephraem des Syrers: Hymnen auf Abraham Kidunaya und Julianos Saba* (CSCO 322–323; Louvain: Imprimerie Orientalische, 1955).

17 A similar motif can be found in the *Hymns on Fasting*, 1:13, though in this instance it is Christ who is the holder of the bond.

18 For this important concept, see Chap. 11.

19 See Mark 10:23–31 (and its parallels in Matthew and Luke) and Chap. 11.

20 Augustine, *Exposition of the Psalms* (33–50), vol. 2, trans. M. Boulding (OSB; Hyde Park, N.Y.: New City, 2000), 133.

21 One should note the fine essays by Michael Root ("Aquinas, Merit, and Reformation Theology after the Joint Declaration on the Doctrine of Justification," *Modern Theology*

20 (2004) 5–22) and Joseph Wawrykow ("John Calvin and Condign Merit," in *Archiv für Reformationsgeschichte* 83 [1992], 73–90). Root argues that the Thomistic understanding of the relationship between human merit (that is, the result of doing good works) and divine grace does not contradict in any essential way the Reformation emphasis on salvation by grace alone. Wawrykow goes even further and argues that on most essential points, Calvin and Thomas are on the same page regarding the value of human merits in the scheme of human salvation. As these two scholars note, everything depends on how we understand the relationship between divine and human agency in the performance of a merit-worthy action. If the achievement of merits is the result of the infusion of the Holy Spirit then many of the worries Protestants harbor about this topic dissipate rather quickly.

22 At this point, the practice of almsgiving shows strong parallels with sacrifice. Early theorists of sacrifice had posited that the exchange made at the altar was a simple quid pro quo—one got back what one put in. But as I have already written, such a theory "fails to account for the asymmetry of the sacrificial process. How is it that the human being can give so little (a single animal) and receive so much (the promise of divine blessing in its many varied forms)? Here one is greatly aided by recent anthropological theories of gift giving: the gods establish their superiority by giving more than they receive. . . . It is in this way that reciprocity can coexist with hierarchy, and that the sacrificial exchange can represent the gods' superiority over men." See my "Sacrifices and Sacrificial Offerings (OT)," *Anchor Bible Dictionary* (New York: Doubleday, 1992), 5:871–872.

23 See St. Anselm of Canterbury, *Cur deus homo*, bk. 1, chap. 20. I shall return to this work in Chap. 12.

24 See St. Thomas Aquinas, *Summa Theologica*, pts. II-II, quest. 32, art. 1. I consulted the *Summa Theologiae: Latin Text and English Translation*, Blackfriars English Translation, vol. 34 (New York: McGraw-Hill, 1975).

25 See my discussion of this in Chaps. 1 and 9.

26 See K. Aland, ed., *Martin Luther's 95 Theses* (Saint Louis: Concordia, 1967), 54.

CHAPTER 11 A Treasury in Heaven

Epigraph: The quotation is from l. 11 of Sebastian Brock, "A Syriac Dispute Between Heaven and Earth," *Le Muséon* 91 (1978): 261–70. The translation is mine. The manuscript probably dates to the sixth century, but the text is certainly older than that.

1 See the Jerusalem Talmud on *Peah* 1:1 and any of the traditional commentaries on the Mishnah. Clement of Alexandria (late second century CE) in his work "Who is the Rich Man That Would Be Saved?" also recognizes the need for prudence in regard to how much money ordinary laypeople would be expected to part with. But also note that Cyprian (third century CE, from North Africa), in his treatise on almsgiving, believes that whatever amount one might give, God is sufficiently generous to sustain and reward one in return. See chaps. 8–13 of Cyprian's "Works and Almsgiving," in *St. Cyprian: Treaties*, trans. R. Deferrari (New York: Fathers of the Church, 1958). As I shall discuss at the end of this chapter, early Christianity proved a more hospitable environment for lavish acts of self-impoverishment.

2 The books of Ben Sira and Tobit are clear on this fact (see Chap. 9) and therefore anticipate the Talmud (see BT *Sukkah* 49b: "Almsgiving is better than sacrifice").

3 This is an important text in the early church from the Syriac East to the Latin West. It

also appears in the Sibylline Oracles (though it is hard to know whether this represents a Second Temple Jewish usage or a later Christian addition). "Whoever gives alms knows that he is lending to God. Mercy [perhaps better: "charity"] saves from death when judgement comes." The citation is from James Charlesworth, *Old Testament Pseudepigrapha* (New York: Doubleday, 1983), 1:347.

4 St. Ephrem takes a comparable position on the role of almsgiving in the Divine Economy. See my discussion in Chap. 10.

5 St. Irenaeus, *Against Heresies*, bk. 4:18; quotation is from ANF 1:486.

6 The linkage of Prov 19:17 and Matt 25:31–46 becomes standard for almost all commentators after Irenaeus. See, e.g., St. John Chrysostom, *On Repentance and Almsgiving*, trans. G. Christo (FC 96; Washington, D.C.: Catholic University Press, 1998), homily 7.24, p. 105; St. Gregory of Nazianzus, *Select Orations*, trans. M. Vinson (FC 107; Washington, D.C.: Catholic University Press, 2003), oration 14, pp. 68–70; Clement of Alexandria *Stromateis, Books One to Three* (FC 85; Washington, D.C.: Catholic University Press, 1991), bk. 3.6, p 290; *S. Ambrosii, De Tobia: A Commentary*, with an introduction and translation by L. Zucker (Patristic Studies 35; Washington, D.C.: Catholic University Press, 1933), 71–73.

7 As Ephraim Urbach already noted ("Religious and Sociological Tendencies Regarding the Rabbinic Understanding of Almsgiving," in *The World of the Sages: Collected Studies* [in Hebrew] [Jerusalem: Magnes, 2002], 20), this tradition is close to one found in the Midrash on Psalms. He writes: "There is a great similarity between the teaching of the church in the Apostolic era and the first few centuries afterwards and that of the rabbis. There can be no doubt that the church was influenced by Jewish thinking. Jesus says: 'Come, those blessed by my father and inherit the kingdom prepared for you. For I was hungry and you fed me, thirsty and you gave me drink, I was a visitor and you took me in, naked and you covered me, sick and you visited me and in prison and came to me.' This entire list of charitable deeds that the church endeavored to uphold reminds one of an anonymous midrash: " 'Open for me the gates of charity *[sedeq]*' (Ps 118:19). 'In the world to come, one will be asked: What was your work?' If he answers, 'I fed the hungry,' then they will say, 'This is the gate of the LORD' (118:20)—Let the feeder of the hungry enter by it. If he answers, 'I gave drink to the thirsty,' then they will say: 'This is the gate of the LORD'—Let the giver of drink to the thirsty enter by it. If he answers, 'I clothed the naked,' then they will say, 'This is the gate of the LORD' (118:20)—Let the clother of the naked enter by it. And so forth." As Urbach has noted, the list of righteous deeds not only overlaps those of Matt 25 but derives ultimately from a list in Isa 58:6–7.

8 As Rudolf Bultmann had noted (*History of the Synoptic Tradition* [New York: Harper and Row, 1963], 124), there are good grounds to see this entire tradition as originating in a Jewish context. The crucial change in the Gospel tradition, he observes, was that "the name of God was replaced by the title Son of Man." If the Jewish tradition that Matt 25 had at its base was a midrash on Prov 19:17, it would be difficult not to see this chapter as representing a rather high Christology, for the figure of Jesus is positioned where the figure of God once stood.

9 Hence the graded sin or purification offering in Lev 5.

10 Cf. the freewill offering and the vow of the sailors at the close of the first chapter of the book of Jonah.

11 Note that one of the mosaics found on a synagogue floor in Sepphoris has the story of Aaron's first offering of the Tamid, or daily offering (Lev 9), in its top register and the sacrifice of Isaac at the bottom (see the discussion in Ze'ev Weiss and Ehud Netzer, *Promise and Redemption: A Synagogue Mosaic from Sepphoris* [Jerusalem: Israel Museum, 1996], 14–31). This should be compared to the midrash which says that every time Israel offers the Tamid, God directs his attention to the binding of Isaac (Weiss and Netzer discuss this midrash on p. 38; see my discussion in Chap. 12). On this reading, it is the sacrifice of Isaac that grounds the temple cult.

12 He is called the rich young man only in the Gospel of Matthew; in Mark he is simply a rich man. But given how popular this title is for the story, I will continue to use it for the Markan version as well.

13 On the nexus between the beloved son and a sacrificial death in the Bible, see Jon Levenson, *The Death and Resurrection of the Beloved Son* (New Haven: Yale University Press, 1993).

14 *Homilies on Genesis and Exodus,* trans. R. Heine (FC 71; Washington, D.C.: Catholic University Press, 1982), homily 8, par. 8, pp. 144–45.

15 See Philo, *Decal.* 121: " 'The second set' of commandments refers to 'the actions prohibited by our duty to fellow-men' whereas the other 'set of five . . . is more concerned with the divine.' " Cited in Dale Allison and W. D. Davies, *The Gospel According to Saint Matthew* (ICC; Edinburgh: T & T Clark, 1997), 3:43 n. 32.

16 As Joel Marcus has shown (forthcoming in his second volume on Mark in AB), there is ample legal evidence in rabbinic sources indicating that the command "not to covet one's neighbor's goods" was frequently understood as "do not defraud."

17 One way to explain this conundrum is to assume that the man was not completely honest with Jesus about his integrity in keeping the law. Many New Testament commentators have been suspicious of his claim. C. E. B. Cranfield, the eminent British scholar of a generation back, wrote *(The Gospel According to Mark* [Cambridge Greek Testament Commentary; Cambridge: Cambridge University Press, 1959], 329): "The man's naïve reply makes it clear that he has not understood the Commandments nor ever really taken them seriously. But he was no more mistaken about the law's real seriousness than were his Jewish contemporaries generally." It is clear that Cranfield has not come upon this position innocently. His skepticism about the man's honesty is a result of a specifically Pauline construal of the law. In Paul's mind, it was one thing to know what the law required and another thing to do it. "For we know that the law is spiritual," Paul avers, "but I am of the flesh, sold into slavery under sin. I do not understand my own actions. For I do not do what I want, but I do the very thing I hate. . . . For I know that nothing good dwells within me, that is, in my flesh. I can will what is right, but I cannot do it. For I do not do the good I want, but the evil I do not want is what I do. Now if I do what I do not want, it is no longer I that do it, but sin that dwells in me" (Rom 7:14–20). If we begin with the assumption of Paul that keeping the law is an impossibility, there is no option but to doubt the veracity of the young man. But surely Joseph Fitzmyer gets it right when he says (in regard to Luke's version of the tale), "Jesus has not denied that the magistrate has actually observed the commandments; he takes the man's answer for what it is and tries to draw him on still further" *(The Gospel According to Luke X–XXIV* [AB 28a; New York: Doubleday, 1985], 1197).

18 See my article "Sacrifices and Offerings," in the *Anchor Bible Dictionary* (New York:

Doubleday, 1992), 5:87–86. I am dependent on the anthropologist Valerio Valeri for this particular gloss of the phrase "do ut des."

19 See Shamma Friedman, "The Primacy of Tosefta to Mishnah in Synoptic Parallels," in *Introducing Tosefta* (Hoboken, N.J.: KTAV, 1999), 99–122; *Tosefta Atiqa* [in Hebrew] (Ramat Gan: Bar Ilan University Press, 2002); and Judith Hauptman, *Rereading the Mishnah: A New Approach to Ancient Jewish Texts* (Tübingen: Mohr Siebeck, 2005).

20 See Lev 19:9–10, 23:22; Deut 14:27–29 (the "poor man's tithe," which takes the place of the second tithe in the third and sixth years of the seven year cycle), 24:19–22.

21 On the form of this Mishnah and its relationship to the Dead Sea Scrolls, see Aharon Shemesh, "The History of the Creation of Measurements: Between Qumran and the Mishnah," in S. Fraade, A. Shemesh, and R. Clements, eds., *Rabbinic Perspectives: Rabbinic Literature and the Dead Sea Scrolls: Proceedings of the Eighth International Symposium of the Orion Center for the Study of the Dead Sea Scrolls and Associated Literature, 7–9 January, 2003* (Leiden: Brill, 2006), 147–73. He argues that among the sect at Qumran the items listed in this first mishnah originally had measures attached to them.

22 The full form of the opening mishnah in tractate *Peah* is: "These are matters that have no specified amount: *peah*, first fruits, the festival offering, charitable deeds, and Torah-study. Regarding the following matters, a man may enjoy their fruit in this world and his principal will remain for him in the next: honoring father and mother, charitable deeds, establishing peace between a man and his friend, [but] Torah-study is equal to all of them."

23 Urbach ("Religious and Sociological Tendencies," 10ff.) argues that part of the reason poverty was so extreme in the land of Israel in the early second century CE was that the temple infrastructure had disappeared and another had not yet arisen to replace it. A similar poverty must have been the case in the Diaspora in Tobit's day. If so, the redirection of money from temple offerings (including the tithe for the poor) to alms would have served an important social function.

24 *The Tosefta* (Jerusalem: Jewish Theological Seminary, 1992), 41.

25 Albeck, *Shishah Sidre Mishnah: Seder Zeraʾim* (Jerusalem: Bialik, 1959), 41.

26 I have edited out a short aside about how little one might give and still have it count as fulfilling one's obligation.

27 There follows a long aside about how much one might spend on other commandments.

28 There follows another long aside on the status of a law that is so diligently pursued.

29 I am not assuming that the entire tractate of *Peah* was authoritative in the second century—that would be highly unlikely—but, rather, that some form of the opening line ("these are the things that have no measure") was already in circulation.

30 The text concludes: "For scripture says: 'Truth springs up from the earth, but almsgiving peers down from heaven' (Ps 85:12). My fathers stored up [wealth] in treasuries that produce no fruit, I stored [alms] in treasuries that produce fruit. For scripture says, 'Almsgiving and justice are the very foundation of his throne' (Ps 89:15). My fathers gathered money but I gathered souls. For scripture says: 'The fruit of a charitable man is a tree of life; the wise man acquires souls' (Prov 11:30). My fathers gathered for others, but I gathered for myself. For scripture says, 'Almsgiving shall belong to you [before the LORD your God]' (Deut 24:13). My fathers gathered in this world, but

I gather for the world to come. For scripture says: 'Almsgiving delivers one from death' (Prov 10:2). Death here refers not to mortal death but to death in the world to come."

31 In parallel traditions in the Babylonian Talmud (*B.Bathra* 10a) and Tosephta (4:19) his generosity is occasioned by a famine. Some commentators explain the presence of this unit in the Jerusalem Talmud on the grounds that his actions were necessitated by these extreme social conditions, in which case the Talmudic dictum about giving only 20 percent might be bracketed. But it is surely significant that this version eliminates those details. Presumably the Jerusalem Talmud knew the Tosephta's account but chose to present its own version.

32 One may object that this discussion concludes on the halakhic (i.e., legal) note with which it began, that is, a distinction between charitable activity in general and the giving of alms in particular. But one should observe two things. First, the distinctions made in this unit are purely formal in nature, that is, charity is better because it is more inclusive, not because it preserves capital. This formal criterion differs from the pragmatic issue that opened this Talmudic unit (see Unit A). Indeed, according to this unit (F), charity includes almsgiving ("charitable deeds are customarily done with *both* one's money and body").

33 Lieberman, "Two Lexicographical Notes," *JBL* 65 (1946): 67–72, esp., 69–72.

34 This is an excellent argument for seeing the Tosephta's belief that almsgiving is equal to all the commandments as older than the Mishnah's counterclaim for the Torah. To my knowledge, nowhere is Torah-study described as *the* commandment. Rabbinic semantics confirm the picture we have seen in Tobit, Ben Sira, and the Gospels.

35 Surprisingly, Howard C. Kee, in his translation in Charlesworth, *Old Testament Pseudepigrapha,* 1:817, was not aware of Lieberman's suggestion. The result is an unintelligible translation: "Someone else commits adultery and is sexually promiscuous, yet is abstemious in his eating. While fasting, he is committing evil deeds. Through the power of his wealth he ravages many, and yet in spite of his excessive evil, *he performs the commandments.*" Because we are dealing with a list of self-contradictory behaviors, Lieberman's suggestion remains much more sensible: He cheats and steals and then uses what he has gained to give alms. For the Greek text, see Marinus de Jonge, *The Testaments of the Twelve Patriarchs: A Critical Edition of the Greek Text* (Leiden: Brill, 1978), 137. De Jonge has provided good evidence that the *Testaments* in their final written form were not Jewish but Christian. Lieberman's argument, however, suggests that this particular verse must go back to a Jewish source.

36 Eliezer Diamond, *Holy Men and Hunger Artists: Fasting and Asceticism in Rabbinic Culture* (New York: Oxford University Press, 2004). Especially valuable is his second chapter, " 'The Principal Remains for the Next World': Delayed Gratification and Avoidance of Pleasure in Rabbinic Thought," which concerns m. *Peah* 1:1.

37 BT *Shabbat* 32a. The translation is taken from Diamond, *Holy Men,* 70, with some slight alterations. Could this motif of drawing down one's treasury in this world be compared to the story of the rich man and Lazarus in the Gospel of Luke (16: 19–31)? I am not aware of any New Testament scholar who has pursued this idea, nor do I wish to push the matter myself. But if this rabbinic motif was relevant, one of the points of Luke would be that the rich man had enjoyed all the fruits of his labors in this world and as a result had nothing left in the world to come.

38 Diamond, *Holy Men,* 70.

39 Just as there are meritorious acts whose benefits one can enjoy both now and in the world to come, so there are sins that are punished in both this world and the hereafter. Tosephta *Peah* lists four sins (idolatry, improper sexual relations, murder, and gossip) for which God will demand repayment in both this world and the next. The contrast to the four special virtues in m. *Peah* could not be more complete. In the case of the four sins, the currency one raises by suffering in this world will not be deducted from what one owes. The entire principal will be transferred to the world to come, where further payment will be demanded. On the symmetry of these two lists of virtues and vices, see Marc Hirshman, "Learning as Speech: Tosefta Peah in Light of Plotinus and Origen," in H. Kreisel, ed., *Study and Knowledge in Jewish Thought*, 2 vols. (Beersheva: Ben-Gurion University of the Negev Press, 2006), 1:49–64. The contrast between items 3 and 4 should be clear: peace between neighbors balances murder, and the study of Torah (the "pure speech" of God; Hirshman, 52) is contrasted with evil speech. Acts of charity (item 2) might not seem to be the obvious counterpart to illicit relations, but note that in rabbinic thought just as almsgiving is "the" commandment, adultery is "the" transgression (Shlomo Naeh, personal communication; it is confirmed by the article of Meir Grossman, "Le-mashma'utam shel ha-bituyyim 'averah u-devar 'averah bi-leshon hakamim," *Sinai* 100 (1987): 260–72). As to the opposition of honoring parents and idolatry, see the comments of Hirshman (51–52): "[One must recall] that in late antiquity religion was first and foremost *ta patria*, those things practiced by your parents, [and thus] idolatry seems to be not only a rebuff to the one God but also an abandonment of the ways of the parents."

40 The text is from Edmund Beck, ed., *Des Heiligen Ephraem des Syrers: Hymnen auf Abraham Kidunaya und Julianos Saba* (CSCO 322–23; Louvain: Imprimerie Orientaliste, 1955).

41 A number of exegetes view the command to give alms as subordinate in importance to the act of following Jesus. Vincent Taylor, in *The Gospel According to St. Mark* (New York: St. Martin's, 1966), 429, speaks for the majority when he writes, "In saying to the man, 'One thing thou lackest', Jesus does not mean that there is *just one act to perform* in order that he may inherit eternal life, for after the command to sell all that he has He adds 'come and follow me'. It is this 'following' which leads to life; the renunciation of riches and gifts to the poor are actions which in his case following entails." Taylor is clearly uncomfortable with the notion that one would be rewarded for a specific *deed*—that would appear too Pharisaic; rather, the command to follow indicates that the most important thing is *faith*. Yet Taylor undermines this declaration in part when he later cites with approval the observation that "Jesus Himself appears to have chosen a life of poverty; He wanders to and fro without a settled home (1:39, Lk 9:58), His disciples are hungry (2:23, 8:14), women provide for His needs (Lk 8:3) and His disciples can say, 'behold we have left everything and have followed you' (10:28)" (Taylor, 429). But there is nothing intrinsic to the Christian tradition that demands such a low appraisal of the deed itself. Indeed, it seems obvious that the possibility of following Jesus turns on the desire to perform this deed. Faith and works are inseparable in this story.

42 There is no need to explain the man's claim that he kept the commandments as disingenuous, as Cranfield did (see n. 17, above). The context suggests that he has spoken honestly and that Jesus believes him. On the specifically Protestant sources of Cran-

field's position (i.e., the presumption that one could really keep the law), see the excellent exposition of Ulrich Luz, *Matthew 8–20* (Hermeneia; Minneapolis: Fortress, 2001), 521–22. As E. P. Sanders has noted, Jesus may have opposed certain legalistic excesses within the rabbinic movement, but in general he "objects to the Pharisees because they are not righteous enough" (*Jesus and Judaism* [Philadelphia: Fortress, 1985], 277). In this narrative about the rich man, Jesus is demanding a strict adherence to the legal logic of the Mishnah.

43 Urbach, "Religious and Sociological Tendencies," 15.

44 Schwartz, "From Priests at Their Right to Christians at Their Left? On the Interpretation and Development of a Mishnaic Story (*m. Rosh HaShanah* 2:8–9)" [in Hebrew], *Tarbiz* 74 (2005): 21–42.

45 Of course some of the apostles (perhaps even the majority?) were married. Nevertheless the narratives about them in the Gospels take no interest in that fact; they are portrayed as having left everything. In the post-apostolic period this renunciation of marriage will become a desirable option for many.

46 Cf. *t. Yeb* 8:7, wherein we read that Ben Azzai declared that anyone who refrained from procreation was like a murderer, for he had impaired [God's] likeness. On the tension between devotion to Torah and family in rabbinic culture, see Daniel Boyarin, *Carnal Israel: Reading Sex in Talmudic Culture* (Berkeley: University of California Press, 1993), 134–26.

47 I have followed closely the translation of Diamond but have changed a number of details. The text is from BT *Taʿanit*, 24a.

48 One wonders whether I Tim 5:8 does not have a similar problem in view ("And whoever does not provide for relatives, and especially family members, has denied the faith and is worse than an unbeliever"). Eleazar of Birta, a contemporary of R. Akiba, would have been roughly a contemporary of the person who wrote I Tim. I would like to thank my student Bradley Gregory for suggesting this to me.

49 Diamond, "Hunger Artists and Householders," *USQR* 49 (1994): 33.

50 Consider, e.g., St. Athanasius's famous treatise "The Life of Antony." After hearing the story of the rich young man in Matthew's Gospel, Antony left the church and proceeded to give away his goods to the poor, retaining just enough of his wealth to care for his younger sister (see Athanasius, *The Life of Antony and the Letter to Marcellinus* (Classics of Western Spirituality, trans. R. Gregg; Mahwah, N.J.: Paulist, 1980), 31.

51 My discussion of the rabbinic sources has been greatly aided by the work of Jonathan Schofer on this topic and our many discussions of these texts. See his *The Making of a Sage: A Study in Rabbinic Ethics* (Madison: University of Wisconsin Press, 2005); "Theology and Cosmology in Rabbinic Ethics: The Pedagogical Significance of Rainmaking Narratives," *JSQ* 12 (2205): 227–59; and "Protest or Pedagogy? Trivial Sin and Divine Justice in Rabbinic Narrative," *HUCA* 74 (2003): 243–76.

52 For a short synopsis of Honi's life as well a list of texts that document it, see the entry in the *Encylopedia Judaica* (Jerusalem: Keter, 1972), 8:964–65.

CHAPTER 12 Why God Became Man

1 I have used the translation of Brian Davies and G. R. Evans, eds., *Anselm of Canterbury: The Major Works* (New York: Oxford University Press, 1998). I have consulted the following works on Anslem: G. R. Evans, *Anselm* (Wilton, Conn.: Morehouse-Barlow,

1989); Evans, *Anselm and Talking About God* (Oxford: Clarendon Press, 1978); and R. W. Southern, *Saint Anselm: A Portrait in a Landscape* (Cambridge: Cambridge University Press, 1990). Other sources can be found in the notes below.

2 Rachel Fulton, in *From Judgment to Passion: Devotion to Christ and the Virgin Mary, 800–1200* (New York: Columbia University Press, 2002), 185, notes that while theologians, in general, have not argued that Anselm drew his analogies from contemporary culture, historians have not been as circumspect.

3 Anselm wrote in his preface that his work proves "by unavoidable logical steps, that, supposing Christ were left out of the case, as if there had never existed anything to do with him, it is impossible that, without him, any member of the human race could be saved." See the translation of Davies and Evans, *Anselm*, 261–62.

4 I have taken this summary from David B. Hart, "A Gift Exceeding Every Debt: An Eastern Orthodox Appreciation of Anselm's *Cur Deus Homo,*" *Pro Ecclesia* 7 (1998): 333–49.

5 And to make matters worse, the debt is of an infinite magnitude because the person who has been offended is God. Joseph Cardinal Ratzinger provides an apt analogy: "Behind this is the idea that the measure of the offense is determined by the status of the offended party: if I offend a beggar, the consequences are not the same as they would be if I offended a head of state. The importance of the offense varies according to the addressee. Since God is infinite, the offense to him implicit in humanity's sin is also infinitely important." See his *Introduction to Christianity* (1968 [in German]; San Francisco: Ignatius, 2004), 232.

6 Hart, "A Gift Exceeding Every Debt," has argued that Anselm's portrayal of the atonement has much in common with traditional patristic theology in contrast to the way many Orthodox theologians have understood him. This particular feature is very close to St. Athanasius. In his "On the Incarnation" (par. 6), he argues that it would be monstrous for God to declare an amnesty and let Adam and his progeny off the hook, for he had threatened Adam with death and he must follow through. "For God," Athanasius declares, "would not be true if, when he had said we should die, man died not." But it would be unseemly if God took such efforts to make man, putting within him an aspect of his very being (man is rational *[logikos]* because a portion of the Word *[logos]* resides within him). It would have been better not to have made man at all than to allow him to come to ruin. "For neglect reveals weakness, and not goodness on God's part." For the text, see E. Hardy and C. Richardson, eds., *The Christology of the Later Fathers* (LCC; Philadelphia: Westminster, 1977), 60–61.

7 This was the position of Gustav Aulén, *Christus Victor: An Historical Study of the Three Main Types of the Idea of the Atonement* (New York: Macmillan, 1951), 81–84. But he is followed by many others. See, e.g., the discussion of Hans Urs von Balthasar, *Theo-Drama IV: The Action* (San Francisco: Ignatius, 1994), 254–55, and Colin E. Gunton, *The Actuality of the Atonement: A Study of Metaphor, Rationality and the Christian Tradition* (Edinburgh: T and T Clark, 1988), 89.

8 The translation is mine. I have used the text found in G. Florentino Martínez and E. Tigchelaar, *The Dead Sea Scrolls Study Edition* (Grand Rapids, Mich.: Eerdmans, 1997).

9 There is a copyist error in the original. See my discussion in Chap. 3, n. 21.

10 *CD* 5:5–6.

11 One can find my first discussion of this problem in "The Status of the Torah Before

Sinai: The Retelling of the Bible in Jubilees, and the Damascus Covenant," *DSD* 1 (1994), 19 n. 35.

12 See n. 26 in Chap. 1.

13 "Term or Metaphor: Biblical *nōśēʾ ʿāwōn/pešaʾ/ ḥeṭ*" [in Hebrew] *Tarbiz* 63 (1994), 149–71.

14 Gary A. Anderson, *The Genesis of Perfection: Adam and Eve in Jewish and Christian Imagination* (Louisville, Ky.: Westminster John Knox, 2001); see esp. 162–65 for a preliminary discussion of the bond of Adam that Christ voided on the cross.

15 Jacobus de Voragine, *The Golden Legend,* trans. William Granger Ryan (Princeton: Princeton University Press, 1993), 1:210.

16 See, e.g., the discussion of Robert Jenson in *Systematic Theology,* vol. 1, *The Triune God* (New York: Oxford University Press, 1997), 187–88. He concludes: "The tale of Christ's victory over anti-godly powers does not so much place the Crucifixion within the biblical narrative as construct a new and independent narrative from bits of biblical and patristic language. The language appropriated is in large part mythological, used interpretively in the Bible and by the fathers along the way of telling the history. But a story constructed directly from this language necessarily comes out a genuine myth. As such, it is independent of the history told by the Old Testament and the Gospels." A similar evaluation can be found in Gunton, *Actuality of the Atonement,* 53–82.

17 See the comments of Hans Urs von Balthasar, *Mysterium Paschale: The Mystery of Easter* (Grand Rapids, Mich.: Eerdmans, 1990), 148: "The more eloquently the Gospels describe the passion of the living Jesus, his death and burial, the more striking is their entirely understandable silence when it comes to the time in between his placing in the grave and the event of the Resurrection. We are grateful to them for this."

18 See the discussion of the theological tension that existed already in Second Isaiah. There, Isaiah wanted to claim that God was not the holder of the bond (50:1) yet was the recipient of the repayment (40:2). On this problem see Chap. 4, n. 12.

19 *Theological Oration* 45.22; the citation is from J. N. D. Kelly, *Early Christian Doctrines* (San Francisco: Harper and Row, 1978), 383.

20 The quotation is from Gerald O'Collins, SJ, *Jesus Our Redeemer: A Christian Approach to Salvation* (New York: Oxford University Press, 2007), 133. By "sacrificial," Käsemann means an offering whose sole intention is to placate the wrath of God. There are, of course, other ways to define "sacrificial," so the term need not (and should not) be stricken from the theologian's vocabulary.

21 As Hart astutely notes ("A Gift Exceeding Every Debt," 337–38), Adolph von Harnack had already made this point in his *History of Dogma.* Hans Urs Von Balthasar makes this point as well in his *Theo-Drama IV,* 255–61.

22 On the distinction between Peter Damian and Anselm, see Fulton, *From Judgment to Passion,* 176.

23 See J. Patout Burns, "The Concept of Satisfaction in Medieval Redemption Theory," *TS* 36 (1975): 285–304. As many commentators on Anselm have noted, it is crucial to grasp his distinction between these two ideas. Many detractors of Anselm have simply folded the notion of satisfaction into that of punishment.

24 See my discussion of Origen's treatment of Adam and Eve in "Is Eve the Problem?" in C. Seitz and K. Greene-McCreight, eds., *Theological Exegesis: Essays in Honor of Brevard S. Childs* (Grand Rapids, Mich.: Eerdmans, 1998), 100–102.

25 The several quotations below come from Joseph Cardinal Ratzinger, *Introduction to Christianity*, 281–82. Emphasis added.

26 Jaroslav Pelikan, *The Growth of Medieval Theology, 600–1300* (Chicago: University of Chicago Press, 1978), 137.

27 Both textual citations come from Pelikan, *The Growth of Medieval Theology*, 137. The first is from Anselm's *On the Sacraments of the Church;* the second from Rupert of Deutz's *Commentary on the Book of Job.*

INDEX OF ANCIENT SOURCES